WHO OWNS FOOTBALL?

WHO OWNS FOOTBALL?

THE CHANGING FACE OF CLUB OWNERSHIP

NICK MILLER

BLOOMSBURY SPORT
LONDON · OXFORD · NEW YORK · NEW DELHI · SYDNEY

BLOOMSBURY SPORT
Bloomsbury Publishing Plc
50 Bedford Square, London, WC1B 3DP, UK
29 Earlsfort Terrace, Dublin 2, Ireland

BLOOMSBURY, BLOOMSBURY SPORT and the Diana logo are trademarks of
Bloomsbury Publishing Plc

First published in Great Britain 2024

A catalogue record for this book is available from the British Library

Library of Congress Cataloguing-in-Publication data has been applied for

ISBN: HB: 978-1-3994-1716-7; ePUB: 978-13994-1719-8; ePDF: 978-1-3994-1720-4

2 4 6 8 10 9 7 5 3 1

Typeset in Adobe Garamond Pro by Deanta Global Publishing Services, Chennai, India
Printed and bound in Great Britain by CPI Group (UK) Ltd, Croydon, CR0 4YY

MIX
Paper | Supporting
responsible forestry
FSC® C171272

To find out more about our authors and books visit www.bloomsbury.com
and sign up for our newsletters

For Laura

CONTENTS

INTRODUCTION

In February 1998, Manchester City faced Bury at Maine Road in what was known at the time as Division One. Bury won 1-0, the goal credited to centre-back Paul Butler. It would turn out to be Frank Clark's last game in charge of City, sacked as they headed towards relegation into the third tier. Bury finished the season five places above them.

In many respects it was a relatively inconsequential game in England's second tier. But the paths that the two clubs would take over the following quarter of a century represent perhaps the two most extreme examples of the significant impact an owner can have on a club.

City were back in the top flight by 2000, then over the following few seasons established themselves as a middling Premier League team, until in 2008 they were bought by Sheikh Mansour bin Zayed Al Nahyan, a member of the Abu Dhabi royal family and owner of the Abu Dhabi United Group, the emirate's investment vehicle. Over the next couple of decades his money ensured City became the dominant force in first English, then European, football, culminating in them winning the treble – the Premier League, the FA Cup and the Champions League – in 2023.

Bury were relegated back to the third tier the following year, agonisingly going down on the final day of the season on goals scored, the Football League having curiously settled on that as a tie-breaker for teams finishing on the same points: had it been goal difference, Bury would have survived. They went into administration in 2002, barely avoiding going out of existence completely, before spending the next 17 years shuttling between the third and fourth tiers of English football.

Much of that time was spent in financial turmoil, all of which came to a head in 2019 with expulsion from the Football League. They were the first club to exit the league for non-sporting reasons since Maidstone United resigned in 1992.

They effectively ceased to exist, although not long afterwards a 'phoenix club', Bury AFC, was formed, which would eventually join forces with the remnants of the original club and started the long road back to the Football League.

In June 2023, five days before City beat Inter Milan in the Champions League final to complete the treble, the FA confirmed that Bury could compete in the North West Counties Football League Premier Division.

The face of English football ownership has changed beyond recognition since the 1800s, when most of the current league clubs were formed. But it's also changed beyond recognition in the last 30 or so years.

In 1992 the Premier League came into being, one of the most significant events in the history of English football and the thing that set it on the path to being the most dominant – certainly in financial terms – league in the world a few decades later.

That was when the money started to roll in, but for the first few years of the division's existence the clubs involved were still being run in much the same way they had been in previous decades. Players were on much higher wages than the average person, but the disparity wasn't as massive as it is now. John Barnes was the highest-paid player in the Premier League's inaugural season, earning £10,000-a-week, while according to Professional Footballers' Association (PFA) figures the average top-flight wage was in the region of £1,500-a-week.

Figures are slightly more opaque now, but at the start of the 2023/24 season the highest basic wage was believed to be earned by

Kevin De Bruyne, who was paid £400,000-a-week by Manchester City. The average weekly wage was around £60,000-a-week.

For the rest of us, the average weekly wage was £264 in 1992 and £627 in 2024. So, to summarise: in the Premier League's first year footballers earned about five-and-a-half times more than the rest of the populace. In its 32nd season it was a little under 96 times more.

That disparity is similarly reflected in the boardrooms. Back then, the people that controlled our football clubs were wealthy, but broadly speaking were what you might call 'normal people', who existed in roughly comparable planes of reality to the rest of us. The list included men who made their money in paint (Leeds United majority shareholder and chairman Leslie Silver), steel (Blackburn Rovers' Jack Walker), caravan parks (Oldham Athletic's Ian Stott), timber (Sheffield United's Alan Laver) and package holidays (Aston Villa's Doug Ellis).

Martin Edwards, then chairman of Manchester United, essentially inherited his position from his father Louis, who had been a successful local butcher. Bryan Richardson, Coventry City chairman, was a former professional cricketer. Different strands of the Moores family owned both Everton and Liverpool, the ultimate source of their wealth being Littlewoods, the retailers who also controlled the football pools.

What is perhaps even more notable is that the vast majority of them were local. Of the 22 clubs who made up the 1992/93 Premier League, all but one owner or majority shareholder was from the UK. The exception was Sam Hammam, the Lebanese property developer in charge of Wimbledon, who once made what he described as 'a lot of money' shipping a particular type of sand to an Arab prince building a palace in the desert.

Even then, you couldn't exactly say that Hammam was a chancer from abroad, lured to the English game by the possibility of making a healthy profit. He moved to south London in 1975 after escaping war in Beirut, and six years later he took over his local club and led them to the greatest period in their history, climbing the divisions to become top-flight stalwarts and FA Cup winners in 1988.

For the most part these owners were from the immediate area, or were at least fans of the clubs they controlled. There were a couple of exceptions: Doug Ellis was from the Wirral and was chairman of Wolverhampton Wanderers before taking over at Villa. Chelsea's Ken Bates was from Ealing, west London, so not a million miles from Stamford Bridge, but he was a Queens Park Rangers fan as a boy and had come to the club via spells in charge of Oldham and Wigan Athletic.

Other than that, broadly speaking most of the people at the top of English football had some form of connection with the clubs they governed, before they governed them.

That has … changed, it's fair to say. At the start of the 2024/25 season, only two of the 20 Premier League clubs were wholly owned by UK companies or individuals. In some ways Tony Bloom is the closest throwback to the previous era: he has been a Brighton & Hove Albion fan for his whole life and his grandfather was vice-chairman of the club in the 1970s. He became chairman himself in 2009, and built the club into one of the most admired and sensibly run institutions in the football world.

Bloom gained the nickname 'The Lizard' from his time as a professional gambler and poker player, because of how cold his blood appeared to run when it came to high-pressure moments. He made his fortune from gambling, having discovered a system that allowed him and his colleagues to identify and take advantage of undervalued odds, mainly in Asian sports betting markets.

From that lucrative business, Bloom begat another home-town owner. Matthew Benham worked as a hedge fund manager in the City of London before entering the world of sports betting when he joined Bloom's company Premier Bet in 2001. There was an acrimonious split in 2004 when Benham left to strike out on his own and the following year he became involved in Brentford, who he had supported as a boy, after reading in a newspaper that they needed investment.

By 2012 he had taken over the club entirely. At that point they were in League One, but gradually over the next decade he implemented similar methods to Brighton, a data-heavy approach taking them up the pyramid until they finally won promotion to the Premier League in 2021. Benham also became the majority shareholder of Danish side FC Midtjylland in 2014, whose approach also brought success in the form of three Danish titles and various appearances in European competitions. Benham sold his shares in Midtjylland in 2023.

Luton would have been a third club, had they avoided relegation, as their majority shareholder is local businessman Paul Ballantyne, who is not enormously wealthy and tends to keep a much lower profile than many owners. But that's it.

The men who took over Tottenham Hotspur in 2001 – Daniel Levy and Joe Lewis – are English, but you would struggle to describe them as a cuddly story of local boys running their local club for the benefit of the local community, given that the ultimate owners are ENIC, a Bahamas-based investment group. Since Lewis was arrested in 2023 on charges of insider trading, which he later admitted and was fined £5 million, Tottenham have been very keen to point out that he is personally no longer involved in the running of the club.

Steve Parish still holds 10 per cent of Crystal Palace, but the rest of the club is owned by American investors Josh Harris, David Blitzer and John Textor. Although, at the time this book went to press, Textor was doing his best to sell his stake. David Sullivan and the family of the late David Gold still hold around 64 per cent of West Ham United, although in 2021 the Czech businessmen Daniel Kretinsky and Pavel Horsky acquired 27 per cent of the club.

And then there's Sir Jim Ratcliffe, who through his company INEOS executed one of the more unusual 'takeover' bids of recent years, acquiring 25 per cent of his boyhood team Manchester United, which included being granted control of the football side of the club. That's a strange thing to contemplate: if you were to tell someone from 1992 this fact, they might quite reasonably ask 'what are the people who have the other 75 per cent doing then?'

But that deal encapsulated perfectly the attitude of the Glazer family to United, following their takeover in 2005. That transaction taught most football supporters the meaning of a leveraged buyout – the method of taking over a company by borrowing money against that company and transferring the debt onto it after the takeover is complete – something most of us had been blissfully unaware of before. In the nearly two decades since probably the most unpopular takeover in modern football history, they have taken an estimated £1.1 billion out of United, mostly in staggering amounts of interest on their initial loans to buy a previously debt-free club.

Ratcliffe's presence is a nod to some sort of local connection, but beyond that they are few and far between. United are one of ten Premier League teams either owned by or significantly controlled by Americans. Stan Kroenke added Arsenal to his portfolio of sports teams by initially buying shares in 2007 and incrementally increasing his stake until completing a full purchase of all the club's shares in 2018.

Chelsea are officially owned by the consortium Blue Co, but are effectively controlled by the American businessman Todd Boehly. Shahid Khan, the Pakistani-American businessman from Florida known by some as 'the tash with the cash' because of his elaborate facial hair and deep pockets, took over Fulham in 2013. Wes Edens, hailing from Montana, co-owns Aston Villa with the Egyptian billionaire Nassef Sawiris. There's also Liverpool, owned since 2012 by Fenway Sports Group, the American consortium of investors that also count the Boston Red Sox and the Pittsburgh Penguins as part of their portfolio.

And then of course there are the nation states. Officially Manchester City are not owned by Abu Dhabi, one of the seven emirates that comprise the United Arab Emirates (UAE), and officially Newcastle United are not owned by Saudi Arabia. But you have to be either astonishingly naive or the Premier League not to recognise who controls these clubs and why.

To summarise, at the start of the 2024/25 season investment groups, consortia or financial speculators of some kind either wholly owned or had significant stakes in 12 of the 20 clubs in the Premier League. Fifteen were owned by people who also held significant stakes in other sports teams. At a push, three – four if you want to throw Ratcliffe in – were owned by people who either supported the clubs or had some form of previous connection with them.

The most frequent industry from which these owners came was finance, in some form, be that investment banking, asset management or hedge funds – things that, if you were to ask the average person on the street to explain the difference between, they might struggle. Other sources of money include real estate, oil, shipping and cars.

As of early 2024, there were no butchers or paint dealers in charge of a Premier League football club.

———

Beyond the stark divergence in their fortunes, the other reason for the comparison between Manchester City and Bury is that it raises an interesting – conceptual, perhaps unanswerable – question: what makes a good football club owner?

It's a surprisingly difficult one to answer. Identifying a bad owner is easy: Bury's financial problems were significant before businessman Steve Dale bought them for a symbolic £1 in 2018, but he was the man responsible for failing to pay players and staff on multiple occasions, the man who was unable to pay the club's tax bill and was ultimately the man at the helm when the club, formed in 1885 by the merger of two local church teams, was expelled from the Football League.

But while the comparison between them and City suggests a clear dichotomy, the placing of the obvious bad next to the obvious good, in reality their situation provides a perfect example of why it's so difficult to properly put your finger on the qualities that makes a club owner 'good'.

For City and most of their fans, the arrival of Sheikh Mansour did not just transform them from a team that was capable of tumbling into the third division to one that reached the summit of the game, but it erased a lifelong existential crisis, the slightly nebulous concept of 'typical City' or 'Cityitis' – the idea that, no matter how well things were going, City would find some way to stuff it up. Under his ownership, which brought with it Pep Guardiola, impeccable infrastructure, some of the best players on the planet and pretty much the smartest people in the football world to run things behind the scenes, they have become an almost unstoppable winning machine, mercilessly rampaging their way to just about every trophy going.

But the question of whether Sheikh Mansour's ownership of City is 'good' in a broader sense is much stickier. Is it 'good' for a single football club to have spent north of £2 billion on players since 2008, skewing the competition and contributing to the vast inflation of transfers and wages? Is it 'good' that this money – combined with significant expertise and skill – has made them so dominant in English football? Is it 'good' that a nation state owns a football club that should be a community institution? Is it 'good' that the nation state in question criminalises same-sex relations, and that City are an undeniable part of distracting from that?

What is more certain is that football club owners have never been so prominent. While we shouldn't get dragged into a whirl of pointless nostalgia for a time that never existed, pretending that the people who ran our football teams in the past did so for the pure love of the game, there was a time when you probably didn't know who owned most football clubs. You probably knew who the chairman of your team was, and you might vaguely have known a few of the more media-friendly chairmen from other clubs, but it was significantly less important.

As far as the casual fan was concerned, the manager of the first team was the person in charge, while the chairman sat upstairs and occasionally signed cheques. Things have changed significantly: today, the people who own our football clubs have never been so prominent and important.

They have the power to turn clubs into the champions of the world, and they have the power to make clubs disappear completely. They have the power to influence geopolitical events and they have the power to make world leaders jump at will. They control football in a way that is unprecedented in the history of the game.

Who Owns Football? will look at how things used to be, from the very start of organised football to the present day. It will look at some of the many different types of owners, and the many different ownership models, considering the strengths and weaknesses of them all. It will consider the consequences of football club ownership; what happens in the real world when something goes wrong. It will look at the strangest tales from down the years of football club ownership; how dictators and warlords have used the game for their own ends.

It will look to the future: what will football ownership look like in five, ten, 15 years' time? Will greater regulation help or harm the game, or will it make no difference at all? And finally it will try, as much as possible, to answer that thorny question: what does a good football club owner look like?

1

A BRIEF HISTORY OF ENGLISH FOOTBALL CLUB OWNERSHIP

'There used to be a football club over there.'
KEITH BURKINSHAW,
FORMER TOTTENHAM HOTSPUR MANAGER

There is a temptation to think of football in the past as a utopian time, of Corinthian spirit when the idea of money or business was alien and everyone was just playing for the love of the game.

Which is true to a point. Most of the very earliest clubs, formed in the mid-1800s, were works teams, or set up around a religious institution of some description, an arm of a broader athletics club designed to make the youngsters of the Victorian day more active. Most of these early clubs weren't really 'owned' by any one person, as such: that would imply there was a significant and robust structure to them, rather than essentially being loose associations of subs-paying members who would gather to play sport.

However, the popularity of football meant that it wasn't long before these nascent clubs became structured like any other company. Because more and more people were showing up to watch these teams play, they needed stadiums to house them all, but stadiums cost money and, as is often the case for anyone who wants a new shiny thing and wants it now, they had to borrow that money.

The problem was that because these clubs were all member associations, if the projects went south and the money couldn't be repaid, the members themselves would be personally liable for it, which most people at the time filed under 'not ideal'. Luckily for them, in 1855 the Limited Liability Act had been passed, which basically meant that if a company was structured in the correct way then that entity would be liable for any debts, rather than the individuals who ran it.

Birmingham City – at the time known as Small Heath Alliance – were the first football club to become a limited liability company, complete with a board of directors and a chairman, in 1888, followed quickly by Newcastle United, Liverpool, Everton, Middlesbrough and Notts County. Over the next 40 or so years almost every club in England went the same way: the only holdout, as Stefan Szymanski points out in his book *Money And Football: A Soccernomics Guide*, was Nottingham Forest, who joined the gang in the implausibly late year of 1982. Which means they won both the league title and two European Cups under Brian Clough, as well as being the first English club to pay £1 million for a player when they bought Trevor Francis, while they were effectively a Victorian sporting association run like a local squash club.

While the early days of the game are slightly murky and it's a bit difficult to properly tell who did what, you could probably make an argument that William McGregor was the first ever 'owner' of a football club, as we would understand it today.

McGregor was a Scottish draper who moved to Birmingham in 1870 and not long afterwards became involved with the nascent Aston Villa, becoming a member of their committee in 1877 and eventually their chairman. McGregor would become notable for a few things, not least being the man who chose the lion which adorns Villa's badge to this day. He was also a teetotaller, who was shocked at the drinking habits of some of the club's players, so formed a sort of coffee club to encourage them to keep the boozing in check a little. He was also among the first chairmen to admit that his players were being paid, as pearls were clutched among the naive souls who still believed everyone was just playing for the love of it all.

At that time the only regular, organised, national football competition was the FA Cup: otherwise fixtures were rather ad hoc – or, to put it another way, completely unreliable. Frustrated at this, McGregor proposed a more formalised competition, where teams would play each other home and away, and points would be awarded for draws and wins. Thus, in April 1888, the Football League was formed, with McGregor its first president and Villa being one of the founder members along with Bolton Wanderers, Notts County, Preston North End, Stoke City, West Bromwich Albion, Wolverhampton Wanderers, Accrington, Burnley, Derby County, Blackburn Rovers and Everton.

At that stage Everton played their games at Anfield, presided over by chairman John Houlding, a Conservative politician and brewer who owned the ground. After the club won its first league title in 1891, a delegation from the Everton board asked Houlding for a long-term lease on the site, to which Houlding responded by increasing the rent.

This, perhaps unsurprisingly, did not go down particularly well, and at a meeting of Everton's 279 members, Houlding was kicked out, so the club sought a new place to call their own, settling on Goodison Park at the other side of Stanley Park. In his book about Liverpool *Red Men Reborn*, John Williams wrote that Houlding claimed that it was not his business plans for Everton but the 'teetotal fanaticism of his political opponents that had forced these actions and produced the split.'

This presented Houlding with a small predicament: he had a football ground but no football club to play on it. So, necessity being the mother of invention, the Liverpool Football Club and Athletic Grounds Company Limited was formed in 1892, by Houlding and a few loyalists – including former Everton manager William Barclay. This is another thing worth remembering when gazing back through time to the early days of football yearning for a more innocent time: perhaps the most romanticised club in England was formed because the owner tried to gouge his original club for rent.

And it wasn't the only example of this, which brings us to Joseph and Gus Mears, a pair of property developers in west London around the turn of the 20th century. Theirs is a story of land speculation and how the birth of two of the biggest clubs in the world can be traced back to a possibly apocryphal story of a dog biting a man on the leg in 1904.

The Mears brothers had bought what they thought could be an extremely valuable plot of land in west London, near to the relatively newly developed District Line and the station at Putney Bridge. The site had been home to the London Athletic Club from 1877, but their lease ran out in 1904 so the brothers Mears swooped and bought the freehold.

They also bought a plot of land next to the old club, leading to fears locally that they had other plans for the site, beyond sporting use. Perhaps they would build housing in what was becoming increasingly valuable land, or rent it to the Great Western Railway company to build a coal yard there.

However, so the story goes, that dog changed everything. A friend of Gus, businessman and sporting enthusiast Frederick Parker, was trying to persuade his associate to continue using the site for sporting purposes during an evening stroll. He wasn't doing particularly well and, while the history books don't record whether it was this weak argument that caused Mears's pooch to sink his teeth into Parker's leg, sink his teeth the hound did.

Legend has it that Parker, despite having a chunk taken from his leg, which perhaps should have required immediate medical attention, reacted rather coolly, prompting an impressed Mears to say: 'You took that bite damned well; most men would have kicked up hell about it.' And then, having reconsidered Parker's arguments in light of his reaction to recent, canine-related events, he continued: 'Meet me here at nine tomorrow and we'll get busy.'

Who knows how true that story actually is. But what certainly is true is that the Mears brothers employed Archibald Leitch, the Scottish architect who would go on to design at least part of most major football grounds in the UK over the following 40 years, to build them a sports venue that would be the envy of the world.

And he delivered: the venue not only had a grandstand for 6,000 spectators and terraces that took the capacity to north of 100,000, but also a running track and a banked cycling track, essentially making it a football ground, an athletics venue and a velodrome in one.

It cost £100,000 (an extraordinary sum at the time: around £10 million in 2024's money), but it would be worth it. Mears planned to hold athletics events there in the summer, just as there had been at the old venue, so all he needed to do was find a football club to play there in the winter.

And as there was a football club just down the road, he had the ideal candidates. However, Henry Norris, chairman of nearby Fulham, baulked at paying the £1,500 annual rent for Stamford Bridge and chose to redevelop Craven Cottage (using Leitch as the chief architect) instead.

So, rather than cast around much further, Mears simply decided to form his own club to play at this gleaming new coliseum. On 10 March 1905, a meeting held in the Rising Sun pub (located just over the road from Stamford Bridge, where it stands to this day, now named the Butcher's Hook) saw the establishment of Chelsea FC.

Gus passed away in 1912, but his brother Joseph took the reins, and both his son Joe and grandson Brian would have spells as chairmen. The club would stay within the Mears family until 1982, when Ken Bates bought it for a nominal £1.

As for Norris, the man who turned down the chance to play at the Bridge, he had bigger things on his mind. Norris had made his fortune as a property developer in west London: the chances are that if you wander around that part of town and see a building that hails from the late 1800s, Norris probably built it.

Norris was known not just for his wealth but, for want of a more elegant phrase, being bloody terrifying. 'Standing at well over six feet tall, invariably with a pipe stuffed into his mouth, he dwarfed his rivals both literally and metaphorically,' wrote Jon Spurling in his book *Rebels for the Cause.* 'Immaculately turned out in a trench-coat, crisply starched white shirt and bowler hat, he would glare demoniacally at them through his pince-nez.'

He combined this physical intimidation with a silver tongue and charisma that got him out of many a sticky situation, and also into the boardroom of a club way on the other side of London. From 1910, Norris and his business partner William Hall had started to buy up shares in Woolwich Arsenal, the club formed as Dial Square by workers at the Royal Arsenal armaments factory in Woolwich, which had fallen on hard times.

By 1912 he and Hall had gathered enough of a holding in the club to suggest some minor changes, such as merging with Fulham, to create some sort of pan-London super club. That idea was blocked by the Football League, but Norris was set on the idea that Woolwich Arsenal needed to move, preferably to a place with a greater population than Woolwich, at the time an outpost in Kent. There were even dark rumours that he stopped spending money on the team to deliberately make them worse, to quell any local enthusiasm for the team and thus opposition to their departure. It worked in one respect, which is to say Arsenal were relegated in 1912/13 having won just three league games all season, but if he hoped nobody would care when he proposed that the club moved to a few acres of land he had found in Highbury, north London, he was disappointed.

The opposition to the relocation was fierce, not just from the residents they were leaving but the ones they were joining, with the local population of Islington not delighted about the idea of more footballing ruffians showing up in their manor. *The Tottenham Herald* urged locals not to go and watch 'Norris's Woolwich interlopers' who had 'no right to be here.'

Predictably, the other established clubs in the area were most vexed too: Chelsea, Tottenham and Leyton Orient (then known as Clapton Orient) all made representations to the FA, but, by happy coincidence, the committee that convened to assess the move featured a number of Norris's friends and it was waved through. Another acquaintance of Norris also proved useful: the land that would eventually house the Arsenal Stadium was owned by the

Church of England and, while there was plenty of ecclesiastical opposition to the plans, this is where being chums with the Archbishop of Canterbury paid off handsomely, and the sale was approved by the highest authority. Well, almost the highest: Norris knew plenty of powerful people, but there's no suggestion that God became directly involved in the switch.

All of which might have been for naught, were it not for the infamous incident in 1919 that saw Arsenal 'promoted' to Division One. They had failed to escape the second tier in either of the two seasons they played at their new Highbury home and then football was suspended after the 1914/15 season because of the First World War, a season in which Arsenal finished fifth and thus, in theory, had not won promotion on merit.

Upon the resumption of the game in 1919, it was decided that the top tier would be expanded from 20 to 22 teams. The assumption was that Tottenham, who had finished bottom in the last pre-war season, would be given a reprieve and the top two in the Second Division would go up. But instead it was suggested that candidates should put their arguments forward to the league and clubs would be nominated for promotion on that basis.

This was where Norris, recently both knighted and elected as a Conservative MP, really thrived. He quite aggressively put forward Arsenal's case, lobbying the FA management committee (apart from the Tottenham directors), suggesting that away trips to London were more appealing than visits to the provinces (Birmingham and Barnsley were among the other candidates), plus that Arsenal should be rewarded for their long service to the league (ignoring that Wolves had been around longer).

There was also talk, never entirely proven, that money and even a house changed hands, along with a variety of other under-the-counter dealings, to ensure the vote not only went Arsenal's way, but did so at the expense of Tottenham. The Gunners were duly elected to the First Division and Spurs dropped into the second tier, where they only stayed for a year, but the irritation turned into hatred and the rivalry that continues to this day.

All of which is a roundabout way of saying: yes, there may well be some unsavoury characters in charge of football clubs now, but don't go thinking the past was a time of pure and upstanding moral characters.

Take Manchester United, and the tale of another ducker and diver, and another dog. Most will know that United started life as Newton Heath in the 1870s and eventually became Manchester United in 1902. They were in financial trouble, about to go out of existence in fact, but the story goes that the dog of the club captain Harry Stafford, Major, found its way to the home of John Henry Davies, a local brewer. The return of the hound led to him being made aware of the club's plight and he invested £500, with three friends putting in the same, to save the club under Davies's stewardship.

After Davies died in 1927, the club was again in financial strife until a textile merchant named James Gibson took over, and the club would remain in his control until his own death in 1951, a few years after he made what turned out to be the pretty decent decision to appoint Matt Busby as manager. Gibson's shares remained in his family, with his wife Violet, although according to Jim White in his book *Manchester United: The Biography*, she kept the share certificates in a draw 'seemingly unaware that they held much in the way of value beyond sentiment.' However there remained some Gibson influence on the club with James's son Alan, who became a director after his father passed away.

By that time though, another family were effectively in control of the club. Louis Edwards ran a successful meat packaging business that he and his brother had inherited from his father, but perhaps more importantly had become friends with Busby not long after the manager arrived at United. Busby had lobbied for some time for Edwards to be added to the United board, but his efforts faced resistance from some of the more conservative directors, not in love with the idea of bringing a man known as 'Champagne Louis' into their fold.

Extraordinarily, the meeting at which Edwards was elected was held the day after the Munich air disaster in 1958, with the then chairman Harold Hartman seemingly such a stickler for procedure that he decided the meeting must go ahead, despite what had happened. Indeed, Edwards could have been among the victims: he was offered a place on the plane, but as he was not yet officially part of the club, he decided it would be inappropriate.

Edwards by that stage had begun buying up shares in the club, via a method that required a little more shoe leather than today: he would find out who held shares – at that point not so much a financial investment as a sort of community certificate, like part-owning the local allotment – and dispatch an underling named James Smart to their houses. Smart would knock on doors and offer people an apparently generous-seeming premium for their shares, given that most people basically deemed them worthless. In reality Edwards had taken advantage of a collective naivety and was on his way to controlling the club for a relative pittance, eventually becoming chairman in 1965.

If there's anything that sums up how different the owners of England's top clubs were, compared with today, where most have made their money in financial services of some description, it's perhaps the prevalence of butchers. Another was one of the most notorious owners of the 20th century: Bob Lord, who controlled Burnley as chairman from 1955 until a couple of months before his death in 1981. Lord made his money in the meat business, starting out as a butcher's apprentice, but after being denied a pay rise, he displayed some of the ruthless streak that would define his later years at Turf Moor. Lord went out on his own, selling meat on the street and undercutting his former employer, to the point that once he had earned enough money, he went back to that former employer and demanded that he sell him his shop. The employer acquiesced, even though Lord was only 20 and at the time a year too young to legally own property. It thus started Lord's mini-empire of butchers' shops, which would eventually earn him enough money and local fame to take a seat on the Burnley board in 1950, with the chairmanship following five years later.

His early years were wildly successful: Lord appointed manager Harry Potts in 1958 and placed huge emphasis on their youth policy, the club becoming something of a production line for talent. More importantly, they were successful: Burnley won the Division One title in 1960, reached the quarter-finals of the European Cup in 1961 and got to the FA Cup final in 1962. For a club that had won the title in 1921 but had been pretty mediocre in the intervening years, these were the glory days.

But rather than the man who brought success to this relatively modest Lancashire club, Lord is mainly remembered as one of the first truly notorious club owners.

'He upset people in droves,' wrote Dave Thomas and Mike Smith in their biography *Bob Lord Of Burnley*. 'Sports journalists, club chairmen, managers, players, officials, referees, fans, committees, and football authorities. Then there were the politicians, television personalities, religions and even entire nations. The list was endless.'

In some respects Lord was extremely progressive. He argued in favour of the abolition of the maximum wage, having listened to a delegation of players who made their case to him. He also advocated the introduction of professional referees in the mid-1960s, some 40 years before they were actually brought in.

But in other respects he, erm, very much was not. He was aggressively opposed to football on Sundays, saying in 1970 that 'If it happens I shall get out of football altogether.' He also strongly advocated against televised football, banning the BBC from Turf Moor when *Match of the Day* started in 1964 because he believed it would harm gate receipts. At least, that was the reason he said he opposed it, but in reality there might have been a more objectionable motivation, vocalised when he said in a speech at a dinner in 1974: 'We have to stand up against a move to get soccer on the cheap, by the Jews who run television.'

Lord was nicknamed the 'Khrushchev of Burnley' for his autocratic tendencies, something exemplified by his habit of banning journalists from Turf Moor if they had written, said or nodded their head in a way that indicated something that he disapproved of. This included Jimmy McIlroy, at the time a correspondent for the *Lancashire Evening Telegraph*, but who was also arguably Burnley's greatest ever player, the key man in their 1960 title win and who has a stand named after him to this day. A group of banned journalists knocked up an exclusive range of ties that bore the legend 'Banned by Burnley.'

Not that he thought of himself as a tyrant, of course, saying in a 1961 interview with *The Guardian*: 'How can I be a dictator? Do you know I never vote at a board meeting? I'm just the captain of the directors. I just advise. Do you know we have our differences but everybody says what he thinks. I don't try to stop 'em. Why am I always in the papers? Because I believe in what I say and think. Too many folk believe in things and won't say so for fear of treading on someone's corns.'

Lord stood out partly because of what he said, but partly because he said anything at all. Chairmen in the days when he first arrived in the game tended to be more demure, unlikely to give interviews to the press and even more unlikely to say anything outrageous in them.

He arguably paved the way for another generation of owners who were more publicly prominent. Like Ken Bates, for example. Bates is mainly known as the man who bought Chelsea for £1 in 1982, threatened to install electrified fences at Stamford Bridge to keep 'hooligans' off the pitch and trumpeted the idea of the 'Chelsea Village' leisure complex, which he promised would provide riches for the club, but, well, didn't.

But Chelsea were the second club he stewarded, having cut his teeth at Oldham Athletic in the 1960s. Bates, a Londoner who had made his money in an assortment of ventures, including land deals in South Africa, property in the Caribbean and quarries in England, became Oldham chairman in 1965, when the club was at something of a low ebb, and was one of the first men to actively seek out the ownership of a club with whom he had no previous connection.

'He is a football fan who decided he would like to see what he could do with a crumbling football club if he had charge of it,' wrote Arthur Hopcraft in his book *The Football Man*. 'He chose Oldham because he took a careful look at the field, just as he might in considering the takeover of a string of shoe shops, and decided it was the only available club with the potential to match his ambition. It was business pragmatism applied to the choosing of a new hobby.'

Bates, even then, was keen to stress the commercial imperatives, arguing that while the football was the most important thing, clubs had to generate as much revenue as possible to facilitate it. 'It is money in the end which makes success,' he argued.

Ultimately he didn't generate much success, Oldham being relegated to the Fourth Division in the final season of his tenure. He had a short spell at Wigan Athletic, before arriving at Chelsea, promising to clear their debts and turn them back into the glamorous club they once were, something that he would certainly argue he did. Bates's record at Stamford Bridge was mixed and his popularity even more so: you could make a reasonable argument that his most significant contribution to Chelsea, and indeed football, was the meeting he took with a Russian businessman he'd never previously heard of in the summer of 2003.

We shouldn't necessarily regard Roman Abramovich's purchase of Chelsea as the moment that money changed football, or indeed football ownership. People who aren't footballers have been making money out of football since the very start, but it was arguably a decision in 1981 that set things down the current path. Until that year, football clubs were not allowed to pay their directors a salary and dividends were capped at 7.5 per cent of the value of their shares. A director could sell their shares and in theory make a profit, but as a rule football clubs weren't viewed as vehicles to generate money: they were, broadly speaking, run as football clubs.

But the rules were relaxed, upping the dividend limit to 15 per cent and allowing directors to be paid. Being on the board of a football club now looked a little more appealing from a financial perspective and that was taken a step further by Tottenham Hotspur in 1983, when they became the first major football club to be floated on the Stock Exchange.

It all started when Irving Scholar, a lifelong fan and Monaco-based property developer, visited White Hart Lane in 1981, ostensibly to peruse plans for the executive boxes in the soon-to-be-built new West Stand. However, he quickly got the impression that this new project was going to saddle the club with millions of pounds of debt, which he thought could be disastrous for both the team and the club, so he quietly began buying up as many shares as he could to get on the inside. By the end of 1982 he had purchased a controlling stake in the club and, because some of the existing board were hostile to him, he installed Douglas Alexiou, the son-in-law of former chairman Sidney Wale, as the new chairman.

The plan was therefore set in motion to raise money, initially to pay for that West Stand – which cost around £4 million – by floating the club, the problem being that despite the relaxation of the rules, they were still hampered by FA regulations. Their solution was simple enough: they formed a holding company – Tottenham Hotspur PLC – of which the football club would be a subsidiary, the club board becoming the board of the holding company. The shares were put to the market at £1.08 each and, according to those involved, they could have sold them four times over. 'Spurs will be showing the lead about the way football should be run and financed in the future,' said Alexiou at the time. 'The present structure of the game is completely outdated and Victorian.'

The Guardian, in one of those quaint turns of phrase that is easy to laugh at in hindsight, speculated that, 'It would not be stretching the imagination too far to see a future takeover bid being made for Tottenham by an industrial giant like ICI or BP.' The club announced the whole thing with a publicity photo of Ossie Ardiles, Garth Crooks and Danny Thomas holding a copy of the *Financial Times*, wearing suits and bowler hats.

Scholar was, to say the least, not especially popular among Spurs fans for many reasons: the commercialisation of football for one, selling to Alan Sugar years later another, but also for the perception that he forced out Keith Burkinshaw, club hero and the manager who had just overseen victory in the 1984 UEFA Cup final.

Burkinshaw left that summer and, the story goes, remarked to the waiting press outside the brand new West Stand: 'There used to be a football club over there.'

Scholar will also be confined to many 'traditional' football fans' personal Room 101s because of his involvement in the foundation of the Premier League, another staging post on the journey to football's explosion into rampant commercialism and telephone-number transfer fees.

He was one of the 'big five' chairmen – along with Manchester United's Martin Edwards, Liverpool's Noel White, Arsenal's David Dein and Everton's Philip Carter – who met Greg Dyke, at that point head of ITV Sport, in 1990 to thrash out the idea that the Football League had simply become too small for these exponentially growing clubs, and that something bigger and more lucrative could be on the horizon.

It took a few years, and the confluence of a variety of factors – the boom in the popularity of football following the 1990 World Cup, the introduction of all-seater stadiums and the decrease of the worst elements of terrace hooliganism – for the whole thing to get started. The FA were on board, at least in part because they were in conflict with the Football League, so having the biggest clubs in the country break away was OK by them. Saatchi and Saatchi were hired to map out what this new league might look like and, after a meeting at the FA, the owners were empowered to basically do what they liked.

The role of Sugar in the whole thing has gone down in legend too. When the live TV rights to this new Premier League were put out for tender, there were two contenders: ITV and BSkyB. ITV's bid looked pretty strong at £262 million but Sugar, whose company Amstrad supplied the satellite dishes that helped beam Sky Sports into people's homes, supposedly instructed Rupert Murdoch to 'blow them out of the water' with a bigger bid. They offered £304million, ITV were duly propelled onto dry land and the 'whole new ball game' began.

That Sugar was there to make that call represents one of the bigger sliding doors moments in English football. When Scholar eventually sold Tottenham, in 1991, he had a couple of potential buyers: Sugar, or Robert Maxwell, the proprietor of the *Daily Mirror* who already had his fingers in the footballing pie in the shape of first Oxford United, and then Derby County.

Maxwell left a few lasting impressions on society before his mysterious death in 1991, but his most notorious contribution to football was the attempt to merge Oxford with Reading in 1984 to form a team that would have been known as Thames Valley Royals. Maxwell announced this wizard wheeze out of the blue, shortly before the end of the 1983/84 season, applying the logic of a ruthless businessman: here were two entities, who in his view were failing financially, so the best thing to do was to merge them.

It works with steel companies or supermarkets, the difference being that the customers of Tesco wouldn't necessarily stage a sit-in if they announced they would be merging with Asda. But that's what Oxford fans did, ahead of their game against Wigan, with around 2,000 fans plonking themselves down on the pitch, delaying kick-off and chanting 'Judas' at their benefactor. Maxwell was not dissuaded and pressed on with the plan, amid more protests by fans of both clubs, and agreed a deal to combine the clubs with Reading chairman Frank Waller.

However, the whole thing was scuppered by Reading director Roy Tranter and their former player Roger Smee, who took out a High Court injunction that would forbid the sale of some of the shares Maxwell would require to complete his takeover. Maxwell was initially belligerent, calling the legal moves a 'side show', but he was ultimately unsuccessful and the two clubs remained separate entities.

Maxwell did leave one other legacy. He didn't actually like football hugely, but even in the 1980s recognised its power and influence, so kept trying to expand his portfolio. He attempted to buy Manchester United in 1984, but didn't come up with the asking price demanded by Martin Edwards, and there was also his run at Spurs in 1989. He was successful in buying Derby in 1987, adding them to Oxford and the 19 per cent of Reading he still kept after the merger failed, but it was his attempt to buy Watford as well that prompted the Football League to bring in a new rule that no one owner could also hold more than two per cent of another club at the same time.

Around the time that Maxwell was failing to gain significant influence over a club that he had little previous connection to, another man was making his first moves towards gaining control of a club he had plenty of history with.

Jack Walker had inherited Walkersteel, a sheet metal business in Lancashire, from his father in 1951 and over the subsequent 40 years had turned it into the biggest provider of steel in the UK. Through that and other business dealings, Walker was an extremely wealthy man by the late 1980s and put his money into two things: an airline called Jersey European Airways, which eventually became Flybe, and Blackburn Rovers.

Walker operated on a different level entirely from the wealthy benefactors that came before him. Walker gained full control of Rovers in 1990, but had been financing signings since well before that, most notably stumping up for the wages of Ossie Ardiles, who slightly implausibly signed for the then Second Division Rovers in 1988.

Colin Hendry and Alan Wright were among the early recruits, and in 1991 they paid their first ever £1 million-plus fee for Mike Newell. By this point Kenny Dalglish, eight months removed from resigning as Liverpool manager, had taken over and led them to promotion (just, via the play-offs) from the second tier, just in time for that first Premier League season, after which the spending really started.

Dalglish was essentially given a blank cheque: they tried to sign Gary Lineker and Roy Keane, Alan Shearer arrived for a then-record £3.6 million, and after they finished fourth and then second, Chris Sutton came in for £5 million and helped them win the title in 1994/95, pipping Manchester United on the final day. The Premier League had been won – or in the minds of many, bought – and the established powers challenged, in perhaps the first real, high-profile indication that a wealthy owner could really take a team from the depths (in their case, near relegation from the Second Division) to the very top in a few short years.

And yet, the figures that Walker was prepared to spend on his team look rather quaint next to the amounts that would come later, in particular after that meeting between Bates and Abramovich at the Dorchester Hotel in London, where the sale of Chelsea was agreed.

And after that, everything changed.

2

INTERNATIONAL RELATIONS: STATE OWNERSHIP

'Newcastle fans haven't chosen to be political and if they don't want to be, it's ok, it's fine. The thing is that they've been used as a political tool. The person who owns their club now is also the one who tortured my sisters.'

LINA AL-HATHLOUL,
SAUDI-BORN HUMAN RIGHTS ACTIVIST

The title of this chapter contains a lie.

There aren't any state-owned football clubs. We know because it says so in the many guarantees given to various authorities by those clubs.

Manchester City are owned by City Football Group, which was established in 2013 and in turn has three different stakeholders. One per cent of CFG is held by CITIC Group, an investment vehicle owned by the government of China. Eighteen per cent is owned by Silver Lake, an American venture capital collective that also has significant stakes in Airbnb, Expedia and Klarna. The remaining 81 per cent is in the hands of Abu Dhabi United Group for Development and Investment, which is a private equity company based in the United Arab Emirates. It in turn is wholly owned by Sheikh Mansour, bin Zayed Al Nahyan, at the time of writing vice president of the UAE and brother of the president, as well as being part of the Abu Dhabi royal family.

It is separate from the Abu Dhabi government.

Newcastle United are owned by three different stakeholders. RB Sports and Media, the investment vehicle of David and Simon Reuben, hold ten per cent. PCP Capital Partners, a company controlled by British businesswoman Amanda Staveley, has another ten per cent. The other 80 per cent is the property of the Public Investment Fund of Saudi Arabia, which is controlled by Crown Prince Mohammed bin Salman, the ruler of Saudi Arabia, as well as Yasir Al-Rumayyan, who serves as the club's chairman as well as the chair of Aramco, the Saudi state-owned petroleum group.

It is separate from the Saudi government.

Paris St-Germain are owned by two different stakeholders. 12.5 per cent is held by Arctos Partners, which is an American investment group 'dedicated to the professional sports industry.' The other 87.5 per cent is held by Qatar Sports Investments, whose chairman is Nasser Al-Khelaifi and is a group established in 2005 by the Emir of Qatar, Tamim bin Hamad Al Thani.

It is separate from the Qatari government.

All of the above is technically true. So technically, these three clubs are not owned by these three states. It says so in the many guarantees given to various authorities by those clubs.

It's January 2024 and the meeting of the European Club Association board is being held in Doha. Geography buffs will have no doubt spotted that Doha is not in Europe, so you might conclude it is thus an odd place to hold such a conference.

Well, yes and no. The meeting was hosted, in more than one respect, by the chairman of the ECA, Nasser Al-Khelaifi, also chairman of Qatar Sports Investments and also therefore the chairman of Paris Saint-Germain.

Occasionally we all think that we would like to live the life of someone in a position of power and influence. The wealth, the travel, the luxuries, the ability to send a dozen people scampering with the flick of an eye.

But if you spend any time watching them at close quarters, there's a good chance you'll change your mind. Al-Khelaifi at times resembles the bird that chooses which direction the flock is going to fly: when he moves, everyone else seems to follow him. You see the commotion before you see the man, a hubbub followed by this slight, ostensibly quite unassuming man, initially dressed in a suit, but who later changes into a thobe, the traditional white robe worn by Arab men. He doesn't have a particularly big retinue, or at least not one that is immediately obvious, but the room seems to move around him.

Everyone wants a little of Al-Khelaifi's time. Fellow executives; assistants; ECA officials; local media; international media; a guy who just walks past the room in which the meeting is held and sticks his head in to see who's there; authors of books on football club ownership. He has that dual quality that many in his position have: when he's on the move, shifting from meeting A to glad-handing opportunity B, he looks straight through you, not in an outwardly rude or unpleasant way but in a fashion that ensures he can move to the next thing without being slowed down excessively.

Yet when he stops, he has that ability to make whoever he's talking to feel like they have his absolute attention: the firm handshake, perhaps the other hand on your elbow, maybe even a hug if he knows you. It's not an uncommon characteristic for those in powerful positions, and indeed it is one that most people who spend their lives talking to people – either trying to persuade having someone to do something, or someone trying to persuade them to do something – have. It looks, to be frank, like an absolutely exhausting existence.

Nasser bin Ghanim Al-Khelaifi was born in 1973 into a moderate, by economic standards at least, Qatari family. He grew up in a house near what was, at the time, the only tennis centre in Doha and started to play seriously after going for a job there as a ball boy. He turned professional in 1992, and while he would give you or I a good thrashing, in the wider scheme of things he wasn't an especially good player: his highest world ranking was 995 and he only played two games on the ATP main tour, losing both.

But for Al-Khelaifi the real trophy was the friends he made along the way. When Al-Khelaifi was 14 he met and started playing tennis with an eight-year-old boy, with whom he would go on to form a lifelong friendship. That boy is now better known as Sheikh Tamim bin Hamad Al Thani – and even better known as the Emir of Qatar, who has since 2013 been the state's ruler.

After Al-Khelaifi retired from tennis, he worked for the Qatar Investment Authority, formed in 2005 to do something with the vast piles of wealth that were accumulating from the state's oil and gas reserves, and the parent company of Qatar Sports Investments. Al-Khelaifi was instrumental in the growth of what was then known as Al Jazeera Sports, a spin-off of the Qatar-based news network Al Jazeera, which would later be relaunched as beIN SPORTS and holds the rights to broadcast just about every football league you can think of to the MENA (Middle East and North Africa) region.

It was in 2011 that the big push was on: Qatar won the rights to host the 2022 World Cup and Al-Khelaifi was named chairman of QSI shortly before they purchased PSG. As part of this role he is also chairman of beIN (although these days he is nowhere near as involved in the actual running of the network as he used to be), overseeing the acquisition of Turkish TV station Digiturk in 2015 and in 2016 the purchase of a 51 per cent stake in Miramax, the American film production company.

He is also involved in the administration of tennis in both Qatar and the Arab world, plus padel – the tennis-esque sport played on a court with walls and with smaller racquets. After a slightly comic morning of chasing him around some of Doha's more ostentatiously opulent establishments (even by the standards of Doha, which often feels like a loosely-strung together collection of ostentatiously opulent establishments), he stays still for long enough to speak to me.

'I wanted to build "a brand",' says Al-Khelaifi, when asked what his primary goal for PSG was back in 2011. 'We wanted to build up the football club. We wanted to have fanbases all over the world.

We wanted to win trophies. We wanted to build the best training centre in the world.

'We wanted to have our youth players coming into the first team, which we are doing now – we never had this before. People thought we would just be buying players, but we invested in our training centre. We want 11 players from our academy – that's our goal. That's our real goal. We want to be here for the long term and this is what it shows. It's our strategy and vision.'

And whatever else you might think of PSG, QSI, Qatar or Al-Khelaifi, it's pretty clear that they have succeeded in building the 'brand' of the club. The 2024 Deloitte Money League ranked them as the third most valuable club in the world, behind only Real Madrid and Manchester City, and ahead of traditional behemoths Manchester United, Barcelona and Bayern Munich.

They opened a shop on London's Oxford Street in 2023, something that Al-Khelaifi was very keen to stress not even clubs in London had. 'That was one of our main objectives,' he says. 'If I had told you before we want to open a store in London you would have said "No, that's totally crazy and impossible." We have them in Japan, Korea, the US – this is also part of our strategy.' This is brand PSG, which is inextricably linked with brand Qatar.

That idea of 'the brand' can be tracked through the three phases of the type of player they signed, none of them especially governed by any sporting philosophy. At first, they recruited big names, players to put them on the map: Edinson Cavani was one of the first, then came Zlatan Ibrahimović and for a brief period David Beckham. The idea was to announce their arrival as a significant power and to have some famous faces to slap on billboards.

Then came the *galácticos* era, starting with the astonishing €222 million purchase of Neymar from Barcelona, a move which was not only the most expensive transfer of all time, but has a case to be called the most consequential too, not just for the impact it had on PSG but for the ripple effects. Barcelona spent the money recklessly and arguably set in motion the chain of events that led to Lionel Messi leaving, for PSG, four years later; that spending spree also provided the funds for Liverpool to re-establish themselves as a true power in the Premier League and Europe under Jürgen Klopp, having used the €135 million that Barça gave them for Philippe Coutinho to help fit out their squad with Alisson, Virgil van Dijk and Fabinho.

Shortly after Neymar's arrival Kylian Mbappé, at that point the most thrilling youngster many of us had ever seen and who had just inspired France to win the 2018 World Cup, was signed. In his private moments Al-Khelaifi wonders if signing Mbappé was worth the trouble, given the grief he caused them over a multi-year flirtation with Real Madrid, eventually leading to him signing for the Spanish giants in the summer of 2024, but at the very least it served a purpose, particularly when Messi joined them in 2021: not only could PSG attract the most famous players in the world, they could get the best too.

Then, in 2023, the focus shifted to young, French talent. The *banlieues* (suburbs) of Paris produce footballers at an astonishing rate: most famously Mbappé, who came from the relatively nondescript Bondy to the north-east of the city centre. But PSG had been pretty bad at actually making us of the hundreds that rise from these multicultural *departments*. The *banlieues* provided 11 of the players in France's 2022 World Cup squad, six of whom have played a first-team game for PSG. That doesn't sound too bad of a hit rate, but there are caveats: Adrien Rabiot and Alphonse Areola came through the ranks and became first-team regulars, but it cost the club something like €300 million to get three – Mbappé, Lucas Hernandez and Randal Kolo Muani – after they left the capital to start their careers elsewhere. But it was arguably the other that hurt the most.

PSG reached their first ever Champions League final in 2020, but they were beaten 1–0 by Bayern Munich, the only goal scored by Kingsley Coman, a Parisien who came through at PSG but was sold before he had a chance to get into the first team, his path blocked by the first wave of expensive foreign signings. Quite apart from the fact it made PSG look ridiculous, it laid bare that they were essentially paying millions to import gold, when there was a mine at the bottom of their garden.

So in the summer of 2023, with Messi gone and Neymar sold to Al-Hilal in Saudi Arabia, they signed three of the best young French talents around – Kolo Muani (a deal Al-Khelaifi completed minutes before the transfer deadline, over the phone from the cloakroom of a Paris restaurant), Ousmane Dembélé and Bradley Barcola – as well Hernandez (also French, but a relative veteran at 27) and the 22-year-old Portuguese forward Gonçalo Ramos.

More than the spending on French talent, Al-Khelaifi's real aim is to produce players. 'My goal for the next few years,' he said in 2022, 'is to have only Parisien players in our team.' To that end, they spent something like €350 million on a new training ground, with all the bells and whistles that such a modern facility should have, in Poissy, to the west of the city centre. To Al-Khelaifi, this is as big a sign as anything else of his, QSI's and Qatar's long-term commitment to PSG.

Another sign that Al-Khelaifi and QSI are more confident in their footing is how they dealt with Messi. The great man joining PSG in 2021 was seen as one of the great coups: they already had Neymar and Mbappé, and now the trifecta was complete, even if not much thought went into how they would actually function together, given that Neymar and Mbappé preferred playing on the left, Messi preferred playing where he liked and all of them preferred not doing much donkey work.

Messi completed a trio of attackers that wasn't so much a forward line, more a set of walking tourist attractions and legitimacy markers. They would sell tickets, shirts and anything else you fancied slapping their names and faces on, but they would also bring with them a sense that PSG were no longer just wealthy upstarts but the real thing, and should be respected as such. And yet they still relied on the names of the players for the brand recognition, rather than necessarily the club: Real Madrid, for example, use their players to market the club, but it's the Real Madrid name that carries the heft and star power. With PSG, that power balance had not yet been tipped: the club needed the stars more than the stars needed the club.

They made their most significant move to try and change that 18 months or so later. Messi was superb for the first half of the 2022/23 domestic season, before the break for the World Cup that he would win with Argentina. After that, his interest seemed to wane, to the point that in May 2023 he missed a training session so that he could visit Saudi Arabia, with whose tourist board he had signed a contract as an ambassador. PSG and Al-Khelaifi were apoplectic about what was effectively a man skiving off work and one who thought he could do so without anyone daring to challenge him.

But PSG did challenge him, suspending him for two weeks. They might not have been so brassy if this had happened in the middle of Messi's contract, rather than as it was running out, but within the club their willingness and ability to stand up to someone who might previously have regarded themselves as too big to be disciplined was regarded as a significant moment.

Messi left for Inter Miami that summer with the sense that both sides had got what they wanted from the arrangement – Messi had kept himself in fighting form for the World Cup, was paid a colossal amount of money and had been given a high-profile home after leaving Barcelona, while PSG got to say they could attract the greatest player of all time – but that it had come to a natural conclusion.

———

The ECA meeting, held at the Fairmont Hotel in Doha (briefly put down this book and Google it: it looks like something that belongs at the gates of Mordor, a colossal three-quarter ring with pointed tips forking into the Doha sky – if you told me it spat out fire every night and the fountains outside ran hot with lava, I'd believe you), winds down and Al-Khelaifi is shuttled to a media roundtable. He lingers, speaking to one of the attendees, and you can easily spot the people who work directly for him because they're the ones whose eyes are nervously darting around and looking at their watches.

Through his positions in football, Al-Khelaifi is probably the most prominent Qatari in the world, besides maybe his friend the Emir, so from that perspective, he's essentially Qatar's ambassador to the world.

'I'm proud to be an ambassador' he tells me, 'I was an ambassador when I was a tennis player. I'm proud of my flag and anything I can do for our country, because I think we have ambition. We have objectives and goals and plans, and we have the right to do it. We have proved it.

'We had the best World Cup, and I think people need to look at Qatar in a very positive and realistic way – not just what they are reading and hearing without being here even. It's not really anything to do with my job, but as a human being, as a Qatari, I feel it when you hear a lot of things before the World Cup and after you saw people give such good feedback. We're very proud.'

If this was a Wikipedia article, there would be a pretty big 'citation needed' next to Al-Khelaifi's claim that the World Cup was the best ever. The spectacle of the astonishing final, with the satisfying narrative of Lionel Messi finally getting his hands on the big one, might allow them to claim that.

But you'd get a different answer if you asked the families of the workers who died building the infrastructure and stadiums that made it possible. Or the workers held in the country and forced to live in cramped, sweltering conditions. Or the gay people who felt unable to exist in Qatar because of the nation's inhospitable attitude towards homosexuality. Right down to the relatively insignificant complaints of those of us who weren't subject to any of those genuinely oppressive conditions, but just found Doha to be a dreary, soulless place where even the Souk Waqif, the theoretical 'old town', was essentially built from plywood (the original souk burned down in the 1990s), adding to the impression that the whole place was just one giant facade.

Those opinions, however, may be in the minority, which could be evidence that their work here is done; that the purpose of all of this has been achieved.

'We don't see it that way,' Al-Khelaifi somewhat unconvincingly claims, when I ask if he thinks the world sees his homeland differently because they own one of Europe's biggest football clubs.

'I think Qatar has changed so much in the last few years, in a positive way. Everything is changing. People came here and said

"Wow, so much has changed here." The infrastructure, stadiums, facilities. It's Arab culture, it's in our DNA: we love to host people, we love to open our houses to people, we love to help and support. This is our culture. It's how we've been educated.

'PSG is owned by QSI: so everyone will talk about Qatar, directly or indirectly. But it's a French club and we're focusing on it and building a French brand.'

The reasons that QSI bought PSG in 2011 are obvious and have been discussed at length. This was soft power, sportswashing, geopolitical influence – however you want to describe it. This is a tiny but fabulously wealthy nation with a population of something like 2.3 million (only 600,000 or so of whom are actually Qatari), with bigger and more powerful neighbours, who wanted and needed a voice on the world stage, and also wanted the global consciousness to think of them as something other than an oil well with a spicy Amnesty report.

Ultimately Qatar's move into football acted as a version of the Streisand Effect, named after the incident in 2003 when Barbra Streisand attempted to use privacy laws to get a photograph that showed her house in Malibu removed from a tiny website about coastal erosion, ultimately suing the owner of the site for $50 million. Before Streisand had brought public attention to the picture, six people had viewed it online, two of whom were her lawyers. Afterwards, north of 400,000 downloaded it. Streisand lost the case.

In Qatar's case, they were a tiny if rich place in the Middle East, which before 2011 not many people could probably have told you much about, other than it was a tiny if rich place in the Middle East. But when they came to the attention of the world through football, suddenly many more knew about alleged human rights abuses and laws against homosexuality. Would your average person have known about the kefala system, the method used by the Qatari state to control workers' movement by withholding their passports and ensuring they remain in the country, were it not for the publicity brought by PSG and, to a greater extent, the World Cup?

The state's move into football raised their international profile massively and with that came greater scrutiny. The bet that Qatar made was they could cope with the negative elements of that scrutiny as long as it brought benefits along with it.

The interesting element to the Qatari ownership of PSG was always going to be what happened after the 2022 World Cup. It wasn't a coincidence that QSI's purchase of the club happened in the same year as the World Cup bid, so the common consensus was that they would lose interest when FIFA and the rest of the world had gone, leaving behind them only a few dog-eared World Cup posters and a selection of ostentatious and capacious football stadiums that would rarely be used. Would they cut football, and by extension PSG, loose, thanking them for their service, having served their purpose?

As it turns out, they wouldn't. One reason is simply that, in terms of a 'brand' and a business, PSG has been undeniably successful. QSI paid something like €70 million for the club in 2011 and, while they have poured Scrooge McDuck levels of money into the club via player acquisitions and infrastructure investments, the purchase of 12.5 per cent of the club's shares in late 2023 by Arctos valued the whole thing at something like €4.25 billion.

Another is a continuation of the original reasons why they bought the club in the first place. They still need influence, they still need soft power, they still need a distraction from a questionable human rights record: in a 2023 report, Amnesty International highlighted 'concerns' with LGBTQI rights, women's rights, citizens' rights to free assembly and forced labour, among others. They also need to future proof their economy: one day the oil and gas will run out, so they need to raise the profile of Qatar as a destination, for business, for tourists and for sport.

But perhaps more than anything else they need an element of geopolitical protection. Because between 2017 and 2021, Qatar was under a wide-ranging blockade from a collection of nearby states, most prominently Saudi Arabia, the nation that is the only one Qatar – this tiny peninsula jutting out into the Persian Gulf – shares a land border with.

The crisis was rooted in a mutual suspicion and rivalry for local influence and power, with Qatar keen to establish themselves as a genuine force in the region, rather than just the little neighbours. But the reason given by Saudi Arabia, along with the United Arab Emirates, Bahrain and Egypt for cutting Qatar off from the rest of the world, was that they 'supported terrorism', specifically groups like Hamas and the Muslim Brotherhood, and were too cosy with Iran for their liking. There was hacking of official government websites and emails of prominent officials on both sides, and an arms deal between Saudi and the USA didn't help matters. By June 2017, the opposing nations announced a severance of diplomatic relations with Qatar, and closed the land border between it and Saudi Arabia, in addition to banning aircraft destined for Doha from using their airspace.

A big part of the crisis was the seemingly outlandish but actually very real threat from the Saudi side to turn the land border between the two states into a canal. The 'Salwa Canal' project proposed by Saudi was, in public at least, said to be a shipping route, but in reality its purpose would have been to literally cut Qatar adrift from the Arabian peninsula, to turn it into an island. They were already legally, diplomatically and ideologically isolated, but this would have cut them off physically too.

The plans were eventually abandoned, but once the idea of something like that is out there, it will always be out there, a constant threat, a huge Acme anvil hanging over their heads on a precarious length of piano wire.

The crisis came to a theoretical close in January 2021, after a summit in the Saudi city of al-Ula. Diplomatic relations were restored and the blockade was officially ended, but many of the more fundamental issues remained unresolved. It was replaced by an uneasy truce and, while there are some small symbolic shows of unity (you can see adverts for the Saudi tourist board at Doha's Hamad International Airport, for example), nobody is under any illusions that the problems have all been solved in the long term.

Which is where stuff like PSG comes in. As long as Qatar has some definitive ties with the wider world, both economically and culturally, then they can count on a certain amount of protection and solidarity. French president Emmanuel Macron, for example, sided with and lobbied for Qatar during the diplomatic crisis: would that have happened had Qatar not owned France's biggest and most successful football club? Of course not. If the countries around Qatar really start to get busy, then will PSG keep Qatar safe? Again, of course not. But it does provide some comfort, some reason for the wider world to care about and notice a nation that, despite its vast wealth, can feel significantly isolated.

———

Part of the reason for meeting Al-Khelaifi in Doha at this time (besides the fact that trying to pin someone like him down to a certain time for an interview is like trying to nail jelly to a wall, so you take what opportunity you can) is because the ECA has become incredibly important to him personally. He took over as its chairman in 2021, shortly after the initial blaze of the proposed European Super League had gutted the organisation: Juventus CEO Andrea Agnelli resigned from his position as ECA chair after that intense Sunday when a bombshell was dropped, without much warning, onto the European game.

Juve were one of 12 clubs – the others being Arsenal, Chelsea, Liverpool, Manchester City, Manchester United, Tottenham Hotspur, Inter Milan, AC Milan, Atlético Madrid, Barcelona and Real Madrid – who announced their intention to break away from the traditional structures of the European game and form their own league. There looked to be no way back, but the whole thing collapsed a few days later amid fierce protests from fans, forcing most of the clubs involved to issue fairly grovelling apologies.

Among the clubs that had no need to apologise were the German giants, Borussia Dortmund and Bayern Munich (who, thanks to the greater tradition in German football of fans voicing their opposition to stuff like this, presumably saw the backlash coming), and PSG. Al-Khelaifi pledged his club's loyalty to UEFA and the established structures, earning heartfelt gratitude from the organisation's president Aleksander Čeferin. 'Thank you from the bottom of my heart to Nasser,' he said in a speech at the time. 'You have shown that you are a great man and that you respect football and its values.'

It was a relatively minor detail, but the ECA needed a new leader. Al-Khelaifi was very reluctant initially and had to be talked into taking the role, but take it he did.

'Before I said: "What the hell am I doing?"' he says when I ask him about taking the role. 'But now, we're trying to build something solid and enjoy what we're doing. It's the base of the whole ecosystem, all our stakeholders working together to protect ourselves.

'For me the most important thing is it's just one family, working together, working for the benefit of football, enjoying each meeting. It's not because of me: before, every single meeting was quiet, there was a lot of negativity – today it's more that people want to work together. Sure, there are sub-divisions, but it's about collective interests more than anything else.'

All very noble sentiments, but Al-Khelaifi didn't just take the role for purely altruistic reasons or just because he cares about the health of the European game. It was a shot at acceptance, at being welcomed into the inner circle.

He still feels like an outsider. He is a man from a Muslim state who bought a club in a country that, to put things delicately, continues to have a tricky relationship with Islam. He is also in charge of a club in a city that has not traditionally been regarded as a 'football town', although many will challenge that idea these days.

He's also from a very different background to essentially everyone he encounters at the top of the European game. Of the people who gathered in Doha for that ECA meeting, only one other – Arsenal's outgoing CEO Vinai Venkatesham – was not white. Football can be an extremely conservative world and newcomers who arrive with lots of money and designs to disrupt and do things differently are often treated with great suspicion. PSG will never, in the eyes of some, be the equal of the more traditional giants.

But by being not just the head of a body like the ECA, but an active reformer of it, he is granted a sense of belonging, of acceptance. That, next to his emphatic alignment with UEFA and Čefarin, has been hugely valuable in consolidating both his and PSG's position.

'When we came in, we wanted to be part of the beautiful European family,' he says, warming to a lyrical theme. 'We have shown we want to be part of the future of European football, it's been amazing, positive. We want to be part of this big success. We're not doing anything wrong.'

If all of this presents the idea of a noble statesman beyond reproach, it is worth pointing out that Al-Khelaifi himself has faced a pretty lengthy list of accusations about his personal conduct.

In 2017 he was alleged to have offered Jérôme Valcke, at the time FIFA secretary general, the use of a luxury villa in Sardinia by way of a bribe in order to win the TV rights for beIN to broadcast the World Cup. Valcke was sacked in disgrace in 2016 over other corruption charges, but Al-Khelaifi was cleared of bribery in 2020 and again in 2022 after Swiss prosecutors appealed the initial decision.

In 2019 he was accused of attempting to 'buy' the right for Qatar to host the 2017 World Athletics Championships, which were ultimately held in London. He was cleared of those charges in early 2023.

In 2023 a French-Algerian man called Tayeb Benabderrahmane alleged that he had been arrested and tortured in Qatar because he held 'compromising documents' related to Al-Khelaifi, who not only denied the accusations but said he was 'amazed so many people have taken their lies and contradictions as credible.'

Al-Khelaifi has not been found guilty of any of these things. But even if you were to take the most generous view and say that this shows a man in his position is a constant target for anyone who takes against him or Qatar, it highlights one of the problems with state ownership. There will always be accusations like this flying around, whether they're true or not.

As more aides start hovering near our table and looking at their watches, Al-Khelaifi switches, unprompted, to the sort of discussions that were around when QSI arrived, about the right of a group previously not associated with European sport, never mind PSG, to take over such a famous name.

'If you want to invest in European football, why not? This is my first question to UEFA when we came in: do you want people to invest in football or not? Do you want the money to go to other sports? It needs solid investors, people who want to be here long term, not short term – which is very important for us – and that's really the most important thing: building something for the long term that benefits the whole family. People who invest in European football, and the players, even outside Europe, it's important to keep – especially in this moment – these investors.'

And with that, he is gone, whisked into one of a fleet of cars to his next meeting. Later, that same fleet will pick him and the other ECA delegates up and a police escort will breezily take them to a game at the Asian Cup, being held in Doha at the same time. It's genuinely like a presidential motorcade, weaving in and out of traffic as the convoy speeds past the everyday people of Doha. It all seems rather stressful, but this has been his life for years. I puff my cheeks out and am thankful for my much quieter life.

When the Saudi Public Investment Fund finally completed their long-running takeover of Newcastle United in 2021, people were literally dancing in the streets.

Mike Ashley, the club's previous custodian, was hated so much (not unreasonably: his parsimonious and distant ownership, which delivered two relegations and years of apathy, had made the place a soulless shell) that someone like Mohammed bin Salman, Saudi Arabia's Crown Prince, was seen as a preferable choice.

A poll conducted by the Newcastle United Supporters' Trust found 97 per cent of their members were in favour of the takeover. When it was formally announced, a Newcastle fan was spotted outside St James' Park with a shirt that said 'MBS 1' on the back. Amanda Staveley, the financier who brokered the deal and took a five per cent share in the club as part of it, was lauded as a hero.

Suggestions that this takeover was perhaps not great, for moral reasons, were generally given fairly short shrift. Another poll, conducted by the fan site The Mag, suggested that while 40 per cent of fans did have concerns about Saudi Arabia's human rights record, 97.7 per cent still thought the takeover should go ahead. One fan, in response to those concerns, tweeted: 'I'll care when someone is beheaded in Eldon Square [in Newcastle city centre].'

A small group of fans did object. 'We've waited a long time to finally be rid of Mike Ashley,' John-Paul Quinn, a supporter from County Durham, told The Athletic in 2021. 'It should be a glorious day but I've dreaded this takeover since it was first mooted.'

But they were very much in the minority. X (formally Twitter) profile pictures were changed to depict the Saudi flag. Fans showed up to games wearing thobes and keffiyehs, the traditional Arabic headdresses. Reporters who asked fans at the ground if they had any misgivings were shouted down – by a minority, it must be said, but a pretty vocal minority.

Newcastle fans were put in a tricky position. As any football fan knows, this is a game that gets deep into your soul and becomes such a part of your life that letting go, whatever the circumstances, is not straightforward. Some fans resolved never to return to St James' Park, but not many, and much as it was for Manchester City supporters before them, it's unreasonable to expect them to simply stop going.

But a pause for thought would be welcome.

Lina al-Hathloul is a Saudi-born human rights activist whose sister, Loujain, was imprisoned by the Saudi regime in 2017. No official reason was given for Loujain's arrest, but she had long been an active opponent of the state's ban on women driving cars, a ban she routinely ignored. She was held until early 2021, but even then only released under a series of punitive sanctions, including but not limited to a travel ban – not just for her, but her entire family. She was free, but not really.

'I think that what should be noted is Saudi Arabia has turned into a complete police state where they don't even have to justify things,' Lina tells me. 'The state security, which is basically the

Crown Prince's private police that was established when he got in power, rules lawlessly and they don't have to justify anything.

'So, for example, regarding my family's travel ban: they found out about it back in 2018. My other sister, who used to live with me here in Brussels, went to Saudi for vacation. When she wanted to leave at the airport, she found out that she's on a travel ban and they didn't tell her why. If you go to the Royal Court, they tell you it doesn't come from them. If you go to the Human Rights Commission, they'll tell you they'll inquire about it, but they don't give you information.

'So, since 2018 they've been asking about why they're on a travel ban almost on a weekly basis and they haven't gotten any, any response. This is how things work.'

A rundown of the other ways that the Saudi state abuses human rights is a grim but necessary exercise. The most famous example is Jamal Khashoggi, the journalist whose 'crimes' included condemning the arrest of Lujain al-Hathloul, and who was killed and dismembered in the Saudi embassy in Istanbul in 2018. The Saudi government initially denied all knowledge of and involvement in his disappearance, then claimed that he had been accidentally killed when a fight broke out in the embassy. Presumably the bone saws used to chop Khashoggi up into small pieces just happened to be lying around.

To date there has been no official recognition of any direct involvement in the murder from the Saudi state: Mohammed bin Salman said he 'took responsibility' for it because it happened 'on my watch', but the state continued to insist that it was perpetuated by a 'rogue' group, rather than at the behest of anyone official.

Then there's the case of Salma al-Shehab, a Saudi student studying at Leeds University in the UK who in 2022 was sentenced to 34 years in prison for having an X account, on which she followed and shared posts by an assortment of anti-government activists. A blogger named Raif Badawi spent ten years in prison and was given 50 lashes for 'insulting Islam', and even though he was released in 2022 he was placed under a ten-year travel ban and prohibited from using social media or even speaking to the press. In 2023 a man named Mohammed bin Nasser al-Ghamdi was sentenced to death by a Saudi court for 'describing the King or the Crown Prince in a way that undermines religion or justice.' In early 2024, a number of football fans were arrested for singing Shia religious songs that were deemed 'sectarian' at a game. I could go on.

The argument is always that none of this has anything to do with football, so why should Newcastle fans care? But that is exactly the point: none of this should have anything to do with football, but by purchasing Newcastle and taking over a clutch of teams in the Saudi Pro League and hiring Lionel Messi as an ambassador for their tourist board, the Saudi government have made it about football. We as fans shouldn't have to care about any of this stuff. It should be a guilt and baggage-free distraction, but it is now impossible to ignore.

'I understand that Newcastle fans haven't chosen to be political and if they don't want to be, it's ok, it's fine,' says Lina. 'The thing is that they've been used as a political tool.

'Saudi Arabia is a very specific case in the sense that the very person who is buying these clubs is also the one imprisoning people. The person who owns their club now is also the one who tortured my sisters.

'In the end, they are being used as a political tool by Mohammed bin Salman to cover up the abuses and to give a different image of what is happening. Because they have accepted it and are silent, Mohammed bin Salman has even more legitimacy; he has even more credibility and power.

'So they, without wanting it, have emboldened someone like him.'

This isn't something unique to Saudi Arabia, but by buying or investing in these clubs, they are also attempting to buy the support and loyalty of that club's fans, who sometimes, in an attempt to morally justify things for themselves, or distance the actions of the states from their club, will either actively or tacitly defend them.

'I think what the Gulf States see in fans,' says Nicholas McGeehan, from the human rights advocacy group FairSquare, 'is they know that you've got this massive bunch of very engaged people who will go to bat for you. The way I think the support base was motivated and energised, really to apply political pressure to the British government [to get the takeover approved], was really interesting and really quite dangerous.'

It's a weaponisation of tribalism, of the sense that exists within most passionate football fans that it's 'us' against 'them'. If an owner can cement their status as one of 'us', getting the fanbase onside by making the club better or just spending a lot of money on players, then any criticism of them will be taken as a personal attack on that fanbase.

McGeehan points to the ferocity of the protests against the Super League as an example of how football fans can use their power if they really want to: when it became clear that the fans didn't want the Super League, that it would not be to their benefit, it was rapidly run out of town and dropped.

The other most frequent argument in favour of allowing states like Saudi or Qatar to own clubs is that the light shone upon and attention brought to their abuses is actually a good thing, that it will help liberalise laws and attitudes. But McGeehan doesn't believe that is true.

'It's based on the assumption that if you shine a light on something, everyone will be concerned about it. It's not the case. You only have to look at Saudi's record since the Newcastle takeover: it was bloody awful before but it's not getting any better and they continue to do the same sort of stuff. People are still being locked up for 40 years for tweeting.'

The concept of sportswashing is a well-established one by now, but Lina al-Hathloul believes that the Saudi state's move into sport – whether that's the purchase of Newcastle or the bid for the 2034 World Cup or LIV Golf or hosting big boxing matches – is about something more.

'I don't agree with people saying that Saudi Arabia does this only to rebrand itself. I think it's much deeper than that.

'Sportswashing is about people thinking of Cristiano Ronaldo when it comes to Saudi Arabia. But also I think it's about normalising a state like Saudi Arabia, that is one of the few states in the world where it's a one-man rule and people can get forcibly disappeared for years without anyone being able to inquire about it.

'I think that it's about covering up and normalising regimes like Saudi for people in the UK or wherever it might be.'

———

One point of view is that state owners are the lesser of a series of evils, a point of view expressed by none other than the UEFA president, Aleksander Čeferin, speaking to Nick Ames of *The Observer* in January 2024.

'I'm not worried about state-owned clubs as long as they respect the rules,' Čeferin said. 'I'm more worried about hedge fund-owned clubs. With hedge funds, you never know exactly who is behind them.

'Where I see a big difference, and maybe this is a bit simplistic, is that state-owned clubs want to win. Whether it's also for name-washing or not, I don't enter into this. But they want to win.'

But Čeferin's argument is a practical one and only really exists on a surface level: it's very easy to think that way about a state owner's motivations if you don't dig down any deeper. Motivation A is to make the club as successful as possible on the pitch, but that is only to feed motivation B, which is everything already discussed in this chapter.

The broader question is whether a nation state, even if you discount sportswashing, should be allowed to own football clubs at all.

For a start, is it really moral to use a nation's money to buy football players? Sheikh Mansour has spent something like £1.5 billion on Manchester City since he bought the club in 2008: Abu Dhabi is not exactly scratching around for cash, but imagine what good that money could have done, had they not decided to boost their image by purchasing a football club? QSI have spent north of €2 billion on transfer fees alone since acquiring PSG.

Then there's the uncomfortable excess influence that comes with owning a huge football club and how a state could leverage that influence, one example being Macron siding with Qatar in their dispute with Saudi Arabia. Is that really how football should be used? Stade Saint-Germain, the club's forerunner that merged with Paris FC in 1970 to form the PSG we know today, was originally founded as an athletics club for youngsters: it's pointless in many ways to complain that football has changed in the last century, but it's stuff like state ownership that illustrates how far the game has strayed.

The counter to this point of view is that we must come to terms with the fact that football is regarded by most as a business, and any significant business interests in a country will influence its diplomatic relations. The outsized cultural significance of football means it is more likely to be used this way than many other significant corporations, but it still follows the same theory.

More than all of this though, is a more fundamental point about the nature of football clubs. They should be community institutions, things that have a sense of place and around which people can gather. They were formed around workplaces or religious institutions or for some sort of social purpose, which is more noble than the interests of a country thousands of miles away. It's probably naive and pointlessly nostalgic to think that the days of purity in football club ownership are ever coming back, or even existed at all, but that doesn't stop it from being a legitimate point of view.

Owners are custodians. They're pausing in the chair, they will be gone soon enough and someone else will take their place. It's the same for managers, players, chief executives – whichever individuals pass through our clubs. What's left is us: the fans. Not you and I individually, because one day we will be gone too, but the collective idea of what a football club actually is and means. The owners aren't the important ones, but they're the ones who wield all the power. And when a nation is able to exploit that kind of power ... well, that's when you have problems.

There's a banner that was made by a Nottingham Forest fan group called Forza Garibaldi a few years ago that carried the simple slogan: 'Whoever's name's above the door, whoever holds the key, they'll never own our football club, it belongs to you and me.'

State ownership is perhaps the biggest single thing that puts lie to that romantic notion: the purpose of the football club has been taken away from the collective, away from the idea that a football club can just exist to be a football club, not for any broader, external purpose.

In 2023 FairSquare wrote a letter to the Premier League about state ownership.

'The arguments against allowing states to control football clubs ought to be self-evident, and result from the powers they can exercise,' they wrote. 'Only autocratic states, with power and wealth concentrated in the hands of unaccountable individuals, are able to sanction the use of sovereign wealth to finance football clubs ...

'Their primary motivation for controlling football clubs is typically the reputational benefits that can accrue. As such they are likely to contribute to systemic instability in the sport, they jeopardise competitive integrity, and they will turn valuable pieces of cultural heritage into branding vehicles for their political interests.'

3

THE DEATH OF A FOOTBALL CLUB

'Football without fans is completely useless. If you keep that at the heart of what you're doing, I'm pretty sure it's going to work out.'
STEFAN SCHUBERT,
CO-FOUNDER, AUSTRIA SALZBURG

Football clubs, in England at least, tend not to disappear completely.

Many face financial ruin. Plenty leave a long trail of casualties. Almost all inspire despair in those that follow them when they do get into trouble. But very few go out of business completely, never to be seen again.

Even those that do disappear tend to reappear a short time later, technically a different entity, sometimes with a slightly different name, but in the same colours and in the same town and often in the same stadium with the same fans.

Take Bury, for example. In 2019 they effectively ceased to exist after businessman Steve Dale took them to the wall. But the remnants of the old club fused with a new club set up by grieving supporters and today they play their games at Gigg Lane, just like the old club, wearing white and blue, just like the old club.

Then there's Darlington, the original version of which was expelled from the Football Association and dissolved in 2012, but a new club bearing the name was immediately formed and became a fan-owned entity, and has since gained three promotions in non-league football.

If you go back further into the dusty annals of English football history, you'll find that some of the most famous names around emerged from the ashes of a predecessor. Leeds United, for example, are effectively a successor club to Leeds City, the original inhabitants of Elland Road, who were kicked out of the league in 1919 for a string of financial irregularities.

But while these clubs tend to regenerate, something had to happen to put them in that position in the first place. And that never happens to the prudently run clubs. It is almost always down to bad owners.

The joke going around Reading supporters was that their owner had taken more points off them than any of their on-pitch opponents had managed. It was 18 points, in fact, deducted by the authorities because of a wide array of financial misdemeanours over three seasons.

It was therefore quite grimly ironic when, during a game against Port Vale in January 2024 in which thousands of supporters invaded the pitch in protest against that owner, Dai Yongge, the club urged those fans over the PA to allow the game to be completed, because otherwise the club would be sanctioned.

They were pretty used to it. The first deduction came in November 2021, when six points were docked for breaching the English Football League's profit and sustainability rules, and not by a small amount either: the rules allowed for a club to lose £13 million a year, but over five years between 2017 and 2022, Reading had lost a whopping £146 million. In 2021, their accounts showed that their wages to turnover ratio was a frankly astonishing 216 per cent. That's two hundred and sixteen per cent. You're starting to see how they got themselves in such a mess.

They were given a further suspended six-point penalty, which would only be applied if the club did not abide by a financial plan agreed with the league: if you'll excuse the highly technical jargon, Reading would basically be OK if they bloody well sorted themselves out. They did not bloody well sort themselves out, so in April 2023 those six points were lopped from their total, which this time had real consequences: they finished the season five points shy of survival in the Championship.

So that's 12 points. At the start of the following season, they were docked a further point for failing to pay their players on time – on three different occasions in 2023/24 – with the promise of a further three to be struck off if they committed the same offence again. Finally, in February 2024 they were issued another two point penalty, for 'failing to meet HMRC payment obligations'. Which brings us to the magic total of 18 points.

But this is what can happen when a club is run badly. Or, perhaps more accurately, run by a bad owner. Because it's easy in football to simply focus on the problems that a bad owner can cause to a football team, but there are real-world consequences in these situations. Even in League One, senior professional footballers being paid late is far from ideal, but is essentially an inconvenience: for club staff who will earn less in a year than those players do in a month, the impact can be devastating.

And some came to view being paid late as a golden age: according to a January 2024 report in The Athletic, a dozen staff were sent redundancy letters in the week before Christmas. Some of those that remained were said to be working in their coats, because the heating in their offices had been rationed so much. Wolverhampton Wanderers Women had to postpone a game that same month a few days after playing Reading because half their team – and Reading's – had become ill, apparently from the food they had been served there. But as it turns out, some dodgy catering wasn't the worst thing that the women's team would suffer. In the summer of 2024 it was confirmed that the financial issues of the broader club meant Reading Women were demoted from the Championship, the second tier, to fifth tier, which are regional leagues. Essentially the club, still at this point owned by Dai Yongge, couldn't guarantee there would be enough money to run the women's team at that level for the season ahead.

It was, by common consensus, one of the worst examples of football club ownership that had been seen in some time. But at least, at the time of writing, Reading still exist. Which is more than can be said for the other two clubs that Dai Yongge and his sister Dai Xiu Li owned.

———

The siblings' club in China went by many names, but for simplicity's sake here we will call them Beijing Renhe, because that was their last moniker. The club had only been formed in 1995, but packed quite a lot into their relatively few years. Initially based in Shanghai, they had moved to Shaanxi in the north-west of China by the time Rehne Commercial Holdings, the Dai siblings' company, had started investing in them. After the move, they were known at various times as Shaanxi Neo-China Chanba, Shaanxi Greenland Chanba, Shaanxi Zhongjian Chanba and Shaanxi Renhe Commercial Chanba, all for sponsorship reasons. But, again, we'll stick to just calling them Beijing Renhe for now.

They got caught up in the Chinese football bribery scandal of the mid-2000s, although it only emerged a few years later: they effectively lost the 2003 league title by a point because a number of their players had taken money to lose a crucial game towards the end of the season. Four of their squad were eventually jailed for between five and six years, in 2012.

The Dai family and Renhe began seriously investing around 2010, a while before the Chinese football 'gold rush' of the mid-2010s, which saw dozens of players, including Paulinho, Oscar, Didier Drogba, Ramires, Carlos Tevez and Nicolas Anelka, move from Europe on astronomical wages.

Renhe were, in some respects, pioneers in that field, admittedly in a relatively minor, home-focused way. They spent big on home stars like Sun Jihai (the former Manchester City defender) and Qu Bo, but they had their sights set even higher. In 2012 they tried to tempt Frank Lampard and Rio Ferdinand from Chelsea and Manchester United respectively, and also made a play for Drogba a few years before he signed for Shanghai Shenhua, dangling weekly wages of £250,000 in front of the Premier League stars.

'I want the best team in China and we are prepared to invest a lot of money to bring Ferdinand and Lampard to us,' club chairman Wang Guolin said at the time. 'Many people here watch the Premier League and know how good the two players are.'

However, the glitzy foreign signings didn't emerge. They managed to recruit Bosnian forward Zlatan Muslimović and a clutch of Spanish journeymen: perfectly fine players, but not exactly Lampard and Ferdinand. What was significant was their next move, taking up an invitation from the local government in Guizhou, some 550 miles south of Shaanxi, where a new stadium was waiting for them.

It used to be relatively common for Chinese clubs to move cities: there isn't quite the same attachment to place and community as there is in most European and South American football cultures, so migrating to take advantage of better commercial possibilities was not unusual. Take Guangzhou City, a club that was ultimately dissolved in 2023: they were formed in Shenyang in 1986, moved to Changsha in 2007 and then relocated twice in 2011, firstly to Shenzhen and then quite quickly to Guangzhou, where they stayed until their last days. However, teams like them and Beijing Renhe remain outliers: you don't usually move more than once.

There followed some actual on-pitch success: under their new name Guizhou Moutai, the Dai siblings' club finished fourth in the 2012 Chinese Super League, thus qualifying for the AFC Champions League, then the following season they won the Chinese FA Cup, beating Marcello Lippi's Guangzhou Evergrande in a two-legged final.

However, the success didn't last. The rest of the league started spending big – really spending big: Evergrande signed Robinho, Shanghai Shenhua snapped up Demba Ba and Tim Cahill, Eidur Gudjohnsen joined Shijiazhuang Ever Bright. The league overtook the club in every possible way and they were relegated in 2015.

The owners reacted to this in the only way they knew how: by moving again, this time to Beijing, becoming Beijing Renhe, their (almost) final form. They did this partly to try reaching a bigger audience in a bigger city (and as ever they were offered incentives from the local government), but it was also because this was their last chance to move: the authorities and the public more broadly had grown weary of the itinerancy, and new rules were due to be brought in, making it much more difficult to do so.

They won promotion back to the top tier in 2017, but in a division that by now was full of even more stars (Hulk, Ezequiel Lavezzi, Yannick Carrasco, Alexandre Pato), they only lasted two seasons, and what's worse they dropped again, losing in the relegation play-offs and falling into the third tier.

And that was it. Players' salaries had gone unpaid and the prospect of football at that level seemingly held no interest to the owners. It remains something of a mystery why exactly the club was dissolved in 2021, but the best guess of those who watched it all unfold was that the owners simply saw no benefit in owning the club anymore. There were no more perks to be gained from local authorities, no more kudos to be gathered. It isn't unheard of for Chinese clubs to simply disband (Jiangsu Suning won the league title in 2020 for example, but a year later were no more), particularly after the government broadly withdrew their support for the idea of Chinese football as an international branding instrument.

But Beijing Rehne were gone and it wouldn't be the only time that this happened to a club owned by the Dai family.

———

In 2016, when things in China were looking relatively promising, the Dais made their first move into Europe. KSV Roeselare were formed in 1999 by the merger of two other teams from a small town, about half an hour south of Bruges. They were a modest-sized club who punched above their weight for a time: they won promotion to the Belgian top tier in 2005 and reached the preliminary round of the UEFA Cup in 2006/07. In terms of relative size, if perhaps not history, think Burnley.

They had been relegated back to the second division by the time the Dais took the club over, this time with Dai Xiu Li taking more of a leading role, but their first season in charge was close to being a big success: they reached the promotion play-offs, only losing to Royal Antwerp, one of the oldest clubs in Belgium who would win the Pro League in 2023. Plenty of investment was made in the squad and the French coach Arnauld Mercier turned them from also-rans into real contenders. The squad also featured François Kompany, brother of Belgian legend Vincent, plus a couple of Chinese players.

However, the season afterwards wasn't quite so hot: Mercier was sacked in September 2017 and was replaced, in what was theoretically a populist move, by the Dutchman Dennis van Wijk: Norwich City fans of a certain age may remember his spell at Carrow Road in the 1980s, but for these purposes he was the man who had been in charge for Roeselare's promotion and venture into Europe a decade earlier.

Yet Van Wijk only lasted a few months, sacked the following January after a disagreement over selection. Which is a diplomatic way of saying he refused to pick the young Chinese winger Jiajun Xu, recruited the previous summer from Hebei FC. 'In my opinion Xu is not good enough,' Van Wijk said at the time. 'My contract stated that there would be no interference from higher up towards selections. If that does happen, then I do not understand why clubs still need a trainer.'

His replacement, Jordi Condom (which is, extraordinarily, his real name), never quite got the hang of the Belgian second division and didn't last the year. The next 18 months saw five further managers come and go, but that was the least of the club's problems.

Stories began to emerge about what we'll call 'cashflow issues', a coy euphemism for wages not being paid on time. Money was owed to outside contractors as well as the club's staff, and they came very close to going bankrupt in 2019.

By this stage Dai Xiu Li's involvement had become even more peripheral and the club was essentially being run by CEO Diederik Degryse and a young sporting director called Jolan Fund. New investment was hinted at. Big plans were suggested.

However, few of these plans materialised and something far more serious came to light when Fund was arrested for sexual offences against youth players at some of his previous clubs. He was sentenced to six years in prison, later reduced to five on appeal.

The club struggled on to the end of the 2019/20 season, by now under the management of Christophe Gamel. Gamel is a gregarious character whose career has taken him from youth coaching in his native France to Qatar, Fiji, Vietnam and a spell as PSG Féminines head coach. When I speak to him, he is working as an assistant coach at Macarthur FC in Australia, having some problems getting his head around the local lingo. 'Do you know what they call "afternoon" here? Arvo!' He shakes his head in bafflement.

Gamel arrived at Roeselare in the middle of what would turn out to be their final ever season, with the sole aim of keeping them in the second division. He managed it, despite more instances of wages not arriving at the appointed time. 'We got paid late, but when you are in, you are in,' he shrugs. 'You continue because you have to get the results. The players never gave up.'

It's not really Gamel's point, but this highlights another way that bad owners essentially get away with this sort of stuff. They are relying on, and even exploit, the goodwill, but more often the competitive nature of footballers and coaches. They're less likely to down tools, because their long-term reputation is often more important than their short-term bank balance. They can even use it as a motivational tool, all of which lets the owner off the hook.

When the season ended, more promising noises emerged. Reports suggested that Dai Xiu Li had approved the previous year's accounts, something that theoretically should have been a formality but was anything but by this stage. What it did suggest is that there might be some more investment in the club and a budget for the following season would also be waved through. All that was required was for the ownership to set that budget and for the league to approve the club's licence, and all would be well.

But as it turned out all would not be well.

'When we knew we were safe,' says Gamel, 'we waited for the owner to renew the licence. We waited and waited. The people at the club were working so hard to prepare everything, but at the last moment the owner dismissed it. That's what killed the club. If the owner had said something earlier, they could have tried to find another solution, another sponsorship.'

In May 2020, the Belgian FA denied Roeselare a licence to play professional football. They were relegated to the amateur leagues. The players, for the most part, were redistributed to various parts of the Belgian system. Club Brugge bought the club's Schiervelde Stadium and now use it for their youth teams. Gamel departed for his next adventure, coaching Paradou AC, a team in the Algerian top tier.

Even then, there remained some hope that the club would be able to continue in some form, but in September 2020 that hope disappeared: KSV Roeselare were no more.

'It was a good club,' says Gamel. 'I feel so sorry for the people there.'

Dai Xiu Li was nowhere to be seen.

'At the time, there was cautious optimism,' says Dave Harris, Reading fan and one of the organisers of the 'Sell Before We Dai' campaign, about the early days of the Dai ownership. 'We knew that he was supposed to be a really rich man. He was going to be putting a lot of money into the club, which was needed.'

The really scary thing about Reading's decline is how quickly they went from stability to bouncing from financial crisis to financial crisis.

'I think it's quite stark as well being Reading. Because up until 2012, we were very much a beacon of how to run a Championship football club, a sustainable football club. And suddenly it has gone massively wrong in the space of ten years and three successive owners.'

That era of stability was under John Madejski, chairman and benefactor since1990, but in 2012 he decided to sell to a group called Thames Sports Investments, headed by Russian businessman Anton Zingarevich. That didn't go brilliantly and by 2014 the threat of administration was real, staved off by the sale of the club to a Thai consortium that included Sumrith Thanakarnjanasuth (who would later go on to become involved with Oxford United), Lady Sasima Srivikorn (who celebrated the acquisition of Reading by recording a truly cringeworthy song called 'They Call Us The Royals') and majority shareholder Narin Niruttinanon.

Alas, despite promises to get the club into the Premier League (they had been away from the top flight since 2013) that trio rather underestimated how much it cost to even run a football club in England's second tier, never mind the outlay required to actually make it good. 'We just couldn't afford it comfortably anymore,' Lady Sasima told the BBC in 2017. 'We're doing this [selling] to save the club and pass it on to better hands. If you don't have very, very deep pockets, it's a struggle.'

On the face of it, the people they sold to did have those deep pockets. Dai Yongge and Dai Xiu Li's company, Rehne Commercial Holdings, owned a large number of shopping centres in China, some of which were built in former air raid shelters. An unusual business but a lucrative one: Xiu Li had been named on the Forbes Billionaires List in 2014, which estimated her worth as around $1.2 billion. She was – sort of – local too: she married an Englishman called Tony Hawken in 2003 (they divorced in 2014) and their family home was in Norwood, south London.

They were also not strangers to owning football clubs, which at the time were both doing OK. On that basic, surface-level appraisal of their candidature to be good custodians of Reading, it looked promising.

It, to say the least, didn't turn out that way. Reading are still there, but only just, and the damage has been done.

Reading were formed in 1871, so they had a century and a half of history behind them before they began circling the drain. Others, however, burn brightly but much more briefly before the flame flickers and is snuffed out.

And so we go from Berkshire, southern England, to a fairly remote part of southern Russia.

Roberto Carlos's career was following a familiar path. Having started out at home in Brazil, he went to Europe to make his name, won pretty much everything there is to win with Real Madrid, had a year and a nice little earner at Fenerbahçe then went back home, signing for Corinthians to play alongside his old pal Ronaldo. It's a path well-trodden, but his career then diverged from the norm when an obscure club in a relatively remote outpost of Russia called to offer him a two-year contract worth something in the region of €100,000-a-week.

Makhachkala is not exactly a tourist hotspot, about as far away culturally, if not quite physically, from Moscow and St Petersburg as it's possible to be and still be in Russia. It's the capital of Dagestan, and the BBC described the city as 'the most dangerous place in Europe' in 2011.

Anzhi Makhachkala were formed in 1991, as the Soviet Union was collapsing. They had reached the top tier of the new Russian league by 1999, but the next decade or so of their existence was relatively unremarkable.

Until, that is, they were taken over by their friendly local billionaire Suleyman Kerimov in 2011. Kerimov was a banker initially, but made most of his money via buying stakes in energy companies like Nafta Moskva and Gazprom, before really striking gold by investing in Polyus, Russia's largest producer of, erm, gold. Through all of that, his family was estimated by Forbes to have amassed a fortune in the region of $10.7 billion.

In that context, Roberto Carlos's contract was a relative drop in the ocean. As was the €1.8 million Kerimov paid for a black Bugatti Veyron, which he presented to the Brazilian legend as a 38th birthday gift.

And as were the millions he lavished on new signings: Diego Tardelli arrived from Atlético Mineiro, winger Mbark Boussoufa came in from Anderlecht, Yuri Zhirkov signed from Chelsea, Willian from Shakhtar Donetsk, Christopher Samba from Blackburn Rovers, Lassana Diarra from Real Madrid.

And then the big one: Samuel Eto'o, just over a year removed from winning the treble with Inter Milan, who signed in August 2011 for a transfer fee of around €21 million and whose reported wage was €20.5 million a year. That's not a typo: €20.5 million a year. After tax. It was, at the time, the highest wage for any player in world football, being paid by a team who had finished 11th out of 16 in the previous Russian Premier League season.

'I asked myself whether I could give faith and hope to a region and really create something,' said Eto'o at the time, floating in a pool of cash and lighting Cuban cigars with a 50. 'The only thing that I want to give is hope and we all know that hope lets us live. There is nothing more valuable than to have the hope of living a better day tomorrow. The club is not only a football club, it represents the whole region and it represents the hope of everything.'

Touching stuff. The whole situation was, however, deeply strange, not least because they played their home games in Moscow, nearly 1,000 miles and a three-hour flight away from Makhachkala. The cartoon amounts of money continued: before Roberto Carlos's debut, a Russian Cup game against Zenit St Petersburg, Kerimov offered a small incentive to the squad.

'The day before the game, Kerimov came into the dressing room and told the players: "If you win this game I will give you a million dollars, to split among the squad however you want,"' the striker Miro Slavov told *The Blizzard* in 2020. 'I was a 20-year-old with no experience, making my debut. It was crazy. And we lost 3–2 – it was a close game!'

They finished third in 2012/13 under head coach Guus Hiddink, just missing out on qualification for the Champions League, and in the same season reached the round-of-16 of the Europa League, knocked out by Newcastle United.

But that summer is when it all started to go wrong. Kerimov's main business by that point was a fertiliser company called Uralkali, which saw £5.5 billion wiped off its value after it withdrew from a trading agreement and caused chaos in the industry. Priorities were shifted, most immediately at Anzhi, whose budget was slashed by two-thirds, although officially and publicly no link was made between Kerimov's finances and those of his football club.

A club statement said that the decision had been taken 'to work on a new long-term strategy for the club' after they had 'analysed the club's recent sporting results.' Other suggestions included a downturn in Kerimov's health and even – adorably – concerns over UEFA financial fair play guidelines. The club's focus was now said to be on youth, with a new academy to be built. The club promised that the decision 'won't lead to considerable deformations in the team's life and in the current structure of our club on the whole.' Which, to say the least, turned out to be a little awry.

Within a month, most of their high-profile players – including Willian, Zhirkov, Eto'o and Diarra, as well as two of Russia's brightest stars, Igor Denisov and Aleksandr Kokorin, who had joined that year – were gone. The games in Moscow were nixed, with the players now based full-time in the slightly less attractive surrounds of Makhachkala.

The following season was a calamity, Anzhi relegated with barely a whimper, winning only three games all season, although they were promoted straight back the following season. Eventually, as had been fairly predictable from the off, Kerimov left in the final days of 2016, quietly, with barely a public acknowledgement.

From there the fall was undignified. Players were paid late, if at all. They weren't given meals on away trips. Attendances plummeted. By the end of the 2018/19 season, which ended in another relegation, their finances were so parlous that they couldn't even come up with the licence fee to play in the second tier. They were thus relegated again, down to the third, but because of their outstanding debts were not allowed to register new players, meaning their squad for the following season consisted almost entirely of youth teamers.

They slowly declined for a couple more years, but the end came in 2022 – and for a club who a decade earlier were handing out Bugattis to their players, it came in bleak, low-key fashion, with a terse press release from the Russian Football Federation. Their continuing financial issues had meant their licence to play even in the regional leagues had not been granted and their appeal against that decision was 'not considered due to a violation of the procedure for filing these complaints.'

All of which poses an interesting question: Anzhi disappeared because of Suleyman Kerimov, but they were only there to disappear because of Suleyman Kerimov. Does that make him a bad owner? A good owner? A good owner turned bad? A bad owner with good intentions? A bad owner with bad intentions?

You could argue that he is a walking cautionary tale, an example of what happens when someone thinks that money alone can make a football club, when in reality money broke them too. Anzhi lived by the sword and died by the sword, the sword in this case being colossal stacks of cash.

You could also view Anzhi as an isolated curio, a brief blip on the football landscape, possibly the most expensive pub quiz question of all time. They were there, for a short time they were a minor sideshow, and then they were gone: a whole football club, who appeared then disappeared without a trace, with not much to remember them by.

Apart from a gleaming Bugatti Veyron, speeding around the streets of Sao Paulo.

There are other ways for a club to die. A club doesn't have to cease to exist for everything that it used to be about, that it used to mean to people, to disappear.

But the good thing about football is that it's full of hope and, that if one thing does end up in the dirt, something else will spring up in its place: after all, excrement can often make the best fertiliser.

The story of how Red Bull started their global football empire is told elsewhere in this book, how they bullied their way into Austria Salzburg and changed the identity of a football club one summer evening in 2005. But two paths opened up that day: down one was a burgeoning worldwide football conglomerate, a network with clubs on four continents who have all been successful to one extent or another, and have developed an extraordinary reputation for spotting talent and nurturing it, but who ultimately exist to sell cans of energy drink.

Down the other is just a football club, something that isn't an advertising vehicle, and just exists for the pleasure of existing and as something for its fans to have some pride in.

Once it became clear that Red Bull wanted to change everything about the old Austria Salzburg, even down to insisting that it was an entirely new club, founded in 2005 and renouncing its previous history (the Austrian league put a stop to that – they were forced to acknowledge it is a continuation of the old club), a group of fans met to form something new. New, and not especially complicated, not guided by anything beyond wanting to have their football club again.

'We wanted a club that played in the city of Salzburg, wore violet shirts and carried on the club's tradition and history,' says Stefan Schubert, one of the founders of the new Austria Salzburg. 'That's about it. There's not that much ideology behind that. It's pretty simple. We just wanted our club back.'

Those early days were pretty wild, very rough and ready. The first problem was reasonably basic: they didn't have any players. So they entered into a partnership with a local club called PSV Schwarz-Weis, who were going through some institutional problems that meant they were essentially about to give up on football but, crucially, they did have players. It's called a *spielgemeinschaft*, which literally translates as 'playing team', but actually means two teams coming together in a mutually beneficial partnership, without it being a full merger.

'The first year was chaotic,' says Schubert. 'Nobody knew the players. Nobody knew the league. Nobody knew the level of play. We hadn't paid attention: we had been following a club in the top flight.'

But eventually they made sense of it all. The path has not always been especially smooth and on occasion has been travelled too quickly: they had made it to the Austrian second tier by 2015, but the club wasn't set up to play at that level yet. Their ground didn't meet the standards of the division and they were forced to play some home games near Vienna, a three-hour drive away. They simply couldn't afford to continue operating at that level and were declared bankrupt, relegated back down to the regional leagues.

By 2023, they were in much better shape and in the early weeks of that season came up against the team who had displaced them.

It was inevitable that Red Bull Salzburg would face Austria Salzburg at some point, and some 18 years after the schism, it eventually came when they were drawn against each other in the second round of the Austrian Cup. Both sides figuratively puffed out their cheeks: while it was a compelling idea for everyone outside the two clubs and for the national and international media that turned out in force, this wasn't something anyone actually involved was looking forward to. It was a game to be endured rather than revelled in. 'It is not a dream draw for us,' said Austria Salzburg president Claus Salzmann at the time. 'I hated it,' Schubert says, speaking a few months later.

There remains a perception about Austria Salzburg that, because of their origin story and the fervour with which they support their team, they are at best ultras, at worst hooligans who roam the streets in balaclavas, defacing anything Red Bull-related, like they're Tyler Durden's Project Mayhem goons from *Fight Club*. Thus, trouble at this most highly charged game was expected by some.

'This was the biggest chance to mess everything up. But looking back at [how it turned out], it's the best that could have happened. We were able to prepare our fanbase and help us shape the narrative for years to come. People expected violence and riots … and nothing happened. It helped us a great deal.'

In reality, their fans are loud, enthusiastic and occasionally aggressive, but rarely actually violent. But the false expectation of violence goes right back to the schism that started all of this off. Back at the start, Red Bull attempted to position themselves as a 'respectable' club, one that would reject what they tried to paint as the 'violent' ultras and fans of the old club. A spokesman told the German newspaper *Der Spiegel* in 2009 that a rejection of violence was 'the reason why we separated from the old fan scene in Salzburg. We lost a thousand followers there in the short term and gained ten thousand in the medium term.' And here is an example of Red Bull's patronising attitude to the fans of the old club, one of the reasons they are so disliked in Austria, as well as Germany and pretty much everywhere else that they operate.

Austria Salzburg were drawn as the home team, but their Max Aicher Stadion was deemed inadequate for the occasion, so they had to stage the game at the home of SV Grödig, about a 20-minute drive south of the city centre. It's an absurdly picturesque venue, in the middle of a few acres of corn fields: one side of the ground is open to those fields and behind that a small mountain rears up from the crops. As the sun sets behind it, you're left feeling guilty for watching the actual football, when there is this much natural beauty right in front of you.

The Austria Salzburg fans turned out in force, armed with banners, pyro and flags. The atmosphere was celebratory, but with the slightest hint of aggression: not the sort where you thought anything was going to spill over into something unpleasant, but just enough to display passion with an edge. They roared for their team, singing long and loud, setting off flares, sporting the historic purple colours of the club.

And that was just for training, the night before the actual match.

The following evening, Red Bull Salzburg rolled into Grödig to be met with yet more fireworks and baying fans. The game itself was barely a contest: it was one of the least competitive encounters you're likely to see, Red Bull winning 4–0. But the occasion was magnificent, heavy with symbolism and meaning: it didn't feel like a game between two football teams, but one between two completely different ideologies, two opposing theories about what football is for.

'It's not just Red Bull Salzburg against Austria Salzburg,' Austria Salzburg's midfielder Rene Zia told me before the game. 'It's Red Bull Salzburg against the rest of Europe.' He was right: good luck messages had come from across the continent. The weekend before the tie, banners had appeared at several games around the country, most notably in games involving Sturm Graz and Rapid Vienna, in support of Austria Salzburg. 'Salzburg bleibt violett' read one

– 'Salzburg is violet.' Another said 'In Salzburg nur die Austria' – 'In Salzburg, there's only Austria.'

'It shows that you can't buy everything,' said Austria Salzburg coach Christian Schaider. 'In my heart, I have a different ideology. My heart burns for Austria Salzburg and my players. It gives you a warm feeling.'

It would be easy to think that Austria Salzburg are defined by what they aren't, as the club that rejected the riches of Red Bull and thus identify as their opposite. But that hasn't been the case for quite a while.

'We have de facto moved away from that a long time ago,' says Schubert. 'It's mostly about us. What they're doing is something different, and we have our own agenda and principles. Of course I like it when they lose, but it's nothing more. We don't do stuff because they don't do it, or the other way around. The difference is deeper because it's a cultural thing. For us, different things are important. What they're doing is a business model, what we do is community.

'On our training field, there's a mural that has a line from our club anthem: "You play for the fans." Football without fans is completely useless. If you keep that at the heart of what you're doing, I'm pretty sure it's going to work out.'

For those that think their club has died, that forces beyond their control have taken away what meant so much, that serves as a message of great hope.

4

FOOTBALL BELONGS TO EVERYONE: FAN AND COMMUNITY OWNERSHIP

'This is true fan ownership and democracy at work.'
ASHLEY BROWN,
FORMER CHAIR OF THE
PORTSMOUTH SUPPORTERS' TRUST

The significant artefacts at most football clubs are usually trophies, or perhaps an important document, or maybe even a pennant exchanged with a prestigious previous opponent.

At Exeter City, one of theirs is a padlock.

It's significant because it signalled the first real tangible piece of control that their supporters' trust had over the club, control that remains to this day as probably the most successful example of fan ownership that still exists in English football.

The idea of fan ownership is something of a utopian ideal for many. The concept that we, the people who genuinely care about the club and theoretically have its best interests at heart, can make the decisions that impact not just the club but the community around it, is incredibly intoxicating. It stands against what many people dislike about the modern game, the idea that the purpose of a football club is to make money and social media impressions and sleeve partners and post-season tours, rather than just being a football club. It allows us to have a more tangible stake in the thing that has been such an important presence in our lives.

It also plays on that little thing in the back of all of our minds, that slight but unshakeable sense that we could do better than the people in charge of our club, given half the chance. Usually this is directed at whoever the manager is, but these days it extends to their bosses too. Why didn't they just buy this player? The first thing I would sort out is the pies. If I was in charge I wouldn't give agents a penny.

And yet, it rarely works. Or, perhaps more accurately at least, in English football it rarely lasts: fan ownership tends to happen when there is nobody else around, when a group of concerned citizens steps in to save things, but after a while a more traditional owner, someone with more money, takes control.

Which is why Exeter are such an interesting case study. Their St James Park home is easy to miss, tucked among rows of houses and overshadowed on one side by a modern block of flats, at the bottom of a shallow valley. The Adam Stansfield Stand, the newest in the ground and partly financed by the sale of Ollie Watkins to Brentford, only runs halfway along one side, prevented from going the full length by the railway line. The St James Road End, where away fans are housed, is a terrace with barely ten steps, the sort of stand over which a lot of errant footballs fly.

In many respects this represents the club nicely: small, relatively unassuming, surrounded by and very much part of the local community, self-contained, no real pretensions to be anything other than what it is. But it nearly wasn't there at all.

In May 2003, Exeter were spiralling. The previous few years had been an absolute circus: the clownish, fun-to-outsiders-but -a-bit-embarrassing-for-them circus elements included a visit to St James Park by Michael Jackson, David Blaine and Uri Geller, the latter having brought the former two as his guests as part of his role, implausibly, as co-chairman. The less fun, trapeze-artist-missing-the-net-and-splatting-on-the-floor bit was the club almost disappearing completely, nearly sunk by rising debts and a pair of rogue owners who were eventually convicted of fraud.

John Russell and Mike Lewis had taken over the running of the club the previous year from Ivor Doble, a local jeweller who had been at the helm for 17 years but who by that point had already ploughed enough of his money into the club and wanted out, pronto. Russell had left Scarborough shortly after they were relegated to the Conference and in 1999 pleaded guilty to two counts of obtaining services by deception. Lewis had previously been involved at Swansea City, but scarpered with them significantly in debt.

Understandably, people were suspicious from the start, particularly when they installed Geller shortly after their arrival. The next year was, to put things mildly, utterly chaotic and the pair left a trail of unpaid bills, angry creditors and despairing fans in their wake. By May 2003, the word was that Lewis and Russell were in trouble with the law.

By that point the Exeter City Supporters' Trust had decided to take matters into their own hands and, rather than simply wringing their hands from afar, made it their mission to save the club. The first step was to change the locks, after a report from the Football Association's financial advisory unit recommended that the club should speak to an insolvency practitioner, became one of many final straws.

As it turned out they need not have bothered: the locks were changed on 13 May and on 14 May Lewis and Russell were arrested, eventually receiving sentences of 200 hours' community work and 21 months in jail respectively.

But those locks remain, as a symbol of how far they have come.

'The reality is you don't understand what you're getting yourself in for,' says Julian Tagg, president of Exeter City, devotee of the club for over 50 years and one of the original members of the Trust that took over the running of the club in 2003. 'If I had understood, perhaps I wouldn't have done it.'

Tagg isn't being entirely serious. Or maybe he is. Either way, he has been a central part of what has in all probability been the most successful and sustained example of fan ownership in modern

English professional football. Progress has not been linear, nor has it always been quick, but when they took over the team was non-league and two decades later they have become established in the EFL.

What they have certainly provided is an element of stability. At a time when some clubs are paying out many more times their annual revenue just on player wages, their finances are relatively secure – or as secure as they can be in English lower-league football. They've also been able to bring stability in a different sense: the first few years were slightly rocky, but between 2006 and 2024 they only employed three permanent managers.

That was partly due to the fact that there is minimal pressure placed on the manager, because their ownership model carries with it an in-built sense of patience. There is an understanding that there isn't a lot of money around, but the trade-off is a steady ship, thus expectations are tempered.

'If I was giving the manager £10 million, I would maybe expect a little more,' says Tagg. 'Those managers – every one of them has tried their hardest and they've all understood the ethos, all understood what's behind it all.'

But maybe more important than that is the knowledge that people who genuinely care are in charge of the club's destiny. The fans can be pretty sure that even when mistakes are made, they are made with good intentions. They can also be sure that the horror stories from elsewhere in the EFL have less chance of being repeated here because they know things are being run prudently.

Boy, has it been a slog, though.

'For as long as 15 or 16 years we were against the wall every day,' says Tagg. 'I think in the last three, maybe four years, we've turned the corner and we reached a financial position which is, if we're very careful, sustainable for a longer period of time than we've ever had. Now, we think of the next three, four years whereas previously for a long, long time, we thought about next Friday.

'So the turning point was very, very late in the day. The panic that went on between myself and a few of the staff when we thought a game was going to be called off was ...' He tails off slightly at the memory of those days. 'You know you're not going to be able to pay the wages on Monday if you don't play the game on a Saturday.'

———

That sort of chaos is something Ashley Brown is very familiar with.

Brown was chairman of the Portsmouth Supporters' Trust between 2011 and 2014, and then from 2015 to 2017. Just written out like that, it doesn't really properly explain his duties, given that between 2013 and 2017 the Trust was not only a concerned group of fans, but the custodians of the club.

There aren't too many occasions when fans take over a club in good shape, but it is worth laying out what an extraordinary state Portsmouth were in, and had been for the seven or so years before the Trust stepped in. Their ownership history in that time is a complex web that includes seven different owners, one of whom was there three times, two administrations and one owner who may or may not have existed, but it's worth recounting if you can follow. Ready? Deep breath.

Their rise from the nether regions of the Championship to Premier League stalwarts came under the stewardship of Milan Mandarić, who was joined in co-control by Sacha Gaydamak (with the backing of his father Arcadi Gaydamak) in 2006. Gaydamak took over fully later in 2006, remaining in charge until the 2009 arrival of Sulaiman Al-Fahim, an Emirati businessman who was initially the face of the purchase of Manchester City by Sheikh Mansour, but was pretty rapidly side-lined by them.

Al-Fahim only remained for a very short period: in October 2009, 42 days after he took control, the sale of the club to Ali al-Faraj was agreed. Al-Faraj was so elusive – he never visited Fratton Park and those around the club only ever reported speaking to him on the phone – that questions over whether he was actually a real person flew around, leading to him gaining the nickname 'Ali al-Mirage'. Those who were there at the time think he probably did exist, but what didn't exist for very long was his ownership of Portsmouth: the following February Balram Chainrai, a Nepalese-British businessman, took control of the club in lieu of repayment of £17 million he had loaned to Al-Faraj.

Shortly afterwards Portsmouth entered administration, thus incurring a nine-point penalty which technically didn't directly result in their relegation (they would have finished seven points from safety even without that deduction), but the whole thing was so demoralising for all concerned that it would be foolish to think it wasn't at least a factor. Remarkably, they did reach the FA Cup final that season, losing 1-0 to Chelsea at Wembley. Chainrai regained control after the club emerged from administration in October 2010, then the following June he sold to a group called Convers Sports Initiatives, headed by Russian banker Vladimir Antonov.

If you want to pause here for a coffee, or to just read over all of that again to make sure you've got it all, please do so.

Any thoughts that Antonov's takeover would lead to peace and stability were scuppered when he was arrested in November 2011 over allegations of asset-stripping of the Lithuanian bank Snoras. Antonov would eventually go on to be jailed in Russia, but the more immediate consequence for Portsmouth was that CSI entered administration and the club was issued with a winding-up order by the British government over an unpaid tax bill. The club were briefly back in the hands of Chainrai before the administrators took over again, this time for more than a year. Meanwhile, another points deduction was issued and Portsmouth were relegated to League One.

The spring of 2013 brought bad news and good news: the bad was that they were relegated again, their third demotion in four seasons, and were now in the bottom division of the EFL for the first time since 1980. But the good was that the Portsmouth Supporters' Trust reached an agreement with the administrators to take control of the club.

'The first year was full on putting out fires and the second year there was a fair chunk of that,' says Brown. 'We took over in May, we had virtually no players, no full-time manager, no kit supplier for the new season, no shop, no training ground.

'As individuals we were all regularly worried [that it wasn't going to work]. The weight on the shoulders is huge because you're fans and because the club means so much to you and you know how much it means to everybody else. You just can't even contemplate failing.'

The structure at Portsmouth was slightly different to a 'pure' fan or supporters' trust ownership, and ultimately ended up as a sort of hybrid between that and a classic 'consortium' of businessmen. Albeit this time, the consortium was brought together by circumstance, rather than by any real design.

'When we set out to raise enough to try and save the club, we realised that we were probably going to need some big chunks of money rather than just people clubbing together,' says Brown.

'So we came up with this 'presidents scheme', where we still targeted Pompey fans, but we targeted wealthy Pompey fans that needed to put in a minimum of £50,000 each. On day one, we had 13 presidents: 11 of those were lifelong Pompey fans and of the other two, one was literally a good friend of a fan and just got talked into the idea. The other one was the local property speculator that we had struck a deal with to develop some of the land around the ground and, as part of that deal, we convinced him to chuck a bit of money in as well.

'The split basically ended up as the Trust had about 48.5 per cent and the others had the rest between them of varying degrees. So the Trust was by far the biggest shareholder but not the majority shareholder. There was no plan – it's just where we ended up with the money.'

And it worked. For four years, there was relative stability. No administrations. No pass-the-parcel changes in ownership. Very little chaos. There was the threat of relegation out of the EFL in 2013/14, but that was avoided and the following September the club announced that they were debt-free. Paul Cook was appointed manager and in 2016/17 they were promoted back to League One.

As the team was celebrating promotion, moves were afoot off the pitch. The Tornante Company had approached the club about a possible takeover, and if the name of that group doesn't ring any bells then the man at its head might: Michael Eisner, the former chief executive of Disney, arrived in town on a warm night that May to give his pitch to the supporters, who had to vote to approve the potential takeover.

His pitch was slick, but pretty cheesy. Eisner suggested that he could do for Portsmouth what Disney did for the careers of Justin Timberlake and Britney Spears: turn them into superstars from humble beginnings.

'I thought it was quite misjudged,' says Brown. 'I just thought "Well, that's not going to resonate." But it did – it got the vast majority of people believing in the hype, I guess. Don't get me wrong: Michael and his family are nice people and in many ways they've been great owners for the club.'

By that stage the club had 16 'presidents', 12 of whom voted in favour of the takeover, as did 81.4 per cent of the standard Trust members. Eisner and Tornante have been in place since, and while nobody has become Justin Timberlake, it's been another extended spell of relative stability.

More than that, even though this was the fans voting that they should no longer be in charge of the club's decisions, in many ways it was a perfect demonstration of what supporter ownership should be. They may have ceded control, but they were deciding the club's future. Part of being a good owner is recognising when someone better placed comes along, which is what they did.

'This is true fan ownership and democracy at work,' said Brown at the time.

The owners of Lewes FC had their own big decision to make in 2023.

Lewes do things differently. They are fan-owned, but not quite in the same way as Exeter or Portsmouth.

It began as many other similar stories do, with years of financial instability. Then, in 2010, a group of six fans who collectively went by the name Rooks 125, decided to take over the club and make it a community-owned entity. It operates as a sort of membership organisation: anyone, regardless of where you are in the world, can buy a membership and thus have a say in how the club is run. 'When you buy a share, you buy it for a year,' says Maggie Murphy, the club's CEO at the time we met, in 2023 (she stepped down in May 2024). 'It's a bit like a subscription business. The key governance responsibilities you have are to vote for directors and you're allowed to stand to be a director. There's no monetary value to your share. We're 100 per cent fan-owned, but we're legally a community benefit society. Everything we do has to have a community benefit.'

In 2017 the club committed to offering equal pay for their women's and men's teams, the first football club in the world to do so. Whereas most clubs who operate teams for both genders tend to be dominated by the men's side, the difference with Lewes is that their men's team is part-time and play in non-league – for most of the time they have been community-owned they have been in the Isthmian League Premier Division, the seventh tier of English football – whereas the women are full-time and in 2018 were promoted to the Championship (they were relagated in 2024), the second tier just below the Women's Super League. So they were equally paid ... but not really.

This produced some fascinating dynamics, such as the people in charge of the men's team occasionally bristling at not being the de facto most important people at the club, which they would be in most other places. But broadly speaking it works and Murphy believes it is only because of their ownership structure that they can do this.

'There's always going to be a corporate reason to justify not investing fully into your women's side. But if you're a community club, you can't say you're only serving 50 per cent of your community.

'I don't have any interest in working for a football team where all you have to do is win. That's just not interesting or important or meaningful. We're constantly looking at football and seeing the bad things the game does, and the toxicity – we have to figure out how you can switch it. You can only really do that when you're about serving people.'

Murphy explains how not being motivated by profit or victory allows them to turn down morally iffy commercial opportunities, whereas other clubs have other imperatives. 'If you're the CEO of another club and you're offered £100,000 from a gambling company, you're going to be crazy not to take it because your principles are only how to win on the pitch, or how to generate more money.'

For a club the size of Lewes, without a significant budget, the community aspect also helps them do things they wouldn't otherwise be able to afford.

'Recently I put a call out in our owners' newsletter saying "I'd really love if there's a skilled owner out there who can put together our impact and accountability report." I had seven emails within an hour from skilled individuals from our network, including someone who works for the UN in Turkiye. Our posters are designed by owners who are graphic designers, whose services we could never afford, but who are committed to the club and offer their services as their social contract as an owner.'

Of course, it isn't all peaches and cream. People sometimes seem to think the club is a charity, rather than a group of teams who would actually like to win some games and progress up the leagues, alongside their social impact. Murphy also has issues related to the old line about democracy being the worst form of government, apart from all the other ones.

'One of the challenges I personally face is the fact that I report to a board that is elected by the fans, which means some of our directors are highly skilled and have strategic outlooks, whereas others I think stand without really knowing what they're getting themselves in for. They stand because they love the club. Sometimes I need more professionalism from my directors. This might not have been an issue when we weren't a professional club, but now TV money and hundreds and thousands are coming in from sponsors, I need a board who reflects that level of professionalism.

'In elections that have gone by, some of the local owners have been more likely to vote for people they know. We've had people elected who used to work for Barcelona: some people have been like, "That's amazing," but others have been more: "How can someone who lives in Barcelona be committed to a community club in England? How many games will she come to?"

'There are a certain number of people who are vociferously opposed to external investment: it's a small number, but they're very noisy. Sometimes I don't like the way they present their arguments and the abuse they level at some in the club.'

Ah yes, external investment. That's where the fascinating decision comes in.

In 2023 an offer was made by a group called Mercury/13, a multi-club ownership group headed by the entrepreneur Victoire Cogevina Reynal, which also included former England international Eni Aluko and ex-Italy goalkeeper Arianna Criscione. They announced in August 2023 that they planned to invest $100 million into women's football clubs in various parts of the world, starting with Lewes.

The offer was to buy 51 per cent of the women's team: the men's team and the broader parent company would remain as a community-owned entity, but the women's team would be majority controlled by Mercury/13.

The question was not just whether to accept outside investment – it was more existential than that. Lewes have been fiercely proud of their community-owned status since it was established, but this would fundamentally change that.

The proposal was put to a vote and in November 2023 the results were in: 67.8 per cent were in favour.

The difference to other clubs accepting outside investment is that this wasn't some financially motivated hedge fund or chancer of a businessman who didn't actually have any interest in football. Murphy and the rest of the Lewes hierarchy ensured some things were clear before they even suggested it to the wider fanbase. 'We made sure we protected some of the key assets,' says Murphy. 'We got reassurances on things like not leaving the Dripping Pan (Lewes's home ground), club colours, all that sort of thing.'

Some weren't happy that this was even being considered. To an element of their membership this went against the whole ethos of Lewes: if they weren't 100 per cent owned by their community, what was the point?

'For some people, their local football club is very much entwined in their identity,' Murphy says. 'So if you bring change, you're inflicting change in someone's identity. Especially if that is a large piece of their identity, their social space, somewhere they go to let off steam. I think therefore there will be arguments against any form of change.

'Some of the arguments that have surfaced are things like "we don't care if we're relegated – we'd rather stay without external investment." My personal feeling is that if we were to get relegated those people would be the first to criticise the club. But I can understand for some people change is difficult and confronting, and it might be a bit strange if the women's team gets more visibility.'

Yet Murphy knew this was inevitable. 'We knew we would reach the point where we would need investment if we were to keep at our current level, never mind grow.'

And yet some, such as the people she mentioned previously, are not particularly interested in 'growth'. They like things the way they are. Which is entirely understandable. So much of top-level men's football is about 'growth', whether that's more money or bigger stadiums or more, more, more football, new competitions popping up around the world to justify someone's existence somewhere. Developing a team at Lewes's level through outside investment and 'diluting' the idea of community ownership isn't exactly on the same hyper-capitalist level as the Premier League, but to some it could look like a similar trajectory.

It's a high-wire act. How do you remain close to the principles of an organisation like Lewes, but still have some sort of ambition and achieve something approaching on-pitch success? Is the idea of fan or community ownership a theoretical dream scenario, that at the same time has a natural ceiling in the modern football landscape? What is more important: the ownership structure or being a football club that wins games and gets promoted? Are those two things mutually exclusive?

It was therefore a pretty dramatic moment when, in November, Lewes announced that the two sides had come to a mutual decision not to go through with the deal.

It wasn't just a problem with the will of the fan owners, nor was it just a problem with Mercury/13 working within that structure. But it was a combination of those things, along with the fact that they were only interested in half of the club. It became too messy.

'Ultimately the easiest way to think about it is that we're complex as a club,' says Murphy, 'because we have a men's side and a women's side and they [Mercury/13] were only interested in the women's side, and because we have principles and values so we're not totally malleable. We have very engaged owners and fans. It's not possible to just do what you like in an entity like Lewes.

'For them to take on their first ever acquisition – we were going to be very complex and they could probably start with another team that isn't so complex.'

It was an emotional moment for Reynal, who we will hear from a lot more later. 'I think we could have figured it out,' she told me, speaking a couple of weeks after the decision was announced, 'but it would've taken time and it would've been incredibly disruptive for the club, and ultimately it became clear that it wasn't a good fit. We're not in the business of trying to force things, and I have enormous respect for everyone there. I had fallen in love with the club and it was heartbreaking the day we went down and told them we weren't going to invest – I was in the car on the way back crying, because I really wanted it to work.'

What was interesting for Lewes, Murphy and perhaps the whole concept of their ownership model, is that in theory the owners were comfortable with ceding some of their control, in exchange for some outside investment.

'We certainly have more information now on where our owners' red lines are,' says Murphy, 'and more clarity on whether the owners would be willing to give up some of their equity.

'But it also throws up some questions about what type of investor will fit with the club. We still believe that the growth potential in the club exists with the women's team and we know there are investors out there who want to invest in women's football. We have to make the case, if we want to find the investment, that investing into a complex club like Lewes is good for women's sport.'

Exeter, Portsmouth and Lewes are three examples of English fan ownership that have worked. But it doesn't always pan out that way. Sometimes, it can be an absolute disaster.

Rotherham United underwent something of a succession crisis in 2005 when Ken Booth, who had used the fortune gained from founding the scrap metal yard adjacent to the team's Millmoor home to prop the club up for the better part of 17 years, sold to a fan-led consortium called Millers 05 Ltd. By their own admission, this collection of lawyers and local businesspeople didn't really know what they were doing, and made a few well-intentioned but ultimately calamitous decisions, including an attempt to build a brand new stand at the ground which ran into financial difficulties and heavily contributed to them having to sell the club just over a year later, the threat of Rotherham disappearing completely being very real at that stage.

That stand, half-built, remains there to this day, along with the rest of Millmoor. The football club left in 2008, eventually building a brand new stadium a few hundred yards down the road. The fan consortium had bowed out by then, the club eventually taken over by Tony Stewart, their current chairman. Stewart had little previous experience, but at the very least had rather more of a business mind, and Rotherham have been on a relatively solid footing ever since, bouncing between the Championship and League One.

Fan ownership is also ripe for disagreement and competing factions. At the very least, when an individual buys a club there is usually a defined purpose, even if that purpose is not always admirable. But that is not always the case when a large group of disparate individuals are making the decisions.

Initially, FC United of Manchester's purpose was clear. It was formed by Manchester United fans who had been disaffected for years and for whom Malcolm Glazer's takeover of the club in 2005 was the final straw. In theory the club was a return to football's ideals, a quite literal reaction to everything that many deemed wrong with the modern game – in this case a financier from the other side of the world buying the biggest club in England, having borrowed the money to do so against United itself and thus loading millions in debt onto a previously debt-free club.

FC United started at the bottom but climbed the divisions, reaching the National League by 2015, but more than that it attempted to represent everything that the bigger United didn't: to return a football club to its status as a community resource, to make it about more than just the game every weekend. By the end of their first decade, they were spending £300,000 annually on community outreach programmes. Their annual 'Big Coat Day' collects warm clothing for those that need it the most. They support charities working to end men's violence against women.

In that respect, they have been a success. But after their purpose-built stadium in Moston, just north of Manchester city centre, went around 25 per cent over budget during its construction, questions started to be asked over that and a range of other issues. On the final day of the 2015/16 season a group of fans invaded the pitch and held up banners that read 'transparency now' and other messages questioning the club's board, who resigned en masse, in addition to general manager Andy Walsh, who had been the driving force of the club since its inception.

'We'd got ourselves into a situation where the majority of supporters weren't really interested in the governance of the club,' Adrian Seddon, who took over as chairman after the resignations, told the writer Connor Whitley.

Fans will often get themselves into these situations with bright intentions and noble aims, but when the actual nuts and bolts and unglamorous stuff about running a football club becomes a reality, enthusiasm, and perhaps more importantly actual skill and know-how, can disappear.

'What happens is they think they're just picking a team,' says the Exeter president Julian Tagg, 'but actually a football club is a microcosm of probably five or six different businesses from hospitality to conferencing, marketing, retail – never mind the football. And then it becomes too difficult, it becomes too onerous in terms of time. They also realise they can't compete because everybody else has philanthropic money coming in. It's much, much more difficult than people imagine.'

The willingness or otherwise of fans to actually run a football club is one weakness of the fan ownership model, but another is that there is a natural ceiling to it in modern football. As of 2024, Exeter are the highest fan-owned club in the men's football pyramid, having finally been promoted to League One in 2022, after almost a decade away.

Heart of Midlothian have been at least partly supporter-owned since 2014 (the fans took over fully in 2021), shortly after their relegation from the Scottish top flight. Luton Town won promotion to the Premier League having been fan-owned in the recent past, but as things stand, and the way the game is structured in England at least, it's tough to imagine that a fan-owned club could thrive or merely exist, even at Championship level, let alone the Premier League.

Is it possible to reach the top echelons of English men's football while being fan-owned?

'Before I thought – maybe naively, maybe not – that we might have a tilt one day at the Premier League,' says Tagg. 'Now I would probably say, if I had to bet on it, that no, it's not possible.

'But then again I never thought that we would refurbish our pitch, or build a £3 million training ground, or sell players for £2-3 million. So it would be foolish to say never, but it's not getting any easier.'

'I'd like to think they could,' offers Murphy. 'But the level of money in Premier League clubs from external sources is just impossible to consider … I just don't think it's viable. I do think fan-owned clubs can progress, but it's very difficult.

That was one of the reasons that the Portsmouth Trust ultimately sold up when Eisner arrived.

'I and other people had said numerous times that, with football as it currently is, we believe we can get us to the Championship, but we can never, without an incredible bit of luck, get higher than that,' says Ashley Brown.

'And although I was being honest when I said that, I think it was in the back of a lot of people's minds that, if we wanted to challenge in the Championship, which is what most people want Pompey to do, then somebody else had to come in and do it.'

Wrexham are another fine example of the fan-owned ceiling. Their supporters' trust had saved the club from potential oblivion in 2011: years of administrations and relegations and threats of being homeless and being passed from owner to owner had rendered the club a shell, technically still a going concern but one that never felt more than a couple of bad decisions away from disappearing.

But goodwill can only extend so far. By 2020, with the club having missed out on promotion from the National League in agonising circumstances a couple of times, and that year only just escaped relegation from it, the strong whiff of stagnation had set in. As had dissatisfaction among the fans: it wasn't as if there was open revolt or strong opprobrium directed at the well-meaning stewards of the club, but just the sense that they had done all they could and perhaps someone else could bring something different.

They probably weren't thinking that someone would be a couple of world-famous Hollywood actors, but in November 2020 Ryan Reynolds and Rob McElhenney bought the club, the documentary *Welcome To Wrexham* became a colossal hit and everything changed, never to be the same again. New players and two promotions followed, but more than that the whole place became re-energised. Few in Wrexham are pining for the days of the supporters' trust.

Perhaps fan ownership can't work at the top level of English football. But it can and does work in other countries, even the biggest in the world.

Because technically speaking, Real Madrid and Barcelona (along with fellow Spanish clubs Athletic Bilbao and Osasuna) are owned by their fans. They're not quite the plucky band of brothers and sisters that saved clubs like Portsmouth and Exeter, holding things together with spit, twigs and a huge amount of good will, but technically speaking they are member-led sporting associations. Fans can purchase memberships, becoming *socios*, which grants them the right to elect the president, who then makes all the decisions. If you're lucky enough to get to the top of the waiting list, you pay a relatively modest membership fee and you're in. For Real, that fee was €150 annually as of 2024 and, if you stay as a socio for 50 years, your fee is waived.

It's a curious but rather nice anachronism that actually required an exemption to Spanish law to remain in place. In 1990 a law was passed that made it mandatory for any Spanish professional football club to be a privately owned company, but they made those four clubs the exceptions, broadly because the *socios* structure of Real, Barça and Athletic were rooted in their regional and cultural identity.

In theory, it's a structure with baked-in oversight and accountability, a democratic way to run a football club: if you don't like the way things are being run, you can vote the person in charge out. On a more ethereal level, it creates a link between the supporters and the club, something that many sets of fans in England would welcome heartily.

It also protects these colossal institutions of football and Spanish society from state owners or leeches like the Glazers. Presidents are not allowed to inject their own money into the club, preventing what Arsène Wenger famously called 'financial doping'. Real and Barça, strange as it might seem given that they both behave like the most rapacious capitalists in the game, are non-profit organisations.

There are drawbacks, of course. Because they have to curry favour among the *socios*, whoever is president at the time will err towards populist decisions, regardless of whether they are financially responsible or not. That's partly why Barcelona got into the colossal financial mess that ultimately led to the departure of their greatest ever player, Lionel Messi, in 2021, and leaving them €1.2 billion in debt in 2023.

Also the idea of democracy in this case is a bit of a mirage: sure, you can vote in the presidential elections every four years, but that's it. You're essentially trusting whoever runs the slickest campaign with the club for the rest of that time, without any say on anything else. Presidents have resigned under significant pressure, notably Josep Bartomeu, who stepped down from Barça in 2020, but it's pretty easy to ignore the fans for most of the time.

That isn't the case in Germany, where a similar ownership structure is mandated by the 50-plus-one rule: simply put, a majority of the voting shares of every professional club in the country must be in the hands of the club, which means its fans and members, with outside investors allowed to hold the rest.

In some respects it's a more comfortable middle ground, where fans have a say and – in theory at least – excessive power is not left in the hands of one person. It also puts in place a slightly curious situation for investors, who can spend as much money as they like on shares, but they will never actually be able to control the club.

That didn't go down well with Hasan Ismaik, a Jordanian investor who spent millions acquiring 60 per cent of the technical shares of 1860 Munich, but only had 49 per cent of the voting rights. To a point he had reason to be annoyed: his investment had more or less saved the club when they were in trouble in 2011, but nationwide sympathy for him was limited after he declared he was going to launch a lawsuit against the 50-plus-one concept in 2017. He did not succeed.

There are some exceptions to the rule in the Bundesliga. Two of them are Bayer Leverkusen and Wolfsburg, who initially existed as works teams for the Bayer pharmaceutical company and Volkswagen respectively, so are owned by those corporations. Another is – or at least was – Hoffenheim, whose benefactor Dietmar Hopp took them from what was a village team in the middle of nowhere to the Champions League. He took advantage of an exemption put in by the football authorities that said if you had consistently invested in a club for 20 years or more, you could be allowed to have full control of it. However, as the years went by Hopp started to step back from direct involvement with the club, and in 2023 announced he would be returning majority control of Hoffenheim to its fans and effectively retiring.

The fourth, and by a distance the least popular exemption, is RB Leipzig. Red Bull started their forays into the world of football with their home club, Salzburg, in 2005, but by 2009 they had reached Germany and purchased the licence of fifth-tier amateur side SSV Markranstadt. They got around the rules by simply forming a new club and prevented anyone other than Red Bull employees from being members. Such is the culture among German fans – who consider the purity of the game as sacrosanct and who are aggressively suspicious of anyone who disrupts the established way of things – that they are pretty much universally despised throughout the country. Even more so than Bayern Munich, the merciless Bavarian winning machine who are unpopular like any dominant force in any country is, but who retain a level of grudging respect for the way they have made themselves into a colossus.

Bayern, however, also expose a flaw in the system. They are financially bulletproof, hoovering up most of the revenue, attention and oxygen in the German football ecosystem: this financial dominance has allowed them to protect their on-pitch dominance (until Bayer Leverkusen's astonishing unbeaten title win in 2024) by nicking the best players from even their closest challengers whenever they like, in the manner of bullies everywhere. The 50-plus-one rule affords them the reassurance of knowing that, with a wealthy group or individual being theoretically unable to take control of and pump money into a competitor, they will probably always retain that financial dominance. The cycle continues and it's difficult to see how that is going to change.

What is perhaps more hopeful and interesting is that the actual power in the direct running of clubs that the 50-plus-one rule gives fans in Germany also extends to a more indirect sort of power. German fans are more influential than any other when it comes to standing up for their rights, and even simply things they hold dear and believe is in their best interests.

Take Monday night football: in England there is an annoyance at, but a shrugging acceptance of, the idea that TV companies will move games around to suit their schedules, with little care for things like how the match-going supporter will get home. In Germany they aren't nearly so passive: in 2018, a series of protests that included but was not limited to Eintracht Frankfurt fans coating the pitch with tennis balls during one game, and Borussia Dortmund supporters simply boycotting another, ultimately led to the scrapping of televised games on Monday nights. This is despite it being enormously lucrative for the TV companies: it was deemed unacceptable by the fans, so it was phased out in the next broadcast rights deal.

Another example came in 2023, when Bayern fans protested vociferously against the club's relationship with Qatar, whose Qatar Airways logo adorned their shirts for five seasons. Eventually the club bowed to the weight of public opinion and decided that they would not renew the sponsorship deal when it expired.

It's naive to think that just because forms of fan ownership work at the top level of the game in some countries, it could also work in others. Like, for these purposes, England. The structures in Germany are so deeply rooted in the history and culture of the clubs involved that it is natural to them. The idea of transposing that to a nation of clubs where it is not so natural is potentially a nice idea, but an extraordinarily impractical one. It wouldn't just be the ownership structures of clubs in England that would have to change: it would have to almost be the very nature of the game itself.

———

It's at this point where fan ownership becomes an interesting philosophical question: is 'progress' – which can be defined in a number of ways, but for now let's say it is climbing up the leagues and achieving greater on-pitch success – more important than the principle of being fan-owned? What is the purpose of what you are trying to do?

This is the quandary that Lewes faced, Murphy and the rest of the club's leadership ultimately deciding that it was better to retain their fundamental identity, rather than extensively compromise in the hope of growth, although the very fact that their community owners voted to continue talks with Mercury/13 indicates that they would be open to it in the future.

It becomes about compromise to one extent or another. What are you prepared to give up? How far will you stretch your principles?

'It all boils down to how much the club sells out,' says Stefan Schubert, from the fan-owned Austria Salzburg. 'You've got to sell out on some level, no matter where you play. Especially if you play with the pros.

'It's about who is in control. If the fans still have the last say, and if the club has the same core values, the details will not matter that much. That sounds awful to some extent, but it's a realistic approach. We have certain values. We'll always do things in a certain way: we won't sell the name of the club, or the colours, we'll keep the interests of the members very high. But we're here to win games and have a proper club. I think that's all possible.

'You can either work with your people, or give all the power to people who don't know your story and don't really care, because they only know about numbers. But if the people who work for the club realise the history, realise why we're doing this … it will still work.'

For Tagg and Exeter, while they haven't faced the reality of a decision in the same way that Lewes did, the answer to the question of whether they would entertain the idea of outside investment or even a full takeover is more straightforward.

'I've seen enough of life and football to never say never,' says Tagg. 'There might be a different group of people in control in, say, 20 years' time. Circumstances might change; it might be inevitable that we have to [cede some control] one day. We might not have a choice. Someone might come in and mess it all up badly.

'But if you ask me that question now, I would say "no". We've never had a realistic proposal, simply because as soon as somebody expresses an interest, we say we're not interested.'

5

FAME: CELEBRITY OWNERS

*'I've lived in north Wales for most of my life and
I think it's probably the best thing that's happened
to it in the last 15, 20 years.'*
OSIAN ROBERTS,
WREXHAM FAN

Stephen Tapp had only been in his new shop for a few weeks when he arrived one Saturday morning to find the back windows smashed in.

He had taken the big step of moving into his own premises, having traded for three years on a market in Wrexham, his home town. He sold sportswear – football shirts, tracksuit tops, t-shirts – and people from all around would send him their trainers to spruce up and customise.

It was going well. Tapp was optimistic. Then the burglars broke in and took, by his estimate, just under £8,000 worth of stock. The loss of 50 or so tracksuit tops and various other items was crushing, but for him the worst part was the trainers – around £2,000 worth were nicked, but it was the fact that his customers had entrusted him with their shoes, which were now gone, that hurt.

What's more, in the whirlwind around the opening of the shop, he hadn't found the time to update his insurance details, which meant that he couldn't even claim back the cost of the stock that had been stolen.

'[Financially] I might have been just able to carry on,' Tapp says, 'but it would have been a really tough period. Mentally I wasn't really there to carry on. If it wasn't for the social media love, which was unbelievable, I would have packed it in. I probably would have put all the stuff on eBay and done something else.'

Then something strange happened. A couple he had met a few times – Kirsten and Ray Webb – saw him post on Facebook about the robbery. They set up a GoFundMe page to raise money to compensate him for the losses. In three weeks, donations from around the world reached a little over £4,000. Not bad. But not quite enough to cover his losses. Then something unexpected happened.

'I was in here on the Saturday morning and Kirsten messaged to say "Have you checked the GoFundMe page? There's a big donation on there …" I thought it would've been one of my friends who had just donated £260, but she said "No, you need to look now." I clicked on it and it said "Rob and Ryan, £3,500". I had to be picked up off the floor.'

Rob and Ryan were Rob McElhenney and Ryan Reynolds. The Hollywood actors had, implausibly, been in control of Wrexham for three years when Tapp was burgled, having completed their takeover in November 2020. Their impact on the pitch has been obvious – in their first full season in charge Wrexham, who had been away from the Football League since 2008, reached the National League play-offs. The following season they won the title with an astonishing 111 points, a record for the division, and got to the FA Cup fourth round for the first time in 23 years. The season after that they won promotion from League Two, at the first attempt.

What's slightly less obvious to the outside world is their impact on the broader community. But it becomes immediately clear if you take a wander around this otherwise unremarkable north Wales town. It doesn't take long before you spot the shops selling t-shirts celebrating Paul Mullin, the club's best player: not places you would expect to sell such merchandise either – there was one available in a photo-frame shop. There's the 'It's Always Sunny In Wrexham' merchandise, a nod to the TV show that made McElhenney's name. The Welch Fusilier pub, about 15 minutes' walk from the Racecourse Ground, Wrexham's home, displays American and

Canadian flags, in tribute to both men. Not far from the ground the logo of 'Welcome To Wrexham', the Disney documentary about the takeover, takes up the whole side of a house.

But the biggest impact has been on people like Tapp. The couple that set up the GoFundMe were Americans, with no other connection to the town, club or country, but who had met Tapp when they had travelled over to see the place they had watched in *Welcome To Wrexham*. That had then come to the attention of Reynolds and McElhenney, who had clearly been tracking its progress: the money they donated was the exact amount to take the GoFundMe up to its target. They hadn't contacted Tapp at all before they donated, and he hadn't attempted to attract their attention in any way. But it's an indication of how closely they – or at least someone working for them – were tapped into the local community. 'It's just baffling that they even know about me,' says Tapp. 'I've got absolutely no idea how it happened.'

Which is something you could probably say about how these two came to own a non-league team in north Wales in the first place. It all started when Humphrey Ker, a friend of McElhenney, recommended that he watch the Amazon documentary *Sunderland Til I Die* during the first weeks of the Covid-19 pandemic in the spring of 2020. McElhenney was inspired by the stories of the ordinary people in the show, as much as the tragicomic escapades of the football club, and wanted to make his own version. So he decided to buy a football club.

He contacted Steve Horowitz, a New York-based investment banker who specialised in putting potential buyers together with sports teams. A few possible candidates were discussed and dismissed, before they finally settled on Wrexham, which fitted their criteria: a team on its uppers who would welcome an outside saviour, in a broadly working-class town that reminded McElhenney of his own home, Philadelphia, and somewhere with a relatively broad catchment area, not overshadowed by a bigger team who would swallow up all the attention.

Pretty soon, McElhenney realised that while he was doing quite nicely for himself, he didn't quite have the cash to do this properly.

He needed someone with a bigger profile, with deeper pockets. '[He] dropped the question in so casually that it sounded like a minor consideration,' wrote Ian Herbert in his book *Tinseltown*, about the takeover, 'not a development that would send this entire enterprise on to another commercial level and create an entirely new dimension. "Would it be a problem if we have Ryan Reynolds with us?" he had asked Horowitz on one of their earlier calls.' It would not be a problem.

The two stars made their pitch to the Wrexham Supporters' Trust, who had controlled the club since 2011. The Trust had been popular but just over a decade of underperformance and disappointment had eroded their support, and people were ready for a change. The timing was also significant: the club had been forced to furlough staff due to the pandemic, and the economic impact was such that the threat of Wrexham going out of business was real.

'Things were at a low ebb long before the lockdown,' says Tapp. 'We'd been sitting in the middle of non-league football. A few players would come in and you'd think "this could be the year", but under a trust ownership you're miles away financially. We were never really competitive in the league.'

Osian Roberts, who has been a Wrexham fan all his life, agrees. 'The fans generally accepted that the Trust was doing their best in the circumstances they were in,' he says, 'but the club was in the doldrums. We had fallen down the leagues, and everyone had forgotten about the club. My reaction [to the takeover] was delight.'

Reynolds and McElhenney promised they would invest not just in the team but the club's infrastructure, while at the same time protecting 'the heritage that has made Wrexham AFC and the Racecourse Ground such a special place to watch football for the last 156 years.' They also pledged not to relocate or rename the team, but did say they would use their 'resources' to 'grow the exposure of the club.' When the proposal was put to the Trust members, 98.6 per cent voted in favour.

There was plenty of scepticism, though, mostly from the outside, but also internally. 'I'm probably similar to everyone else; at first you think: "Nah, no way,"' said Shaun Pearson, the club captain at the time.

'Some people were saying "leave us alone, we're Wrexham, we don't want this foreign investment – we're better off not being owned by them,"' says Roberts. 'But that wasn't the majority opinion.'

The pair were pretty up front about why they had bought the club – to make the documentary, but also to get in on sports ownership at a relatively affordable level, the idea being to purchase a club for a lowish price and take them up the leagues, thus increasing its value. The latter idea made sense, particularly with the two being used to the structure of American sport, where the top levels are essentially inaccessible unless you already have a club in the major leagues, which are prohibitively expensive to even invest in, much less buy. To them, the idea that you could buy a club and theoretically get them to the top via sporting means was extremely attractive.

However, the idea of the documentary came with a fear that this would all be a bit of a joke on their part, that it would be a hilarious 'Hollywood stars arrive in slightly run-down Welsh town and oh how we laughed' culture clash/fish out of water caper. The fear was that the gag would be on Wrexham as a club and a town.

The early 'content' that the two produced suggested that those fears had some substance to them. There was a skit they put out on social media involving Ifor Williams Trailers, who had to that point been Wrexham's main sponsors, in which McElhenney said: 'You may have never heard of Wrexham, the Racecourse Ground or Ifor Williams. But you will.' The sense that it all may have been a publicity stunt was growing.

The honeymoon period among the Wrexham fans even showed some signs of ending prematurely, after activity in their first transfer window in charge was limited.

Gradually though, the fears were assuaged. On-pitch success helped: they finished that first season just a point outside the play offs, having been 13th when the Trust vote happened. The next season they finished runners-up, losing in the play-off semi-finals, and reached the final of the FA Trophy at Wembley. And then the season after that they were involved in one of the most extraordinary title races in years, slugging it out with Notts County and winning promotion back to the EFL. Paul Mullin, the striker who had been top scorer in League Two and helped Cambridge United to promotion in 2020–21, dropped down a division and scored 79 goals in those first two seasons, becoming a hero not just in the town but way, way beyond that.

The documentary, when it eventually came out in August 2022, turned out not to be quite the ego trip or comic caper that it might have been. Reynolds and McElhenney featured heavily, of course, but more often than not the main narrative thrusts of the episodes concentrated on the personal stories of the players, or staff at the club, or characters in the local community.

The Turf Hotel, which backs onto the Racecourse Ground, and its jocular landlord Wayne Jones, became crucial to the story and the pub is now a pilgrimage destination for fans of the show: go in there before most home games, and you'll hear American accents, people who watched *Welcome To Wrexham* and crossed the Atlantic to visit the town.

Shaun Winter, a painter-decorator who appeared to be at something of a low ebb when we first met him in the show, became the sort of voice of the fans. There's Michael Hett, member of local band the Declan Swans, who wrote a song called *Always Sunny In Wrexham* and went on to support Kings Of Leon when they played at the Racecourse Ground, whose fight against cancer was shown in one of the early episodes. Kerry Evans, who at the time of the takeover worked as the club's disability liaison officer on a volunteer basis, had her role made permanent. An episode of the second series was based around Millie Tipping, an autistic teenager whose support for the club helps keep her life stable. That episode also featured Mullin talking about his son, Albi, who had been diagnosed with non-verbal autism the previous year.

It's also worth pointing out that, even with the caveat that they're both successful actors so could just be doing a very good job of faking their commitment, both Reynolds and McElhenney seem to have become genuinely emotionally invested in the club.

During the promotion run-in at the end of the 2022/23 season, McElhenney developed a stress-related stye next to his right eye. He also started collecting a little bit of grass from the pitch every time he attended a game at the Racecourse Ground, which he would put into a series of little plastic bags and keep in his office. After a while, his wife Kaitlin Olsen had them mounted into a presentation frame commemorating each individual game.

All of which is not to say that the takeover has been universally popular or positive. The other teams in the National League, for example, were not especially impressed at the idea of one club gaining such a significant advantage because two famous men wanted to make an entertaining documentary.

There is a genuine problem, though, that exists on a couple of levels. For a start, Wrexham's 'exposure' through being a hit on American TV meant that they attracted sponsors and revenue that simply wasn't available to their peers: you wouldn't catch United Airlines or TikTok sponsoring Rochdale, for example. The advantage this gives them is extraordinary: their projected revenue for the 2023/24 financial year, when they would play in League Two, was in excess of £20 million – for context, Preston North End, who have played in the Championship since 2015, reported a turnover of £13.8 million in the previous year.

This gives them a huge advantage over clubs of a similar size, who have not achieved any less on the pitch, but simply didn't have the good fortune to be taken over by two extremely famous men. Every club has its advantages, but this one is a whopper.

But more than that is the relationship between football and money. For many people, the benefit of supporting a club further down the football pyramid is that it exists in opposition to the Premier League, where generally speaking the rich clubs win and everyone else picks up the scraps. The National League, even the lower reaches of the EFL, in theory should not follow the same route. Of course it happens, with teams like Salford City among others, but it doesn't mean people have to like it when it does.

There's also the issue of who Wrexham really belongs to. The first few years of success will naturally keep the fans happy, with the owners' commitment to the local community beyond just success on the pitch helping that contentment significantly too. But it's inevitable that, as Wrexham's success grows and particularly their international following increases, the club will feel less and less like theirs.

Take those American accents you hear in The Turf: nobody has a problem with them and most are actively welcome while it's a novelty, but if these 'tourists' start to gobble up tickets and make it more difficult for local fans to attend games, you wonder how warmly they will be embraced.

It also raises the question of whether a football club should largely exist to be a source of content for two Hollywood actors. Is it really respecting the idea of the club as a community institution if the town and stadium is turned into a Disney documentary set? Apart from anything else, what happens if the show is cancelled, or they simply lose interest? The latter question is something that will only become clear years down the line, but will remain a concern.

'There is a fear of "how long is this going to last?"' says Roberts. 'But I think even if they pulled out, or the documentary ended, they will be returning the club to a better position than it was. And that fear is present in other places: I'm sure Manchester City fans feel the same. Football clubs aren't really profitable entities. Whichever club you support, if there's a rich owner, you always have the fear of something changing, the club being sold.'

But as for the rest of it, does the original intent of the ownership really matter? The team has been successful, and, if you talk to anyone from Wrexham, they will tell you that the takeover has not only significantly impacted the club, but the town generally.

'It's brought people to life again,' says Tapp. 'The fact we're getting people coming into the town now – that would never have happened before. We've been put on the map by these two men.

'I have three or four American families in the shop every week, before home games. I had a guy in who had been over for a week. It's completely bonkers.

'A lot of them say it's a connection to where they grew up. Sport is more of an entertainment thing rather than a passion thing over here. It's a different feel and the atmospheres are completely different. Wrexham isn't the smartest and it's not the poshest, but it's got lovely people.'

Tapp pauses, remembering the robbery. 'Well, the majority of the people are lovely.'

Roberts concurs: 'It's surpassed anyone's expectations how much they have put Wrexham on the map, what they've done for the community, how much attention the club has had. A lot of these clubs have rich benefactors and owners, but this is completely different.

'I've lived in north Wales for most of my life and I think it's probably the best thing that's happened to it in the last 15, 20 years.'

'I was a member of the supporters' trust,' says Tapp. 'I always remember Spencer Harris, who was head of the Trust, said in one meeting "We need to kick on, but it's going to be a struggle – no sugar daddy is going to buy this club."'

If the sight of McElhenney and Reynolds at Wrexham was one of the stranger sights you'll see in football, then Michael B Jordan holding up a scarf and striding out onto the pitch at Bournemouth wasn't far behind.

The man most will know more from Marvel's *Black Panther* films, rather than his involvement with a mid-range football club on the south coast of England, was announced as a minority shareholder in the club in December 2022. Bournemouth's social media feed tweeted a picture of the actor with a graphic featuring his image and the statement 'Welcome to #afcb, @michaelb4jordan' as if they were unveiling the signing of a new left-back.

'I'm really excited about that venture,' he said a couple of months later when, as a guest on Graham Norton's talk show, he was asked the not unreasonable question: erm, why? 'The team is awesome. The town is amazing, and I'm just ready to kind of maximise potential, see what I can bring to the table, help bring the popularity of the players in the team up.'

Of course, Jordan won't be at board meetings to discuss planning applications for a new training ground or poring over WyScout footage to assess potential new signings. Bournemouth's long-running takeover saga finally came to a close at the end of 2022, when Bill Foley, an American businessman who also owned the Las Vegas Golden Knights ice hockey team, led a consortium to take over the club.

That consortium – Black Knight Football and Entertainment – consisted of a wide range of investors, but oddly not many of them featured in the same amount of stylishly filmed social media content as Jordan. Which gives you an idea as to his role in the whole thing.

'Mike is a great guy,' said Foley at the time. 'He's a very down-to-earth, common individual. He hasn't got stars in his eyes. He loves football. He will be involved on the marketing side, on developing new gear … He'll be here on Saturday, he'll be on the pitch waving at people and talking to them.'

'Jordan's first substantive contribution to the club came in July 2024, when two special edition kits were released, billed as a 'collaboration' with the actor, and which they wore in their pre-season games in California. "Having the opportunity to design a kit has been a project I have been excited to work on since joining the club, and I can't wait to see them out on the pitch this week," he told the club's website.'

Jordan isn't the only absurdly famous and wealthy American star to inexplicably pop up as part of the ownership of an English football team.

LeBron James has been involved with Fenway Sports Group since 2011: initially that came about when John Henry's investment consortium became the marketers for his image rights, a deal which came with a two per cent stake in Liverpool – which doesn't sound like much, but in 2023 Forbes valued the club at around £4.6 billion, making his shares worth something like £90 million. Not bad. He became a full partner in FSG in 2021.

Like Jordan, LeBron's main involvement with Liverpool is as a marketing tool, especially in America. You can buy, if this is your thing, a pair of LFC X Lebron Air Max Nike trainers from the Liverpool shop, RRP a mere £164.95. Also available are a full range of LeBron/Liverpool crossover merch, including shorts, hoodies, t-shirts and basketball vests.

A little further down the food chain, Birmingham City were bought by the US-based Knighthead Capital Management, via their investment vehicle Shelby Companies Limited, in the summer of 2023. A month or so later, at the start of the Championship season, there was an unusual visitor to the Roost pub, just over the road from St Andrew's, as Tom Brady popped in (with his bodyguards and a film crew) for a quick pre-match pint and a spontaneous and natural chat with the locals. Who, to be fair, did seem quite pleased and impressed by the whole thing.

Brady had entered into a partnership with Knighthead which meant he would become a minority shareholder and join – later chair – the club's advisory board. A press release at the time said that Brady would 'apply his extensive leadership experience and expertise across several components of the club, including working alongside the sports science department to advise on health, nutrition, wellness, and recovery systems and programs.'

'I know I like being the underdog,' said the seven-time Super Bowl winner and five-time NFL MVP. 'Maybe you're asking, "What do you know about English football, Tom?" Well let's just say I've got a lot to learn. But I do know a few things about winning and I think they may translate pretty well.'

Would Birmingham become a club that prioritised celebrity and big splash announcements over sensible sporting decisions and a genuine relationship between the fans and the team? Perhaps only time will tell, but one of their first acts was to get rid of manager John Eustace, who had taken a shambles of a club to seventh the previous season and only just missed the play-offs, and replace him with Wayne Rooney, whose DC United team finished 12th out of 15 in the MLS Eastern Conference.

Three months and 15 games later, Rooney was sacked. Birmingham had only won two of those games, going from sixth in the table and in the play-off places when Rooney arrived, to 20th and six points off the relegation zone upon his departure.

They were ultimately relegated at the end of the season to League One, having got through another couple of managers in the interim. Even by the standards of some of the most calamitous owners in football history, the sheer speed of the drop-off under Knighthead was almost impressive. It later emerged that Brady's 'minority' stake in the club was extremely minor: 3.3 per cent, to be exact, with no voting rights.

And then there's JJ Watt, the NFL star who, along with his wife, the former US international Kealia Watt, bought a minority stake in Burnley in 2023.

'America is craving football content,' Watt told ESPN in 2023. 'There's a large group of people that still don't have a great knowledge base, so they're still trying to find their squad. They're still trying to find who they're supposed to support. I think it helps us a lot that more eyeballs come over. We just direct those eyeballs up to Burnley.'

And so, here we have again the global reach of the Premier League, whose piercing and overpowering light has become powerful enough that even already astoundingly famous and wealthy American stars want to bask in a little corner of it.

And they in turn want to use their own glow to attract US sports fans to a specific part of the Premier League. James and Jordan and Brady and Watt are essentially billboards with wallets, chucking a nominal handful of coins into the pot, knowing that their role in the whole business is to smile for the cameras and encourage sports fans from Boston and Baltimore and Boise to direct their passions to, erm, Burnley and Birmingham and Bournemouth.

While many of these ventures in the men's game have the glitter of celebrity sprinkled on them, a new American team that came into being in the summer of 2020 was built on that glitter.

The bare facts of Angel City's beginnings were that their founders were awarded one of the American National Women's Soccer League expansion franchises in 2020 and played their first game in 2022.

But that underplays their origin story quite significantly. They were the brainchild of the venture capitalist Kara Nortman, who at a lunch in 2018 was evangelising the US Women's National Team's fight to be paid equally to their male counterparts. On the other side of the table was Natalie Portman, Oscar winner and star of films that, as of 2024, cumulatively grossed almost $10 billion. Portman was enthused by Nortman's enthusiasm, and wondered if she could leverage her celebrity and get some famous friends to help the cause.

So she invited a selection of pals, including Eva Longoria, Jessica Chastain and Jennifer Garner, to the friendly between the USA and Belgium in April 2019, and from there the idea was born. At the time Los Angeles had two men's teams – LA Galaxy and LAFC – but hadn't had a women's club since Los Angeles Sol had folded in 2010.

'I didn't go into this thinking I would build a team for LA,' Portman told The Athletic in 2020. '[Kara] introduced me to Becca Roux (director of the USWNT players association) and a handful of USWNT players to see if there was a way for my actress friends and soccer players to support each other. At the [Belgium] game, they too could meet the amazing players I'd gotten to know and see them in action.

'Shortly thereafter, the USWNT won their second consecutive World Cup title. Then TIME'S UP and the players' association joined forces to host a pay equity workshop in Los Angeles prior to the first Victory Tour game. The more time I spent with these women, the more I learned and the bigger impact I wanted to make.

'It was just so obvious — we needed to see these women play in LA. We needed a team here.'

It was a more or less instant success, off the pitch at least. They were valued at $100 million before they had even played a game and by 2023 that had shot up to $180 million, according to Sportico. They had managed to build a brand before actually having a team, reversing the traditional way a football team might leverage its image for profit: for them, the image came first and the football afterwards.

'Those values were all estimates at the time, but they were made real in July 2024, when they were bought for around $250 million by Bob Iger, CEO of the Walt Disney Company, and his wife Willow Bay, the journalist and TV presenter. That made them the most expensive women's sports team in the world.'

In April of 1975, Elton John ran into a record shop in New York and asked if he could use their phone. Important information was waiting at the other end of that phone line, across the Atlantic, just outside London. Watford were at home to Walsall in the last game of the season in the old Third Division: they needed to win in order to avoid relegation to the fourth tier, but the lad who grew up as Reggie Dwight, watching Watford from the Vicarage Road terraces, was told the bad news. A 3-2 defeat. The Hornets had sunk to the bottom of the Football League. John sunk too, onto the floor of the record shop and burst into tears.

He was already involved with the club in a loose way, having been named as vice-president a year earlier after raising money by giving a concert to help out his beleaguered club. A couple of years later, when the team had failed to escape the clutches of the Fourth Division, John was asked in an interview with *Playboy* magazine whether there was anything else he wanted to achieve.

'My real ambition,' he answered, 'is to make enough money to retire and become chairman of my local football club, Watford.' History doesn't record whether the journalist laughed, scoffed or wrote it off as the eccentric spoutings of an eccentric pop star, but John wasn't joking.

He didn't retire, but when the long-standing chairman Jim Bonser decided he'd had enough in 1976, he gave the club to John on the condition that he cleared their debts of around £200,000. 'I didn't need to think about it,' John told John Preston for his book *Watford Forever*. 'I was so keen to accept.'

John immediately declared that he wanted to take Watford to the First Division, and while he was viewed with incredulity at the time, as it turned out his prediction was modest. He initially didn't sweep in and make big changes, leaving manager Mike Keen in charge for a season after he bought the club. But after another season when they didn't threaten to challenge for promotion, Keen was dismissed in 1977. John's first choice for Keen's replacement was Bobby Moore, captain of England's World Cup winning team 11 years earlier. But eventually he settled on a young manager who came recommended by Don Revie, at the time England manager.

Graham Taylor was climbing towards the top of Division Three with Lincoln when John called him towards the end of the 1976/77 season. Taylor turned him down, with half an eye on a First Division job, but after meeting John and instantly hitting it off, along with the promise of a very generous salary for such a lowly position, Taylor accepted.

That began one of the great chairman-manager relationships in English football. 'I had exactly the same sort of feeling with Graham as I'd done when I met Bernie Taupin,' John said about his immediate rapport with Taylor. The next two seasons saw back-to-back promotions into the Second Division, where they paused for three campaigns before making it to the top tier for the first time in their history in 1982. This was all done with some of the players who had been there right from the Fourth Division days, like strikers Ross Jenkins and Luther Blissett, but also with new blood like the brilliant John Barnes.

Astonishingly, Watford finished second in the top flight in their first season there, qualifying for the UEFA Cup, where they would reach the third round. The following season they got to the FA Cup final, losing 2-0 to Everton at Wembley.

It remains one of the great underrated success stories in English football, a team going from the murky depths of the Football League to almost winning the league title, inside six seasons. But more than that it was one of football's great love stories, a professional and platonic bond between two men that created something astonishing.

Taylor left to take over as Aston Villa manager in 1987 and later that year John sold the club to a property developer called Jack Petchey. The two things were not unconnected. 'I still loved the club,' John told Preston, 'but there had been a serendipity, a magic, about the two of us together and I couldn't conjure up that same magic without him.'

The two would come together again, a decade later, when Taylor returned as manager (winning promotion to the Premier League, of course) and John had got back involved although not as sole owner this time. But it was that first spell, 11 years when a shy boy who became a global pop star did what many of us dream about by bringing unimagined success to our club, that has a case to be the greatest single tenure by an English club owner. In terms of success when measured against expectation, combined with the emotional aspect of having a home town hero at the helm, there aren't many that can match it.

While Elton John's custodianship of Watford was an emotional decision rather than a financial or even logical one, the other famous faces who have become involved in football over the last few years are doing so because football is a growth industry, something fashionable and lucrative to be part of.

All of which feels quite strange for those of us who started watching football in the 1980s when the game, in England at least, was a pariah sport. Or, as a 1985 editorial in *The Sunday Times* put it, a 'slum sport played in slum stadiums and increasingly watched by slum people, who deter decent folk from turning up.'

But it should tell you plenty about the power that football holds, and the commercial possibility that people looking to expand their portfolios see in it, that these worldwide stars are so keen to become involved in it. There are plenty of other ways to make money, plenty of other ways to grow your assets, plenty of other things to hook yourself to for the reflected glory. Ryan Reynolds doesn't need to own Wrexham. Natalie Portman doesn't need to own Angel City. LeBron James doesn't need to (part) own Liverpool.

And yet they all do. They all actively got themselves involved in football, taking the seats in director's boxes that used to be occupied by successful local butchers or the proprietor of the factory just down the road. You can see why they do it, but should football welcome them with open arms?

In the case of Portman in Los Angeles and Reynolds and McElhenney in Wrexham, the impact has been undoubtedly positive. Even if you don't really pay attention to the financial success, that Portman was able to help bring a women's team to Los Angeles when, somewhat ridiculously, there wasn't one there before can only be a positive for the game in America. Likewise Reynolds and McElhenney have saved a football club and re-energised a town, so while you can shift slightly uncomfortably at the idea of them using Wrexham as a pseudo reality TV show set, how much do their intentions truly matter when the outcome has been so uplifting?

It feels slightly different with the likes of Brady and Watt and James. They are semi-passive investors, watching the performance of these football clubs like a stockbroker might watch the NASDAQ ticker. You can argue about what the purpose of these football clubs was intended to be, but one thing they definitely weren't meant for is to be part of an investment portfolio, and something you occasionally pop up and promote like an Instagram influencer trying to sell you a nutritional supplement.

Maybe those conclusions are too outcome-based. If things had gone badly on the pitch at Wrexham, the idea of them being bought mainly to feature in a documentary would be used as the biggest of sticks with which to beat them. If Angel City had been a financial dud when they were launched, people might have asked what an actor was doing in the game.

But ultimately, while it might be a little odd to see these famous faces in control of clubs, the same sentiment applies to them as it does to any owner: some are good, some are bad. Applying a judgement across the board doesn't make much sense.

6

THE DISRUPTORS – OR THREE PEOPLE WHO DO THINGS DIFFERENTLY

'We haven't done anything wrong: we've just done something that a lot of people don't understand.'
SPENCER OWEN,
HASHTAG UNITED FOUNDER

'We're a football club that is doing something very different,' said Dale Vince, owner of the green energy company Ecotricity and, more importantly for our purposes, owner and chairman of Forest Green Rovers, in 2022.

This book is full of many different types of football club owner. But after a while they do start to blend together. Rules are followed. Archetypes repeated. Money changes hands. Millions are spent on wages. 'Traditional' methods are followed.

But every now and then you come across people who genuinely are doing things very differently. And not just running their football clubs in a non-traditional manner, but approaching the whole business from a different place, changing the way we think about football club ownership and possibly giving the rest of the game some hints on how to make change possible.

A team that began life as a YouTube channel. Cryptocurrency and NFT speculators who promise to fix what they view as a broken system. An environmental activist using his club to promote, in his words, a 'green agenda'.

These are the disruptors. They're not necessarily good owners, they're not necessarily bad. But they are different.

———

Luton Town were in the Premier League in the 2023/24 season. The division's evangelists will say it's the best league in the world, but while that's subjective, deeply arguable even, it's less so to say that it's the most prominent, the most famous, the one that attracts the most attention.

The renewed domestic TV rights deal, announced in late 2023 and covering 2025–2029, was worth around £6.7 billion. Between 2022 and 2025, its international rights brought in a little over £5 billion. It is broadcast in over 200 countries and territories around the world. There was a time when the English fan would struggle to find somewhere to watch their team while on holiday abroad, unless a pub called the British Bulldog had a dodgy satellite feed, but these days wherever you are on the planet you won't have much trouble finding a live broadcast of Bournemouth v Wolves.

You might therefore think that a team like Luton would automatically benefit from its burning spotlight. It's always tricky to properly measure these things, to gauge the worldwide popularity of a football club in some sort of tangible way, but you could do worse than their social media following.

Midway through their first Premier League campaign, Luton had a little over 203,000 followers on X, another 368,000 on Instagram and 534,000 on TikTok, along with 103,000 YouTube subscribers. Less tangibly, everyone who follows football in England and a fair chunk in the wider world will at least have heard of them, if only as the club with the cramped ground you have to enter through someone's house.

Hashtag United, a club founded in 2016, are very much not in the Premier League: their men's team competed in the Isthmian League Premier Division while Luton were facing Liverpool, Arsenal and Manchester City. But they had 230,000 followers on

X, 505,000 on Instagram and 382,000 on TikTok, plus a whopping 639,000 YouTube subscribers.

This is a club that had a following before they had even played a game. Which is thanks to their founder, Spencer Carmichael-Brown, better known by the name Spencer Owen, a wildly successful YouTuber who made his name playing esports – FIFA in particular – and who was part of a wider online community that included the Sidemen, a collective that includes occasional boxer KSI.

It's a world that is a mystery to many football fans, particularly those above a certain age, but one that has become increasingly difficult to ignore and, crucially, is no less valid because a bunch of 40-year-olds don't know about it. But that is perhaps the reason why Owen's venture into the tangible football world hasn't always been especially popular.

In 2016, Owen and his brother Seb set up their own club. Initially it was populated by them and their friends, playing 11-a-side football at the weekends just as thousands of other Sunday league teams across Britain do. The difference was that your standard Sunday league team didn't have access to a massive worldwide audience: at the time, Owen personally had around a million YouTube subscribers, a number that has since surpassed two million. Plus, they had the brothers' ambition behind it.

'Our vision was to create a club, but we didn't know the best way to do it,' Owen says. 'It's always been my dream to run a football club, but I thought it might be at the end of my career – if I had the money I would buy a club, like a lot of people do.

'When YouTube started to take off we thought there was a chance to short-cut that. The initial idea was that we would get a sponsor to give us a load of money up front to buy a non-league team, then we would document ourselves running that club as a YouTube series.'

That would have been an unconventional way of doing a fairly conventional thing: football history is littered with examples of men either making or being given money and spending it on a football club. But the more they thought about it, the less they actually wanted to do it like that.

'To do that we would have to buy an existing club and take over its history, and draw some critics for that. We wondered if we could enter the pyramid as a new club, so we created a new club that we played in. It was all about growing the audience first, and for want of a better word the "brand" of the club, then take that into non-league once we've got the support.

'We did two years of exhibition matches in some amazing places, based purely on our YouTube following, not our football ability, because we were pretty average.'

They played games in seven different countries, including a tour to America. Those exhibition matches were against, among others, a Comedians' XI, a team of former professional footballers and the Great Britain deaf team. Owen created a competition, the Wembley Cup, in 2015, which was a charity tournament and initially a vehicle for a team put together by him – Spencer FC – to face one representing the Sidemen. Hashtag United played in and won the 2017 edition with a team that featured former USA international Jimmy Conrad, who became a YouTuber after retiring from the game.

In 2018, they started to formalise things a little more, and took advantage of a new league being created in the south-east of England, meaning that they could enter the pyramid without taking someone else's place, something that had been playing on Owen's mind. From that point, their rise was rapid: they won promotion from the Eastern Counties League Division One South in 2019 and were flying high in the Essex Senior League in 2019–20 when the season was cancelled due to the Covid-19 pandemic; they were promoted again the following season and had two seasons in the Isthmian League North Division before rising to the Isthmian Premier in 2023.

Hashtag United are unconventional in a variety of ways, one of which is that they are not tied to a place. Basically every other team you can think of, in Britain certainly, has sprung from some sort of local community institution: back in the 1800s and early 1900s, when most teams in the English football pyramid were founded, clubs would form from works teams, or from religious institutions, or were rooted in some kind of physical community. Hashtag are rooted in a community, but it's not physical: it's online. You're just as likely to follow them if you live in Essex, south-east England, where they play their home games, as if you live in Essex County, New York.

'You have to find your people,' Owen says. 'For most clubs it's a geographical location and you start off with that, you find a catchment area and you try and make those people support your club. Then if you're really successful you look beyond that and try to build your brand worldwide. We sort of reverse-engineered that: we had people watching us in every country in the world, but we didn't necessarily have people in the local area coming to our games, so we had a different challenge.'

Their lack of significant ties to a locality might also give them more licence to ignore one of the most stridently adhered-to rules in English football: thou shalt not move. While American readers might find the idea of people losing their minds at the prospect of a team shifting to a different town or city rather curious, given that it happens so often in US sports, the idea that clubs should not relocate is sacrosanct in England. Milton Keynes Dons are still pariahs to some, after the original Wimbledon FC moved from south-west London to Milton Keynes in 2003. But that is because of most clubs' origin stories, their groundings in a certain place, their role as a community asset. Hashtag are also a community asset, it's just a different community, one that isn't grounded in or restricted by (depending on your point of view) geography.

That online community is, in part, the source of the club's name (plus the fact that Owen used to work as a social media manager), which as you might expect divides opinion. And it does, initially at least, sound pretty stupid. 'Gimmicky' would perhaps be a generous interpretation of it. This isn't just limited to grumpy old football fans: when they were promoted into the Isthmian League, they were told they had to change their name because it didn't conform to the guidelines as it didn't refer to a place. But Owen fought his corner, finding a few other examples of clubs whose names didn't do that either: Port Vale, for example, or Forest Green Rovers.

But while the name has been unpopular in some quarters, it has done the job that any 'brand' needs to do: attract attention.

'I think it's our secret sauce,' says Owen. 'Everyone who thinks we need to change it doesn't understand that, without the name being such a divider of opinion, the BBC would never have put us on TV [which they did when Hashtag beat Soham Town Rangers on penalties in the qualifying rounds of the FA Cup in 2020], because nobody would have thought we were special. Every response we've ever had, all the coverage – it's all come from the name.

'I realised: actually it doesn't matter if people don't like us because of our name, it doesn't matter if people don't understand what we're about because of a generational thing or whatever. It's actually a good thing. It's better to divide opinion than for people to have no opinion on you.

'I'm a West Ham fan. When we were founded we were an ironworks team. So when Hashtag started, the name did the exact same thing that Thames Ironworks [West Ham's original name] did – it told everyone who the people who played for the team were.

'The name may change one day, if it's a good choice for the club. But the main thing it does is what I'm saying now – it makes a club's identity central to its value, at its core. For us it's about people who come from the internet generation, understanding what a hashtag means and understanding why there's a different way of doing clubs that doesn't have to be local first.'

Their worldwide fans follow Hashtag's fortunes via the range of clips they post to YouTube, centred around the 20-or-so-minute wrap-ups of their games. Owen commentates on these clips, which has led to the odd raised eyebrows from fellow owners and chairmen: the convention is for the top brass from the competing clubs to hobnob before and during games, but Owen is typically otherwise engaged.

That's where Owen has delegated and brought in people with a little more traditional football background. He has a couple of co-chairmen who deal with the glad-handing. In 2019 they hired Jay Devereux, a non-league veteran who had previously managed Dagenham & Redbridge and East Thurrock, to be their manager. They diversified too: they have expanded to over 40 teams, including a women's team, youth teams and a more casual Sunday league team. In 2020 they merged with two teams – AFC Basildon and Forest Glade – and subsumed many of their teams into the broader Hashtag empire.

And their YouTube audience gives them significant advantages over many other clubs at their level, not least the revenue it brings. They have been sponsored by Football Manager and Adidas, something that clearly would not have been possible without their audience.

Despite them being a team of the internet, whose spiritual ownership belongs not to a physical place but to an intangible one, the club is a personal endeavour for Owen. It's one of the reasons that he decided to launch his own club, rather than taking over an existing one. This is something that he and his family built.

'The fact that me and my brother played in our club's first ever game, that my dad [who has been a physio in non-league football for years] has been involved, that my mum and my other brother are involved, and there's nothing that came before us – it's pretty special.'

There have been multiple backlashes. As you can imagine, some of the more traditional members of the non-league scene in the south of England were not delighted that a bunch of YouTubers showed up to muscle in on their patch, or at least what they perceived to be their patch.

You also wonder how sustainable the whole thing is. This is a long way off, but if they continue to grow and get promoted up the divisions, pretty soon they will reach a point where they will run into broadcast rights considerations that will make their highlights clips on YouTube trickier, to say the least. Does the sort of revenue they can earn from being an 'online' club have a ceiling? Will they, at some point, become like any other club in the lower reaches of the English football system?

Maybe. Thus far Hashtag United have been disruptors in a world that is typically quite conservative. There are rules, some written, some unwritten, rules that teams like Hashtag don't tend to adhere to. As the attention on them grows, so will the opprobrium. But perhaps one of the things that football needs is for people to ignore conventional thinking, to do things differently.

The locality of many clubs is their grounding, the source of their most loyal support, but it also restricts them. Take Bowers & Pitsea, the club that shares the ground Hashtag play at: with the greatest of respect, who is realistically going to care about them, beyond the people in their local community, if something goes wrong? Hashtag don't have a physical anchor, which could be a weakness (not least if the time comes when matchday income from people actually attending games becomes more important), but the fact that they don't rely on a location for their support and even revenue is equally a potential strength.

'As a football chairman, your job is not to make everyone like you,' Owen says. 'Nobody has ever succeeded with that in the history of football. No team has been supported by everyone. It's the opposite of that.

'The reason we're in non-league is not to tell everyone else how to do things, it's because I love non-league football and I've always wanted to be part of it. All I want with Hashtag is that I think we deserve a seat at the table, because we've shown there's a different way of doing it which is actually more economically sound.

'I maybe could've taken some of the negativity that came our way better. Even though it was unfounded. We haven't done anything wrong: we've just done something that a lot of people don't understand.'

———

Another group who arrived from a place that many in the often conservative and stuffy world of football don't understand – the internet – are called WAGMI, which stands for 'We're All Going To Make It.' WAGMI are a consortium of NFT (non-fungible tokens) investors, who arrived at Crawley Town in 2022 with grand and brash plans to take them to the Premier League, by doing things differently.

Crawley is a fairly nondescript town about 30 miles south of central London, right next door to Gatwick Airport. Aside from its proximity to a major international hub, its primary claims to fame are as the location of Britain's largest branch of Poundland, and as the home town of Gareth Southgate and Robert Smith from The Cure. Without wishing to be unkind to the fine people of Crawley, it's the sort of place kids complain about growing up in and escape from as soon as they're able.

Its football team, Crawley Town, does not have the most illustrious history: they reached the Football League for the first time in 2011, having only gone full-time professional in 2005. However, what they do have is quite a spicy ownership history.

In 1999, when the club was in the Southern Premier Division (the regional league below what was then called the Conference, now the National League), they went into administration for the first time, after which they were taken over by John Duly, a local businessman. He then sold Crawley to a local hospitality and retail company called SA Group in 2005, who announced at the time that they were 'looking to do great things' with the club.

Which they sort of did, taking them fully professional for the first time, but a year later they were in administration again, with the added complication that Chas Majeed, the chairman, was revealed to have been declared bankrupt in 2004, which at the time was one of the few things that could bar a person from owning a football club. His brother Azwar, the ultimate owner of the club, defended Chas, but he had bigger problems: a few years later he would be jailed for tax fraud, having used money from his various businesses as a 'piggy bank', according to prosecutors.

It also emerged that the club was £1.8 million in debt, a significant sum for a non-league team, and they came within hours of being forced out of existence entirely. Eventually the club was returned to the hands of Duly, before an ex-banker and Crawley fan named Vic Marley took it over in 2008. Then in 2010 they were taken over yet again by another local businessman, Bruce Winfield, who was backed by what he would only describe at the time as 'Far East' investors. Crawley subsequently went about making themselves just about the least popular club in non-league by spending, relative to their competitors at least, lavish sums on players.

Their popularity wasn't helped by the appointment of Steve Evans, who we'll delicately describe as an 'abrasive' character and who had been banned from the touchline for a cumulative 25 games in the previous couple of seasons. More seriously, in November 2006 Evans had been given a one-year jail sentence, suspended for two years, after being convicted for his part in a tax fraud scheme while manager of Boston United.

Still, it worked: they were promoted to the Football League for the first time in their history in 2011 and, despite the departure of Evans, they were promoted again the following season. After some up-and-down seasons, they were taken over again in 2016, this time by Turkish businessman Ziya Eren, who made his money in the steel business and already owned Kayseri Erciyesspor, a club that at the time was in the Turkish second tier but has since gone out of business.

Crawley remained in League Two throughout Eren's tenure and he was broadly speaking respected, if not perhaps loved, by the support simply because he kept the club afloat throughout some tricky years.

And then the club was brought screeching into the crypto age, whether they liked it or not, when WAGMI bought Eren's stake in the spring of 2022. WAGMI had attempted to buy Bradford City the previous year, but that deal fell through after they essentially announced their takeover was happening, only for the existing chairman, Stefan Rupp, to reiterate that he had only received an emailed bid for control of the club, which as it turns out did not constitute a binding contract.

Scepticism was rife. But they were certainly confident, if rather brash, when they took control of Crawley. 'Crawley Town Football Club is a club with more than 125 years of rich history that we revere and respect,' began their statement after the deal was confirmed, before going on to say: 'However, a conventional approach to ownership hasn't worked, and the club is losing hundreds of thousands of pounds while its fans suffer through year after year of uninspiring results on the pitch.'

WAGMI's front men are Preston Johnson, a former betting analyst for ESPN, and Eben Smith, whose background is in cryptocurrency and NFT trading. But these were just the most prominent of Crawley's new owners: WAGMI is a collective with an indeterminate number of investors from the internet, and it would appear that Smith and Johnson are simply the frontmen, who personally own no more than ten per cent of the club. Indeed, it would appear that no one person owns more than ten per cent, meaning there isn't a person of 'significant interest', which the Football League requires their clubs to publicly declare.

The fact that it's not entirely clear to outsiders who owns Crawley isn't ideal, but that's not the main reason people seem to be suspicious of them. Their crypto background is the main factor, but there's an innate suspicion about American owners in English football – especially ones that give the impression that they can come over and teach the Brits a thing or two about how to run a sports team. That is a little unfair, and while their opening salvo smacked of arrogance, they did have a point: football clubs in the lower reaches of the English Football League haemorrhage money, and there is thus at least an equal level of arrogance in the idea that things should just go on as they are regardless, and that new ideas shouldn't be tried, much less embraced.

Their plans essentially consisted of two things: that they would raise money to help the team through issuing NFTs (although they have repeatedly insisted that this was to be an occasional endeavour and not the club's main source of funds) and they would also use advanced statistics and analytics to gain an edge on their competitors.

Anyone who purchased one of the NFTs would get a Crawley shirt and the rather vaguely defined ability to vote on club matters, which they hinted would even go as far as which players they should sign, or who should play in some games. The first rounds of NFT releases were pretty successful: just over 10,000 were sold at £400 a pop, meaning that even before they got started they had raised £4.1 million. In football, people excel at creating money from thin air, but even by those standards, this was pretty impressive, even if it wasn't clear exactly how much of that would go to the club.

All that said, they didn't help themselves. Before they arrived at Crawley, Smith gave an interview to *The Washington Post* in which he said: 'We are going to try a bunch of unconventional stuff but will be pretty much led by the numbers from an analytical perspective. And our hope is that it works. There's not much downside if it doesn't.'

Not much downside, apart from the potential ruin of a football club. This was, not unreasonably, seized upon by those suspicious of both their motives and their methods, and served as evidence that they didn't really know what they were buying. WAGMI gave the impression they just wanted to buy a football club for giggles, as a sort of experiment, and they would try a few funky things, but if it didn't come off then they would just move on to their next one. There seemed to be little regard for the mess they might leave behind if they failed, but plenty for the idea that if it did work, they could hail themselves as the geniuses that defeated convention and cracked English football. They talked about a football club as if it was a petri dish, something they could play around with and then toss away. They appeared to, initially at least, have very little idea that they weren't just buying a sports team, but a community institution.

There were other, smaller gotchas: for example, one of the group's social media accounts carried a banner that said 'Crypto's road to the Premiership', hastily changed after someone pointed out that the top division of English football hadn't been called the Premiership since 2007.

They were certainly dealt a rough hand immediately after arriving at Crawley. Barely a month after the takeover was completed, manager John Yems was accused of racist behaviour towards his players by the FA, and one of WAGMI's first acts was to suspend and then sack him. Yems was later found guilty of 17 charges and was initially given a 17-month suspension by an independent commission, which the FA appealed, and the ban was extended to almost three years.

'We planned to come in for a year with stability and learn, see what works, what doesn't, how things work,' Johnson told me in January 2023. 'We weren't afforded that opportunity and we were kind of just thrown into it, and we had to make quick decisions on an entire new staff.

'We've made mistakes and we have to take responsibility for them for sure. But if anyone has the book on how to handle it when, within two weeks of you arriving, the manager gets that thrown at them: send it to me.'

Nonetheless, they seemingly couldn't help but make things difficult for themselves, Before their opening game of the season, a trip to Carlisle United, WAGMI put out an inexplicable video which featured a man dressed as a devil (Crawley's nickname is the Red Devils), complete with horns and red-painted face, trash talking their opponents. 'First of all, their nickname is the cum brains,' quipped the devil, 'riffing' on Carlisle's nickname being The Cumbrians. 'You're not going to win a whole load of soccer matches if your brains are full of cum.'

People weren't so much offended as absolutely baffled, but an apology was issued anyway. 'We want to apologise to the fans who found a video posted earlier to be in bad taste,' they said. 'We've heard you, we need to do better and promise that next week's Leyton Orient preview will be more on-brand for English Football.' Crawley lost to Carlisle, 1–0.

Then came the publicity stunt in September 2022, when they said two of internet collective the Sidemen – Tobi 'TBJZL' Brown and Manny Brown, as well as their brother Jed Brown – would be taking part in training, with Johnson sincerely expressing the hope that one of them might impress enough to take part in a game. The purpose was apparently to introduce Crawley to 'millions of potential new supporters', but it was the most on-the-nose example of their tone deafness, the sort of stunt that someone writing a parody of a group of cryptocurrency speculators taking over a football club might have discounted on the basis of being too obvious. Jed Brown, a decent amateur footballer, did actually sign for Crawley and was on the bench for a few EFL Cup games, but never actually played in a game.

Things reached a nadir in the middle of the 2022/23 season, around the time that Matthew Etherington resigned as Crawley manager, meaning WAGMI were looking for their fifth manager since they arrived, not much more than eight months earlier. Yems was the first, a situation that even their harshest critics would not blame WAGMI for. Then came Kevin Betsy, appointed from the Arsenal youth system, but he lasted 12 games (of which he won one) before he was sacked.

Lewis Young, brother of former Manchester United and England winger Ashley, who had been at Crawley for eight years as a player and a coach, stepped in and on the face of it did pretty well: he was only in charge for seven league games of which they only lost one, but he was dismissed partly on the basis of the owners' statistical analysis, which noted that Crawley had been outshot 87–28 over those seven games, figures which were not seen as sustainable.

Etherington then came in, but he only lasted 32 days, taking charge of just three games, before he resigned. The suggestion was that the owners were micromanaging, something Johnson denied, but it seemed that a series of irritations had managed to build up over the month Etherington was there, which led to his departure.

It was at this point that Johnson decided to take matters into his own hands: he flew to England from America for a game against Stevenage, and took the potentially unwise, if well-intentioned, decision to sit in the dugout. He insists it was simply to show some support to Darren Byfield, who had taken charge on a temporary basis, but with the suggestions of interference in the team still hanging around, plenty jumped to conclusions.

It wasn't helped by the Stevenage stadium announcer tweeting after the game, which Crawley lost 3–1, that: 'Tonight's highlight was Johnson asking the fourth official at half-time how subs work. Whilst sat on the bench. All the best, Crawley fans.'

Johnson, who when you talk to him comes across as an ostensibly confident but ultimately quite fragile character, was at something of a low ebb.

'I genuinely get emotional thinking about how they all dislike me now,' he said, 'and it's tough for me to handle that part for sure, because genuinely every decision I've made has been at the heart, what can we do to make Crawley special.

'I feel like we've done a good job earning some of the fan trust, but now we've lost it. And so it's my responsibility to gain the trust back and that's why I'm here and that's why I'm trying to stabilise things.'

Things did stabilise after that, but there was more high staff turnover, some departing due to what they perceived to be a chaotic working culture and, perhaps more seriously, believing that promises had not been kept. The slapdash nature of some of their planning meant that people hired to do one job would frequently end up doing one, two, three others on top of their primary duties.

At the end of their eventful first season, it was reasonable to ask how exactly they were disrupting things, in a positive way at least. Before they took control of Crawley, WAGMI published a manifesto with three broad points. Their goals were: '1) To reinvent broken legacy sports management models. 2) To give fans a meaningful voice. 3) To take Crawley Town FC, the smallest team in the English Football League, to the Premier League.'

The fact that the club only avoided relegation from League Two by three points in that first season, ten places and 15 points worse off than the season before WAGMI arrived, suggested that they had at best underestimated how difficult it would be to revolutionise the running of a lower league football club, at worst didn't have the first idea of what they were doing.

But then came the second season. Manager Scott Lindsey arrived from Swindon in January 2023 and would later say that he found a club in disarray, with players unable to do such basic things as arrive to training on time. Results were patchy in the first half of the following season and by the middle of

February they were languishing in 15th place, closer to relegation than promotion.

Then something strange happened. They started winning games. And then more games. By the start of April they were in the play-off places, which is where they stayed. MK Dons, who had finished eight points ahead of them in the table, were expected to make short work of them in the play-off semi-finals, but Crawley destroyed them, winning 8-1 on aggregate and 5-1 in the away leg. They were underdogs again in the final against Crewe Alexandra, who had beaten them twice in the league, but Crawley dominated the game and in the end ran out 2-0 victors.

Preston Johnson sounded slightly emotionally exhausted when I spoke to him again, a week or so after that playoff final victory. Exhausted, but vindicated.

'We came into this trying to figure out how can we take these online communities that were forming around NFTs and actually give them something to root for every week, like a real English football club.

'What we found out pretty quickly is that if you're losing football games, it's really, really hard to get international fans to engage and care about a club that all the fans hate, and hate the owners, and are tweeting and posting and commenting about every negative thing possible.'

Part of the problem was that Johnson and WAGMI had to worry about irritating the existing fans, rather than bringing in new ones. They took some steps to mitigate that by dropping ticket prices, which resulted in a boost in attendance figures for home games, but in the end it all came down to winning games.

'The relationship with the fans was a little strange, because I feel like some of them actually appreciated what we were trying to do. When I was there in person people always treated me pretty kindly. I never felt threatened for my safety.

'These last few months, multiple people have come up to me and apologised for how things were last year, and were really pleased with the direction of the club – this was before we even made the playoffs or got promoted.

'One of the most important parts of my whole experience in the last two years is the relationships I formed with a few fans that really cared and supported me even through the bad times. They kept my head up, kept things positive because there were multiple times in the back half of last season when I did not know what I was doing – I thought we knew what we were doing, but like "Why am I still here? My wife and family are at home thousands of miles away. It's an 11-hour flight. I had to leave a couple of days after Christmas because Matthew Etherington just quit and we're trying to figure this out. Everyone hates me. They're telling me to leave the hotel in Crawley and go to London because there are people waiting out front, ready to beat me up." Like ... what am I doing here?

'There were definitely a few fans that helped me get through that. I can frankly say that without them, I might not even have done this second season.'

Johnson puts their success in that second season down to the appointment of Lindsey, changing a few things about how they approached dealing with the English game, but mostly by simply continuing with the ideas that they initially wanted to bring in. 'We didn't actually implement, to anything close to the degree we wanted, our data-driven approach [in that first season],' Johnson says. 'Ultimately we just bet on ourselves, which is also just a bet on the maths and a model that we hope could do a much better job than, than last year.

'It's just maths, combined with Scott and his staff, that just absolutely killed it with a bunch of players that were either already here, or new players that were coming from lower leagues or were back-ups elsewhere.'

They recruited 13 players, including Danilo Orsi, Liam Kelly and Ronan Darcy, who would all prove to be crucial in the play-offs, using mostly statistical models and relying on Lindsey to help persuade some of those who had doubts about joining that the club wasn't an enormous basket case. And it worked.

The question from that point is whether it will work in the future. Perhaps it will, perhaps it won't, but Johnson and his fellow owners certainly learned lessons after their chastening first season in charge.

The plan now that Crawley have been a little more successful is to capitalise on their promotion and actually winning some games, to expand their global audience – to make them 'the internet's team', as they promised they would. Which is where they might run into a few more problems.

Is it good that a football club's leadership structure is so opaque? Probably not. Is it good that Johnson, Smith and the others appeared to treat Crawley as an experiment, even if they ultimately became much more emotionally involved and improved the way they operated? Again, it's not ideal. But equally their attempts to do things a little differently, to change the way that lower league clubs were operated, should be embraced to a point: teams in the EFL lose money at unsustainable rates, so in theory anyone who has a new way of trying to stop that should be welcomed.

However, the real question is perhaps more fundamental than all of this, and comes back once again to what football clubs are for. Should they even be trying to make Crawley 'the internet's team'? Is that a thing that we actually need in football? Is it not enough for a team just to exist in its local area, to be a community institution rather than a vehicle for speculation and expansion? Maybe it's too late now to complain about things like that, but the fear with the promises to make a club like Crawley bigger, more international, is that the locals inevitably get left behind.

―――――

Nailsworth isn't the sort of place you'd expect to find one of the world's most interesting football clubs. It has a population of about 5,000, which roughly equates to the away supporters' allocation at some of the bigger stadiums in England. It doesn't have a train station: if you want to get there on public transport you'll need to get the train to nearby Stroud, then hope there isn't too much of a wait for the No.63 bus.

When you get on that bus, you'll drive through the Gloucestershire countryside, along a relatively narrow road, a canopy of trees overhanging the route. You'll get to a roundabout, and if you go left you'll reach the modestly sized Morrisons supermarket, or you can go right, up the hill. You'll keep going as the gradient seems to gradually increase – not the sort of incline you'd need crampons to traverse, but one that will certainly keep a cyclist's thighs burning.

The first real indication that you're approaching a professional football ground is at the top of the hill when you look left, through a gap between a couple of houses, and you see what could be a largish warehouse, but is actually the East Stand at the New Lawn. On the side there is a large banner, which looks like half a Union Jack but with the colours changed from red, white and blue to green, slightly darker green and white. 'We are FGR' is written across it.

Dale Vince didn't so much take over Forest Green Rovers as, in his own words, 'bumped into' it. He wasn't even really much of a football fan before he arrived at the club: he played when he was a kid and watched England games, but didn't have a club team and the broader football world didn't really impinge on his consciousness.

Then in 2010 he read in a local newspaper that the club was in trouble. Forest Green were founded in 1889 and spent most of their existence playing in the local leagues around Gloucestershire and the south-west of England, reaching what is now called the National League in 1998, but never rising higher than that.

But they encountered problems on and off the pitch: they only escaped relegation in 2009/10 because Salisbury City were demoted instead, having failed to exit administration. Not that Forest Green were in a happy financial place themselves: they needed around £30,000 to get them through the summer of 2010 and as a local resident and the founder of Ecotricity, the green energy provider that generates its entire electricity supply from windmills and other sustainable sources, he was tapped up as a potential saviour. Initially he only got involved because he thought it was a pity if this

120-year-old club went out of business, but pretty soon he realised he could use football for a slightly higher purpose.

'We reasoned that football fans were passionate people,' Vince wrote in his autobiography *Manifesto*, 'and if we could reach them with our sustainability messages we could harness some of that passion and point it towards the environment – and make eco fans out of them. And not just in our own club. We thought we might be able to reach the wider world of football and even sport itself.'

You'll often see Vince referred to as an 'eco-warrior', mainly by people who still think people concerned about the environment and the climate crisis are cranks and grubby hippies strapping themselves to trees. But while the term is reductive, the broad sentiment is fairly accurate: Vince founded the Renewable Energy Company, the precursor to Ecotricity, in 1995, and has committed himself to green activism for most of his life, which includes donating to protest groups like Extinction Rebellion and Just Stop Oil.

And that's how Forest Green is run. They get all their electricity from solar panels at the stadium and from a windmill just up the road. There are charging points for electric vehicles just outside the ticket office. Even the lawnmowers that the groundsman uses on the pitch are electric. Their kits are made from sustainable materials. They don't fly anywhere. And, perhaps most famously, they only serve vegan food, to both fans and the squad: players aren't required to be vegan, but essentially any food the club pays for is vegan. They were certified by FIFA in 2018 as the world's first carbon-neutral club.

'Almost every game I come to, someone tells me they've gone vegan or vegetarian,' Vince said in a documentary called *Another Way*, made about the club in 2022. 'You can see the ethos permeates everything. We have sustainability in our DNA. This tiny little village football club is doing all of that.'

While the club's approach does sometimes invite mockery (the terrace ditty 'You can shove your fucking carrots up your arse' is not uncommon from visiting fans), it has resonated beyond their little corner of Gloucestershire. They have in the region of 120 fan clubs around the world. Their principles serve as a point of difference, something to attract people looking for anything slightly out of the ordinary in a football club.

That includes Héctor Bellerín, the former Arsenal full-back, who in 2020 became the second-largest shareholder in the club. 'The way the world is built nowadays, there are going to be many times when you have to compromise,' Bellerín told The Athletic at the time. 'It's very hard to live a carbon-neutral life today. You can be more conscious of the choices that you make, but it's also about what we have available.

'A lot of the time we blame society, we blame ourselves: "We're using too much plastic, we're flying a lot." But they're not giving us another choice. We need to not just push society to do better, but push big industries to give us another choice.'

It's easy to forget that there is a successful football team among all of this. They had never played in the Football League before Vince arrived, but were promoted to League Two in 2017 and then to League One, as champions, in 2022. They do things differently in other respects too, rather than just their green approach: in the summer of 2023 Hannah Dingley, the head of their academy, was promoted to caretaker manager of the first team while they searched for a full-time replacement for previous boss Duncan Ferguson. Dingley was eventually replaced by Southampton coach David Horseman, but the decision prompted accusations of tokenism and a 'PR stunt' from the dimmer lights of the commentariat. In reality, it was simply a practical choice as she was the club's most qualified coach, but at the same time it was a choice that others might not have made.

Additionally, their squad often consists of players that other teams weren't interested in, for a variety of reasons. 'It's not necessarily a financial decision, although that comes into it,' then director of football Rich Hughes said in 2022. 'We like players with interesting stories. We like these broken toys that we can pick up, put them back together and help them get on with their careers.'

Things have been slightly stickier in recent seasons: they were relegated back to League Two in 2023 and a year later slipped out of the league. Horseman left after half a season and was replaced, briefly and disastrously, by former Watford striker Troy Deeney. He was in charge for six matches, none of which they won, and was eventually sacked after a remarkable series of interviews in which he said he would 'rather watch the *Antiques Roadshow*' than his team, and also ripped into his players, including the particularly unfair singling out of Fankaty Dabo.

The full-back had played for Coventry City the previous season, and missed a penalty in the shoot-out in their Championship play-off final defeat to Luton Town, leading Deeney to say that 'Six months ago that kid had a kick to go to the Premier League. Now he won't get a game in the National League.' Weaponising that sort of traumatic moment in a player's career, for which Dabo received racist abuse, was one of a few steps too far, and Deeney was swiftly dismissed.

Around that time it was interesting to see that they had entered the broader consciousness for their football, rather than the green/vegan approach. Of course, it helped that Deeney was a famous name, but it was a signal that they had become part of the furniture and were not just a novelty anymore. Although you wonder whether Vince thought of that as a good or a bad thing.

Because while Vince wants success for the team, the reason for that is not simply for either glory or even financial gain, it's to increase the size of his platform. Winning games and being promoted serves the dual purpose of making the club more successful, and allowing him to reach a broader audience for his activism.

'Our mission is to be a football club, have fun doing that, but to carry a serious message,' he told the *Another Way* documentary. 'The advantage we take from the PR coverage is to spread the message. We want to promote the environment, get other clubs on board, change how the game works. And we can do that best when we get lots of PR.

'Essentially what we're trying to do is use football as a platform to communicate to people about the climate crisis and what they can do about it, the changes they need to make in their lives. Our fans haven't just put up with the green agenda we have – they have embraced it completely and they have changed how they live. It shows me that we can take sports fans and we can make them fans of the environment.

'People take their cues from football. They follow football clubs, they follow football players, and they influence the lives of billions of people. So let's use that for good.'

7

THE MULTI-CLUB GROUPS

'We have to convince people that we are losing our independence. We don't know who they are. We have to convince people that multi-ownership is a danger for us, and French football. The club is not the same as it was. The atmosphere has changed.'

MATTHEW KITTEL,
RACING STRASBOURG SUPPORTER

There are a few benefits to living in the cheese wedge-shaped apartment block just off Rue Etienne Dolet. It's convenient for the Metro, Garibaldi station being a few minutes' walk away. It's near the Paris ring road, making getting around this notoriously traffic-unfriendly city a little easier. It's also not far from the Stade de France, so if you fancied popping along to watch Les Bleus, you'll be home before Kylian Mbappé has had the chance to take his boots off.

The main benefit, though, is free football. The block looks out over Stade Bauer, home to one of Paris's 'other' clubs Red Star FC, so if your apartment is on the right side of the building, you can watch games without the inconvenience of having to pay an entry fee.

And the residents often do, many availing themselves of the opportunity to provide forthright feedback on how Red Star are doing. One resident in particular, Sylvie, is notorious for heckling while leaning out of her third floor window – what she refers to as her 'VIP box'.

Red Star are very much 'of Paris', in a way that their critics will say Paris Saint-Germain, way over on the other side of town in the rather more well-to-do 16th arrondissement, are not and never will be. Those at Red Star like to say that PSG are the big-money blockbuster, but they are the art house film.

Their history certainly stretches back further than that of PSG, who only officially came into being in 1970 after the merger of Paris FC and Stade Saint-Germain. Red Star were formed in a Paris cafe in 1897 by a young lawyer who would go on to have a slightly bigger impact on the world of football than merely founding a relatively niche club in the suburbs. His other grand scheme was the formation of a football tournament to determine the best international team on the planet, and while the trophy no longer bears his name, most people will know Jules Rimet more for coming up with the idea for the World Cup, rather than forming Red Star.

But in many respects it was no less noble an enterprise. Rimet's vision when he and some like-minded friends founded the club was to encourage an institution that would 'work the body and feed the mind.' Rimet wanted a club that welcomed everyone from every background, that recognised football wasn't just a sport but a vital cultural and societal force, an ethos that continues to this day.

The club runs a programme called the Red Star Lab, which is in part designed to help the players in their youth team adjust to life away from football, to expose them to as many cultural experiences as possible. On the walls of the club's offices there are a series of photos of their young players at places like the Palais Garnier and the Musée d'Orsay, the idea being to help produce rounded human beings, so that if they don't make it they are not simply launched back into society without much clue of what the world is like. The kids have made documentaries, they have made their own jerseys, they have completed photography courses, they have worked with architects. All of which is designed to fit with Rimet's vision of a football club that should be more than merely a football club.

That sentiment fits with the political leanings of their fans too. You would perhaps think that the name Red Star was chosen because of some stout commitment to the communist cause, when in fact it was chosen because when Rimet was young his family had an English governess called Miss Jenny, who would travel back home on boats operated by the Red Star Line shipping company.

Nevertheless, Red Star's fans do, to say the least, lean to the left. The Stade Bauer is in the Saint-Ouen district of Paris, which historically has been a staunchly working-class area, although gentrification is working its way through it now. Immigrants from all over the world settled there and it was known to be a hub of communism, something reflected in the causes some of the club's ultras support. Rino Della Negra, a hero of the French Resistance who was shot by the Nazis in 1944, played for the club and still features on flags and banners held up by the club's fans. François Hollande, the former socialist French president, is a lifelong Red Star fan and has spoken of the club being an embodiment of 'a diverse and multicultural France'.

In many respects, Red Star are theoretically the anthesis of many disliked aspects of the modern game: anti-capitalist, grassroots, fiercely proud of their history, lauding socialist heroes.

You can probably see where this is going. In May 2022 Red Star, in the third tier of French football at the time, were subsumed into the Miami-based, multi-club ownership group 777 Partners, who just beat a consortium led by former Barcelona defender Gerard Piqué. At that stage Red Star were one of four clubs wholly owned by 777, along with Vasco da Gama in Brazil, Genoa in Italy and Standard Liège in Belgium. They also held a minority stake in Sevilla; then later in 2022 they took 19.9 per cent of Melbourne Victory; the following year they bought 64.7 per cent of Hertha Berlin; and then, in September 2023, announced they had agreed the purchase of Everton, or at least Farhad Moshiri's 94.7 per cent stake of the club.

Maybe there are some things that are further from the ideals of a club founded to be a pillar of the local community and once described as 'France's only openly communist club' than becoming part of an investment portfolio, but it's tricky to think what they might be.

The takeover was, initially at least, broadly opposed on philosophical grounds, the idea that becoming just a small part of a profit-making entity – no matter what that entity actually was – was anathema to the whole concept of what Red Star were supposed to be.

A banner was held up at the game after the takeover was reported that read '777 Not Welcome' – in English, so the American investors really got the point. The club had to play behind closed doors after a game against FC Sète was abandoned due to pyrotechnics being thrown onto the pitch in protest. Several politicians signed an open letter that was sent to *Le Monde*, which reiterated that Red Star 'is a common good that cannot be sacrificed on the altar of profit.'

But the fans might have had even more cause to be upset after details of who 777 actually were emerged. The group was founded in 2015 by Steven Pasko and Josh Wander, and they initially built their fortune via a variety of businesses that included, according to a report by *The Washington Post* in September 2023, a company called Liberty Settlement Funding.

They specialised in 'cash advance' deals, usually for people who have been awarded compensation for something or other. Say you have an accident at work, your company is found liable for your injuries and you are awarded a settlement of £1 million, paid in a series of smaller instalments. A company such as Liberty would offer you an immediate lump sum, always much lower than the eventual amount you were due to receive, in return for the full annuity. If someone has an immediate financial need, for whatever reason, a deal like that can look pretty attractive.

However it has led to accusations that they preyed on the vulnerable and the desperate. 'In terms of the bad human component, it's up there with the worst I've ever seen,' a lawyer named Edward Stone told *The Washington Post* about the case he was working on, in which a woman called Lyndsy Noell alleged that representatives for 777 facilitated her heroin addiction and then threatened to expose it, during the process of trading around $793,000 of an injury settlement for $180,000.

777 have, at one time or another, owned various similar companies, plus a couple of low-cost airlines in Australia and Canada, and the London Lions basketball team, and held a minority stake in STX Entertainment, a film production studio.

———

Their first foray into the football world was that stake in Sevilla, purchased in 2018, followed by Genoa, Vasco da Gama and the rest. Their involvement initially seemed to result in something of a curse for the clubs involved: Genoa were relegated from Serie A (then promoted the following season), Vasco were promoted but struggled for most of the following season in the top flight, Hertha were relegated from the Bundesliga, Standard Liège's fans protested against a perceived lack of spending and ambition, Red Star blew promotion to Ligue 2 and a little over a month after their deal to buy Everton was announced, the club was docked ten points for breaching profit and sustainability rules.

Clearly, you can't exactly blame 777 for all of those things, but none of them were likely to boost the value of the assets they now had on their books, which itself exposes one of the potential weaknesses of their model.

That model is to take on clubs that are not quite distressed assets, but clubs where the up-front price is relatively cheap, with the aim of growing their value. Red Star were thought to have cost €19 million, but according to reports by Josimar, the investigative news website, the actual price may have been much less than that. Genoa were acquired for the symbolic sum of €1. Former Hertha owner Lars Windhorst admitted in 2023 that 777 had agreed to pay only €15 million up front for his shares in the club, the deal sweetened by a promised €35 million bonus payment … if Hertha won the Bundesliga. Given he said this a couple of months after they were relegated, 777 probably don't have to budget for that bonus in the immediate future.

The deal to buy Everton was supposed to be worth anything in the range of £500–600 million, depending on which figures you believe, but for a historic Premier League club with a new stadium on the way, when the admittedly much bigger and more successful Chelsea went for £4.25 billion, it did look like a bargain. The deal is that 777 will have to manage the debt that the clubs carry. In Genoa's case, at the time 777 acquired the club, that stood at something like €290 million.

The aim for 777 is then to both increase the potential earnings of their clubs, thus increasing their value, and also use their new captive audiences – or football fans, as they are sometimes also known – as fresh sales demographics.

They look for clubs that have 'done a horrible job of commercialising the product,' according to Wander, the implication being that they can do much more to bring money in and thus increase the value of their investment. 'We have a strong view that there's a new wave of commercialisation coming to football,' Wander told the *Financial Times* in August 2023.

Also in that interview Wander claimed that the fanaticism of most football supporters meant that 'they want to be monetised' putting forward the proposal that in addition to selling 'hot dogs and beers to our customers' they would at some stage sell them 'insurance or financial services or whatever'. In response to apparent suggestions that 777 were 'not serious' about their investments, Wander said: 'We bought [stakes in] seven clubs in the last 18 months. Is there anyone in the world that's been more serious about buying football clubs in history than Josh Wander?'

Who indeed? It is worth clarifying that he meant acquiring seven clubs in a year-and-a-half was a good thing, rather than seeming like … well, a bit of a rush. Another basis on which Red Star fans – or supporters of any club in 777's portfolio, for that matter – might oppose their takeover is that there wasn't actually much evidence that they knew how to run a football club. They have spoken about bringing in new areas of expertise in player recruitment, and in theory being part of a network of clubs can be beneficial in terms of sharing best practices, increased knowledge of other leagues and sharing actual players.

For example, when Watford were taken over by the Pozzo family, also custodians of Udinese and Granada, it became a running joke that their squad would be stuffed with players on loan from the

Italian club. Maybe it looked a bit fishy from the outside, but they didn't massively care when Matěj Vydra and Odion Ighalo, signed (both on loan, although Ighalo's move was made permanent not long afterwards) from Udinese, scored a third of their goals in the 2014/15 season when they got promoted to the Premier League.

But the point is there was proof of concept, with the Pozzos, evidence of some experience in football. With 777, however, they had nothing that said they could deliver some of these benefits, because they hadn't given themselves the time to do so. The way most multi-club models work is this: you buy one club, make a success of that, apply your knowledge to the next, and so on.

Maybe if 777 had been a little more circumspect, then things wouldn't have unravelled at quite the pace they did in the summer of 2024. The regulatory approval of their takeover of Everton was supposed to take around 12 weeks, which in theory meant that it should have been waved through by Christmas 2023. But as the end of the 2023/24 season approached, the approval was still pending. By June 2024, the takeover had collapsed.

The reason? In short, it was because 777 couldn't prove they had the requisite funds. Or, really, any funds of its own at all. In February 2024, their Bermuda-based reinsurance business, 777 Re's, one of their major sources of income, was downgraded and was eventually seized by regulators. Then A-Cap, the American insurance group that was another source of funding for 777, went a similar way. Throw in a few lawsuits, and suddenly 777's primary concern was to keep its head above water, not acquire new clubs.

Perhaps if they had done what the Pozzos did then they would have had better luck. Or if they had followed a similar approach to the Mexico-based Orlegi Group.

———

Maybe part of it is that Orlegi didn't start with the intention of being a multi-club project. In 2006 the owners of Modelo, the crisp and light Mexican beer, appointed Alejandro Irarragorri to be the president of Santos Laguna, a slightly down-on-their-luck but relatively young outfit that was formed into the club that exists today in 1989 by the merger of two other clubs.

Irarragorri didn't have any background in football, having spent most of his career to that point in a variety of other industries. So rather than running Santos as a sort of hobby or vanity project, as many other Mexican club presidents did around that time, he instead chose to run it as a business, applying cold logic to every decision and investing in off-pitch facilities.

Then in 2013 Modelo were bought by a Brazilian beer company who decided that they wanted to divest their sporting interests and concentrate on the icy cool refreshing booze game. This was around the time that Manchester City's owners had started to diversify, purchasing a Major League Soccer expansion franchise that became New York City, the start of what would become the City Football Group. Red Bull had also been in the multi-club game for a few years, so Irarragorri and a few others took inspiration from them and set forth a management buyout of Santos, the intention being for it to be the first club in their own multi-club group.

'We thought if our methodology is working, it might also work in a multi-club structure,' says Martin Hollaender, Orlegi's chief financial officer and director. They bought a second-tier Mexican club, Tampico Madero, which they sold in 2022, but the big one was when they took over Club Atlas, one of Mexico's biggest clubs, in 2019. Then in 2022 they expanded to Spain, taking over second-tier side Sporting Gijón.

This is the part where we should explain the great secret to their success, the magic bullet that allows Orlegi to get ahead of the competition and juggle their various clubs, but there isn't one really. It is, by Hollaender's own admission, not particularly exciting.

'We've taken out a lot of functions in the club, and put them in our holding company,' he says. 'You can reduce your headcount at a club: for example, instead of having a scout [for a certain region] at each club, you have a scout for the whole group. It's the same with administration, fiscal experts, and we can cross-sell to commercial partners. On both the income side, and the expense side, there are huge benefits.

'We have a long-term vision: it's not to buy a club then sell it in two years. For us it's not enough to generate cash or win on the pitch, it has to be something better. We want to contribute to the society around the club, so it's a huge responsibility. So the sellers can be sure that we're in it for the long run.

'I don't want to speak badly about anyone else, but if you see an investment group come in with no management experience, and suddenly they buy up four or five clubs in 18 months, you think – how is that possible? It takes time. We've been growing slow and steadily.' Who could he be talking about?

And it all seems to work pretty well. Before Orlegi arrived Atlas hadn't won a major title since the 1960s, but they won both of Mexico's league championships in the 2021/22 season. Santos won the Mexican league's Clausura in 2008, 2012, 2015 and 2018, the Mexican Cup's Apertura in 2014 and the Campéon de Campeones in 2015, plus they reached the final of the Concacaf Champions League in 2012 and 2013. After a sticky first season, Sporting only just missed out on promotion to La Liga, losing in the playoffs to Espanyol.

Part of the model is raising funds with smart player-trading. For example, at Santos they bought Uruguayan midfielder Fernando Gorriarán from Ferencváros for €2.5 million in 2019, and sold him to Tigres four years later for €12.2 million. The most they have ever paid for a player is the €6 million that Diego Valdés cost in 2019: they sold him for €10.6 million in 2022.

It's a similar story at Atlas. In 2021 they took Colombian striker Julián Quiñones on loan from Tigres, signed him for €2.6 million a year later, then a year after that flipped him for €9.1 million. The same summer, winger Ozziel Herrera, a youth product, went to Tigres for €7 million. Buying low and selling high is one of those things that sounds gloriously simple but is actually incredibly difficult to do: Orlegi, however, appear to have cracked it.

Part of the reason it seems to be boring but effective is that decisions are not left to a single figurehead.

'We want to kill the hero,' says Hollaender. 'People want a "hero", but we don't need that. It's so institutional: player-trading and financial decisions are done by committees. It sounds boring, and many times the fans don't want to hear about it because it's not exciting, but in our case it's working.

'We don't have this "figure", the sporting director, that is the face of the group and makes all the decisions. In Spain, a lot of fans found that difficult, because they were used to both praising and blaming those individuals.

'Fans have the luxury of being irrational. We don't have that luxury. It's good fun if you're a fan, but on our management floor it isn't. We have facts and information and data.

'There's a lot of passion in some owners, but we are a little bit more boring. That requires education of our own people, so when we grow in the future we can send two or three people to the new club and they know how we operate. But that's our way: everybody can have their own way, but this has worked for us.'

Do you live in the USA? Did you live there between 2002 and 2014? Did you, in that time, buy a can of Red Bull or could plausibly say you might have bought a can of Red Bull? If your answer is 'yes' to any of those questions, then you may have missed out on an absolutely free $10.

In 2013 a man named Benjamin Careathers filed a lawsuit against Red Bull, in which he stated that their advertising campaigns were dishonest. Red Bull did not, Careathers contended, actually 'give you wings', as their slightly irritating TV commercials of the time claimed. And in one of those great occasions when the scales of justice came down on the side of the good guys, the judge agreed with him.

Disappointingly Careathers didn't actually argue that Red Bull were literally saying their product would cause you to grow actual wings and flutter off towards the horizon, but that the implication was the drink would give you a bigger hit of caffeine (and thus energy boost) than your average cup of coffee. He argued that 'such deceptive conduct and practices mean that Red Bull's advertising is not just "puffery", but instead deceptive and fraudulent and it is therefore actionable.'

The judge agreed and found in favour of Careathers, and although Red Bull themselves admitted no wrongdoing, they did agree to compensate anyone who drank a can of their product and felt deceived with a crisp $10 bill. You didn't even have to give them proof of purchase. Just fill in an online form and start thinking about how to spend your money. Alas, the option is no longer open: you had to put your claim in by March 2015.

Careathers might have found kindred spirits in Salzburg, on 4 June, 2005. On that day the general assembly of a football club teetering between two identities was held. Austria Salzburg were at one time one of Austria's brightest and most successful clubs, having won the title three times in four years in the mid-1990s, reaching the final of the UEFA Cup in 1994 where they were beaten by Inter Milan.

But latterly they had fallen on harder times, finishing second bottom of the Austrian Bundesliga in 2004/05, and the club was in some significant financial trouble. They needed a saviour and in the shape of the local company who had become a worldwide behemoth, it looked like they had found one. Red Bull had actually begun life as a Thai energy drink called Krating Daeng – which translates as, get this, 'red bull' – until a Salzburg-based marketeer called Dietrich Mateschitz discovered its sickly sweet charms and thought other people might like it too. He was right: according to the company website, Red Bull sold 12.1 billion cans of the stuff in 2023.

Initially, the idea was that Red Bull would merely invest in their local club, giving back to the community where their global headquarters still resided. Thus, they were welcomed by many fans, some of whom might have even been able to stomach a name change: after all, Austria Salzburg had been known by other names down the years, including Casino Salzburg and Wüstenrot Salzburg, both for sponsorship reasons.

But they still wanted it to be their club. At that general assembly, there was an insistence that the team's colours – violet and white – not be changed, so that some identity would remain. No dice. It quickly became clear that Red Bull didn't just want an investment, not even merely to take the club over completely, but they wanted to change its identity entirely and make it the first in a worldwide network of football teams that would in effect be a colossal global marketing exercise for their product.

The pleas to keep Salzburg's colours were ignored. The new iteration would play in red. 'The red bull can't be violet, or else we couldn't call it Red Bull,' said an indignant Mateschitz, which in the view of the old club's fans summed things up nicely: the branding was infinitely more important than the identity of the club.

A token attempt at placating the masses was made: in a solemn nod to the club's traditions, Red Bull graciously conceded that the goalkeeper's socks could be violet, as well as the captain's armband and the logo of Adidas, the kit manufacturers. Like a mugger tossing you a few coins for the bus after they've stolen your wallet, this was regarded as an insult, as was Red Bull's initial insistence that, officially speaking, the club was born in 2005 and all previous history was to be disregarded.

So instead a group of the original club's fans decided to start their own team, named Austria Salzburg, who would play in violet and in some way still have some connection to the fans and the club they once loved.

For Red Bull, meanwhile, this was just the start. The year after they purchased Salzburg, they acquired the New York/New Jersey Metrostars and simplified their name a little, to the New York Red Bulls. The year after that they established Red Bull Brasil, starting out in the regional leagues but with a plan to reach the Brazilian Serie A inside ten years. In 2008, Red Bull Ghana was founded, although that was more of a youth academy than a 'proper' senior team.

Then in 2009 came what would turn out to be the big one. Red Bull were keen to get themselves into Germany, and initially wanted to repeat what they had done in Austria and New York, to acquire an established club and improve them, rather than starting from the ground up. They looked at Fortuna Düsseldorf, 1860 Munich and

St Pauli, among others, but their proposals were rejected by them all. On counsel from no less an adviser than Franz Beckenbauer, they focused on Leipzig, the second-biggest city in the former East Germany (behind Berlin), the place where the DFB (the German football federation) was founded and one of the host cities at the 2006 World Cup, but a city that didn't have anything close to a top-level football team. They hadn't had a Bundesliga team since 1994 and not even a fully professional one since 1998: VfB Leipzig, formerly known as Lokomotive Leipzig, who reached the European Cup Winners' Cup final in 1987, had recently gone out of business.

They tried to acquire a fourth-tier side called FC Sachsen Leipzig, but pulled out of that deal after a restaurant where a group of the club's fans were celebrating their Christmas party was attacked by ultras from Lok Leipzig, a phoenix club formed from the ashes of the former Lokomotive/VfB Leipzig. Red Bull wanted no part of anything like this and shelved their Leipzig plans for a few years.

That wasn't their only problem. While a German club was very much their goal, they had an obstacle in the shape of the 50+1 rule, a provision introduced in 1998 that technically requires all clubs in the German system to be majority-owned – at least 51 per cent – by their fans, the idea being partly to prevent an oligarch or a nation state or an energy drinks company from taking over one of their biggest cultural assets.

Not to be deterred, Red Bull got around the pesky rules by returning to the Leipzig idea and purchasing the licence of a virtually dormant, fifth-tier club in the city called SSV Markranstädt for around €400,000, then neatly tap-dancing atop the rules by officially making it a member-owned and member-led organisation – but all those members are employees of Red Bull or are linked to the company in some way. Thus, in reality, Red Bull controls the club just as many other companies control clubs in many other countries.

Another rule they had to lightly skip around was that, unlike their other clubs, the German authorities decreed they could not include the name 'Red Bull' in the name of the team. Which is why the official name of the Bundesliga club that has the Red Bull logo on their shirts, play at the Red Bull Arena and is known to everyone as being part of the Red Bull sporting portfolio, is RasenBallsport Leipzig – RB for short – which literally translates as 'Lawnball Sport'.

They aimed to reach the Bundesliga in eight years, but such was their financial backing and expertise gathered from around the world that they got there in seven. They have since established themselves as perennial title challengers and Champions League regulars, and were thus broadly welcomed in a city starved of top-class football since not long after the reunification of Germany.

But in a country that prides itself on protecting the identity of its football clubs, where the principles of what those clubs stand for are sacrosanct, they are roundly despised by everyone else. The reaction of many German fans was summed up by Matthias Gartner, from the advocacy group Bundnis Aktiver Fussballfans, who said at the time of the Leipzig takeover: 'Right now the devil himself could come. If he has a few million with him, he would be welcomed with open arms.'

It was the final, biggest piece in a global jigsaw, a fluid conglomerate of football teams that all serve the greater good, rather than just themselves. Coaches move easily between the clubs, with a clear hierarchical path, leading to eastern Germany. Jesse Marsch has taken charge of the clubs in New York, Salzburg and Leipzig. Marco Rose had a sabbatical at Borussia Mönchengladbach and Borussia Dortmund between his spells in Salzburg and Leipzig. Gerhard Struber swapped New York for Salzburg in 2023.

Players routinely move between the clubs too, usually stepping up from Salzburg to Leipzig, a list that includes Dayot Upamecano, Naby Keïta, Hwang Hee-chan, Dominik Szoboszlai, Konrad Laimer, Amadou Haidara, Benjamin Šeško and Marcel Sabitzer.

One of the earliest to move between the clubs was goalkeeper Thomas Dähne. He was making his way through the youth ranks at Salzburg just as the empire was broadening, but while nowadays Leipzig are very much at the top of the tree, back then they weren't.

'At the beginning, Salzburg was the top priority for every player,' says Dähne. 'We knew there was a club in Ghana, there was a club in Brazil, there was a club in New York, but that was just to develop young players and bring them to Salzburg. Leipzig were in the fifth division in Germany, so at the time it wasn't such a big deal.

'Then they got promoted and promoted and promoted, and suddenly they were in the 2. Bundesliga. Then it got more and more interesting for the young, talented players.'

It was at this point that Dähne, after a spell at Liefering, was offered the opportunity to move to Germany.

They didn't quite tell their young players directly that Salzburg were effectively becoming a feeder club for their German cousins, but you didn't need to read particularly closely between the lines. 'Red Bull gave them this idea that, if you perform well in Austria, there's a chance you could play in the German Bundesliga,' Dähne says. 'It was like an open secret. In my case, I was on vacation, the sporting director called and said "Do you want to join Leipzig?"'

By this point, even though Leipzig were only in the 2. Bundesliga, it became pretty clear that they were now the golden child.

'Leipzig were only playing in the second league,' says Dähne, 'but then everything changed when they got to the Bundesliga. They had this "joker" card: "Maybe we don't play in Europe, but we are in the top league."'

'Salzburg felt like a big family. But when I moved to Leipzig, everybody was just looking for themselves. Players didn't always help each other, just every player wanted to play. It was pretty hard to get used to it. If you go to a club where the coach was like your father and you have a really good relationship with them, this strict German football mentality was really something new for me.'

It all could barely have gone better from Red Bull's perspective, in Europe at least. Salzburg have become the dominant force in Austrian football, winning the title every season from 2009 to 2023, apart from 2010/11 and 2012/13. Meanwhile Leipzig got to the Champions League semi-final in 2020 and were one of the few consistent challengers to Bayern for the Bundesliga title.

At this point it is important to point out that FC Red Bull Salzburg are no longer technically owned by Red Bull. As both they and Leipzig became more successful, it was inevitable that they would participate in the same European competition at some point. Given that it is against UEFA's rules for two clubs with the same owners to face each other in Europe, for obvious reasons, something had to be done.

So in 2017 Salzburg were restructured so that technically they were no longer part of the Red Bull group. This meant they were both allowed to play in the 2017/18 Champions League, and were in fact drawn against each other in the 2018/19 Europa League group stages, when Salzburg won both games.

But, again, they're not part of the Red Bull group. They are just called Red Bull Salzburg, their nickname is 'The Red Bulls', they play at the Red Bull Arena (where you can get a can of Red Bull at the Bull Corner Cafe), while wearing shirts with the Red Bull logo across the front, train at the Red Bull Training Centre and you can send your kids to play at the Bullidikidz-Club next to the stadium. Red Bull are now simply their primary sponsors.

It is, admittedly, one of the better sponsorship deals.

'We told ourselves it was only rumours. We didn't want to accept it was a reality.'

Matthew Kittel, along with his fellow Racing Strasbourg fans, had read the stories. They had heard that something might be in the offing. But nobody was saying anything. Nobody from the club. Not club president Marc Keller. No confirmations, no denials.

Nobody would tell them whether the talk of BlueCo, the owners of Chelsea, taking over their club was true or not. Whether they would no longer be an autonomous club, in control of their own future, and would rather be subsumed into the portfolio of someone bigger and richer, a club from another country controlled by men and women from another country still.

'Everything was hidden,' says Kittel. 'We felt like it was a betrayal. To sell the club, it was the opposite of the old approach of Keller. He said we have to be patient, we have to wait for a new stadium, a new academy. We were OK being patient.'

The deal was confirmed on 23 June, 2023. 'This is an important day for Racing,' said Keller, who would officially still be running things. 'We've built a club that's healthy at every level and well-managed. Although there was no financial urgency, we were aware that we had reached the ceiling of our model.

'If we wanted to continue driving Racing forward and projecting it into a new dimension, we necessarily needed to be accompanied by a solid structure capable of supporting our development and our ambition.' The fee wasn't disclosed but it was reported that BlueCo paid around £65 million for a non-specific majority control of the French club.

For their part, BlueCo said: 'This strategic investment will further our presence in European football, alongside our ownership of Chelsea. We believe it will create huge opportunities to share knowledge and expertise.'

Racing Strasbourg were founded in 1906. At the time, Strasbourg was part of the German empire and known as Strassburg, and the club were initially called FC Neudorf. After the First World War the town became part of France again, but during the Second World War, when the region was once again occupied by the Germans, the players were among the men forcibly conscripted into Nazi forces. Most of them suddenly declared themselves ill, so they could be deemed ineligible. One took a large slug of cognac and insisted that a teammate break his arm. When they played a game against a team made up of SS officers, Strasbourg eschewed their usual colours of sky blue and white, to wear deep blue shirts, white shorts and red rocks, the colours of the French flag.

They won Ligue Un for the first time in 1979. They had won the Coupe de France in 1951 and 1966, and would win it once again in 2001. Two of France's 1998 World Cup-winning team, Frank Leboeuf and Youri Djorkaeff, played for Strasbourg. A rangy midfielder who had grown up as the son of a local pub landlord ended his playing career with a few games between 1978 and 1981: he didn't make much of an impression on the pitch, but then again Arsène Wenger made more of an impact as a manager than a player.

It's a club with a history. An identity. But even if it didn't have some famous old boys, and had never won a trophy, and didn't form part of the Resistance, it would still be a football club, a passion passed down from parent to child. It meant more than being just a subsidiary, part of someone's investment strategy, and not even the most important part either.

'We have to convince people that we are losing our independence,' says Kittel. 'We don't know who they are. We don't know who is responsible for the decisions. We have to convince people that multi-ownership is a danger for us and French football. The club is not the same as it was. The atmosphere has changed.'

This is one of the problems with the multi-club idea. Or at least the version of the multi-club idea that Chelsea are trying to grow. Strasbourg were the first in their collection, but the aim was to mirror the City Football Group model, which started life as the brainchild of its chief executive while he was at Barcelona.

At that point, Soriano's idea was to create a sort of worldwide network of Barcelona academies, but it was only when he got to City that he was actually able to realise his plan.

They began in America (where Barcelona had been in talks over a team in Miami while Soriano was there), purchasing an 80 per cent stake in a Major League Soccer expansion franchise, New York City FC becoming the league's 20th club. The New York Yankees baseball empire owns the other 20 per cent and the team occasionally plays games at Yankee Stadium.

Then Australia, where they purchased the A-League side Melbourne Heart, promptly rebranded to Melbourne City FC. After that they purchased a minority stake in the Japanese club Yokohama F. Marinos in 2014, then three years later wholly took over Club Atletico Torque in Uruguay, again rebranding them to Montevideo City Torque. Also in 2017 they bought 44.3 per cent of Girona in Spain, making them co-owners with one Pere Guardiola, brother of Pep. In 2019 they took a 46.7 per cent stake in Chinese side Sichuan Jiuniu (who have subsequently rebranded as Shenzhen Peng City), and in the same year they bought 65 per cent of Mumbai City, handily named so they didn't even require a rebadge.

In 2020 they took an unspecified majority stake in Belgian side Lommel SK, then they came to a similar arrangement to purchase Troyes in France (both of those clubs were in significant financial difficulties at the time), and in 2022 they bought an 80 per cent stake in Palermo, at the time playing in Italy's Serie B. And then in 2023 their portfolio was completed (for now) with the full acquisition of Bahia, a historically successful Brazilian club that had fallen on hard times in recent years. They also signed up Club Bolivar, from Bolivia, as a 'partner club' in 2021, although they don't have an ownership stake in them.

It has been a busy decade. In summary, as of 2024 that's a stable of 12 clubs, in 12 different countries, (13 in 13 if you count Club Bolivar), across five different continents. At the time of writing they have no presence in Africa, but that's not for the want of trying: they have looked at a number of clubs and, in 2023, Soriano suggested that they were looking to expand still further.

It also means that the group is extraordinarily valuable. In 2015 a Chinese investment group called CMC holdings paid $400 million for a 13 per cent stake in CFG, which valued the whole conglomerate at something like $3 billion. Then in 2019 the US investment group Silver Lake paid $500 million for 10 per cent of CFG, purchasing shares from both Abu Dhabi United Group, the investment arm of the Abu Dhabi royal family, who initially bought Manchester City in 2008, and CMC, and over the following years acquired more and more of CMC's stake to the point that it was negligible. As of 2024, ADUG controls 81 per cent of CFG and Silver Lake have around 18 per cent.

———

Maybe the central flaw in this version of the multi-club model (although CFG will probably not regard it as a particular flaw) is that everything is in service to the club at the top of the tree. It's not the only priority of the group, but ultimately the point of the whole thing is to make Manchester City even stronger than they already are. Or, to put it another way, many of the clubs in the group essentially act as feeder or farm teams to City, something that CFG haven't been particularly shy about admitting.

'One of my biggest frustrations is that in this country we still haven't recognised a greater ability to develop young players from the age of 18 to 22, and the loan system can be very hit and miss, it can create more problems than it solves,' Brian Marwood, CFG's managing director of global football, told The Athletic in 2020.

'In an ideal world we would rather have a B team or a feeder club, but we can't do that in this country, so we have to look at other opportunities. With Lommel, we can give opportunities to young players and allow them to grow and develop properly.

'We run the risk of losing that young talent. So we try to create platforms with some of our clubs and give these young players an opportunity.'

The trouble here is that with one club at the top, and the rest subservient, the smaller clubs naturally lose some of their identity – literally the case with some of the clubs in CFG, the ones who had their name changed to crowbar 'City' into it somewhere, and the ones who changed their club crests to more closely resemble Manchester City's. It's football-empire building: when Octavian defeated the armies of Cleopatra and Marc Antony to conquer the Ptolemaic Kingdom in 30BC, he wasn't doing it for the benefit of the Egyptians – it was for the glory and benefit of Rome.

This is why those Strasbourg fans objected to being subsumed into Chelsea's portfolio and it's why CFG's move to consume the Dutch side NAC Breda failed in 2022. City already had a more informal arrangement with the club whereby they would send players on loan to the Netherlands: 16 of them in all between 2014 and 2021, and sometimes in bulk. In the 2016/17 season, six City youngsters played for NAC, routinely all being on the pitch at the same time and thus comprising over half of their team. A deal to not just formalise the arrangement but fully take over the club, at the time in the Dutch second division, had been agreed and looked like a fait accompli, but they faced a fierce backlash from the club's supporters.

Games were boycotted. Some fans travelled to Manchester to display a banner outside the Etihad Stadium which read 'Stay out of our territory, NAC is not a City Group story.' Other groups of fans drove to Lommel and Troyes, their potential CFG stablemates, to display similar messages. More banners appeared at their home stadium during matches, one with a slightly pithier message: 'FUCK CITY GROUP'.

'The takeover wasn't in the interest of our club,' Leon Deckers, editor of a Breda fanzine, told joe.co.uk at the time. 'We cherish the bond between club and fans and our community very much, and we didn't want to be part of some big international private equity group.

'Football makes sportswashing possible and we cannot be part of that, either. Once you do that, once you take that money, you can never give an opinion about anything anymore.'

This isn't the case across the multi-club board. 777 doesn't have a single team at the top of its pyramid. Mercury/13, the group founded in 2023 specifically to invest in women's football, were established with the original purpose of being a multi-club group, rather than evolving into one and having a 'figurehead' club.

'It's a meritocratic hierarchy,' Mario Malave, Mercury/13's co-CEO, says. 'If you have a club that is outperforming the others, you don't want to constrain them if there's a club that's crushing it.

'There's going to be important differences between leagues: a club in the right league is going to have much more chance to grow and attract the best players and have a gravitational pull for talent. If that happens organically we're not going to stop it, but we're not going to have an explicit "Hey, this is *the* club and all the others are in service to this club."'

The counterpoint to this, and one of the arguments that CFG would put forward, is that their clubs benefit from being part of the broader group. They have access to better facilities, scouting networks, money, players through loans from elsewhere in the group and institutional expertise. Which isn't just theoretical: most of the clubs in the portfolio have done pretty well since joining the group.

Melbourne City's men's team won the A-League in 2021, 2022 and 2023, as well as the Grand Final (the one-off game between the teams that finish first and second in the division, that decides the Championship) in 2021. New York City won the MLS Cup in 2021. Yokohama F. Marinos won the J-League in 2019 and 2022. Bahia won the Campeonato Baiano, their state championship, in 2023. Mumbai City were Indian champions in 2021 and 2023.

Arguably the most extraordinary story of them all came at Girona, the tiny club in Catalonia that became part of CFG in 2017, who had been playing amateur football as recently as 1999 and only in 2006/07 were in the Catalan regional leagues. They had spent much of their history in the third and fourth tiers, but almost went out of business completely in 2013.

Their path under CFG was not smooth: they were relegated to the Spanish Segunda División in 2019, a couple of years after CFG bought their stake. But they won promotion back to the Primera División in 2022, and the following season finished a creditable 10th, but it was 2023/24 when the miracles really started to happen.

Under head coach Míchel, they spent much of the season ahead of the traditional giants of Spanish football, Real Madrid, Barcelona and Atlético Madrid, who had split every league title between them since 2005. They eventually finished third, ahead of Atlético, and thus qualified for the Champions League. It was just their fourth season in the Spanish top division, ever.

A direct way that CFG's presence has been felt is in player recruitment. Two of their key men that season were the Ukrainian internationals Artem Dovbyk and Viktor Tsygankov, the latter of whom also happens to be represented by Pere Guardiola.

'We obviously have the capacity to scout those kinds of markets because we are under the City umbrella,' Girona sporting director Quique Cárcel told The Athletic. 'In those two cases [Tsygankov and Dovbyk], I can tell you it was not easy. Both were Ukrainian internationals, so we had to make a bold move. That's the great advantage of being close to CFG, who support us and are brave when it comes to making calls.'

They have benefitted from many players on loan from City down the years, but the interesting thing about their squad in 2023/24 was that they only had one directly borrowed from Manchester. That said, one of their key men was the Brazilian winger Sávio, who had been bought by Troyes in 2022, but loaned to Girona the following year.

And while Girona have been one of CFG's great success stories, it's the Sávio situation which leads into the story of one of its failures. Troyes, who were gathered into the warm embrace of the CFG family in 2020, were promoted to Ligue 1 in 2021 but went down again in 2023, and to pile on the ignominy and increase the disquiet about their ultimate owners, were relegated again in 2024. For those unfamiliar with the French league structure, the third tier is partly comprised of semi-professional teams: not quite the sort of thing CFG probably wanted for one of their portfolio.

Their supporters grew increasingly furious, their ire partly projected onto head coach Patrick Kisnorbo, who had previously been in charge of Melbourne City, another CFG club. Kisnorbo had been parachuted in to replace Bruno Irles, a broadly popular coach who had established the team in mid-table of Ligue 1. Kisnorbo's time went from bad to worse, they were relegated to Ligue 2, but he managed to survive until November of the following season, by which point the damage had been done. But Kisnorbo was a symptom rather than a cause: the basis of the fans' objections was that they had become CFG's lost club, a minor outpost of their empire that was being neglected.

As an illustration of their point, at that stage their two record signings – the aforementioned Sávio and midfielder Metinho, both recruited from Brazil – had never played a game for the Troyes first team. Sávio was loaned immediately to PSV Eindhoven, then to Girona. Metinho spent a season with the Troyes second team, who played in the French fifth tier, and then was lent to first Lommel, another CFG club, and then Sparta Rotterdam in the Netherlands. The next name on that record arrivals list, winger

Amar Fatah, played once for Troyes before being loaned for 18 months to Lommel. It was hard to escape the impression that Troyes were essentially being treated as a sort of shell company, used as a vehicle for player trading rather than a football club in its own right. The circle was completed in 2024, when the transfer of Sávio to Manchester City was agreed, presumably after some pretty fierce negotiations.

In response a fan group called Magic Troyes 1997 organised a boycott of their games, which they named 'Objective: Empty Stadium! Save Our Club.'

'Going to the stadium, knowing beforehand the result of the match is no longer possible!' the group said. 'It is about time that the players and the management take responsibility for the club's catastrophic situation. Recognising your errors, is that really a failure? It is for this reason that as of today, we, as a group, have decided to boycott home and away games.'

It seemed to work. Attendance at home games dropped. An away fixture against Ajaccio – admittedly a tricky trip because it involves travelling to the island of Corsica – saw just two fans in the away end. Troyes lost 1–0.

Kisnorbo was theoretically an example of talent sharing within the broader CFG family, but he arrived when they were 13th in Ligue 1 and was sacked with them 17th in Ligue 2. Another flaw in the model was highlighted in an interview given by Bruno Irles, Kisnorbo's predecessor, who was sacked in November 2022, to French newspaper *L'Equipe*: 'For the management, the sporting project had to go more quickly towards the City project. There was a difference in points of view.'

Troyes and Strasbourg provide the counter argument to the virtues of the multi-club idea because their fortunes tanked after being consumed by the larger beast. But more fundamental than that is the idea of identity. Every football club has its own character, its own history, its own stories – good and bad. The years create texture and every club's is different. Like a finger print, every club is unique; every club has something that no other club has.

That is eroded by the multi-club model, in which football teams are subsumed into one broader entity, their individuality and character gradually snuffed out, so that they all become a slightly different version of the same thing, like McDonald's franchises. Some will be managed well, others not so well, but after a while they will all start to look basically the same. The same style of play. The same colours. The same club badges. The same coaches, passed between the clubs, allocated a set amount of time to do things the same way, like they're supply teachers.

Sure, some clubs may benefit from being part of a bigger group, from the expertise handed down by people who operate on a higher plane, but firstly that's not always the case, and secondly is it a good thing? Are these clubs not just being standardised, stripped of their individuality and becoming subservient to the godhead?

Red Star Paris are the club of the revolutionary and the working class, of Jules Rimet and a broader sense of community, not an item in an investment portfolio. Austria Salzburg were a proud representation of their city, not a travelling advertising board for an energy drink. Racing Strasbourg were a club of the Resistance, not somewhere for Chelsea to test out loanees.

Troyes, to be absolutely frank, don't really have any of these stories to recommend them to the outside world. They were only formed in 1986, from the wreckage of another club in the town, and in the intervening few decades there aren't many stories to tell, beyond winning the 2001 Intertoto Cup. But in some respects that's the point: they weren't for the rest of the world, they were for Troyes. They existed for the benefit of their town and their community, and didn't have to serve a broader purpose; they didn't have to be relevant to everyone else.

Perhaps nobody really cares about this. Perhaps all people are really bothered about is winning and anything that helps them along that path is acceptable. Perhaps this is the inevitable and unstoppable way the game is going. But multi-club groups have made football a less rich, more homogenised thing.

8

'INHERENTLY A SOCIAL JUSTICE MOVEMENT': THE WOMEN'S GAME

'These clubs are sitting on these massive brands that are being underutilised on the women's side.'
MARIO MALAVE,
CO-CEO OF MERCURY/13

If there is one name that perhaps encapsulates how much football ownership has changed since the days of local factory owners and butchers in Victorian England, it's probably Natalie Portman.

Portman's journey to becoming one of the more unlikely owners of a football team began in 2015, although she didn't know it at the time.

It was the final of the Women's World Cup in Vancouver. The United States of America, who were aiming to become the first team ever to win the tournament three times, were playing Japan. It turned out to be a slightly madcap game, not the sort of encounter you'd expect from such a high-pressure scenario when nerves often override attacking intent.

The US ended up winning 5–2, with a hat-trick from Carli Lloyd, one of which was an audacious chip from the halfway line that left Japan goalkeeper Ayumi Kaihori scrambling and embarrassed. It was not just a thrilling game but a thrilling occasion, and was just one of the many times that team, featuring not just Lloyd but Megan Rapinoe, Alex Morgan, Abby Wambach and various other legends of the game, inspired someone.

That someone wasn't Portman. She wasn't there. Kara Nortman was, though. Nortman is a venture capitalist who started her professional career at Morgan Stanley, then was part of a group called Hatch Labs, from which the dating app Tinder sprang, but really made her name in the financial world as part of Upfront Ventures.

After the game, which Nortman attended with her husband, daughters and parents, she tried to buy a US replica jersey. She traipsed around nine shops in Vancouver without luck. And with her capitalist head on, the germ of an idea started to form, born from annoyance that this incredible event was being underexploited commercially.

A few years later both Nortman and Portman became involved in Time's Up, the organisation founded to raise money for victims of sexual harassment, in response to the Me Too movement and Harvey Weinstein's crimes. They became friends and in 2019 Nortman invited Portman to an event that a number of the US players attended.

Nortman had been involved with the team's long battle with US Soccer over pay equality with their male counterparts, which eventually concluded in 2022 after six years of lawsuits and battles. The parallels between that and Time's Up became obvious to Portman, who began to see the power that football could have as not just a sport, but a social justice movement.

All of which led to more and more conversations about football, going to more games, and ultimately coming to a head when Portman asked in 2019: why isn't there a National Women's Soccer League team in Los Angeles?

The answer wasn't obvious. There were two men's Major League Soccer teams there – LA Galaxy and LAFC – but at the time the closest women's club to one of the biggest media markets in the country was the Utah Royals, nearly 700 miles away in Salt Lake City.

So, they started one. Angel City were born.

The founding trio was completed by the businesswoman Julie Uhrman. Money was raised though Portman's Hollywood connections – Jennifer Garner, Eva Longoria, Uzo Aduba, Jessica Chastain and America Ferrera were all in the first group of investors – plus co-founder of Reddit and Serena Williams' husband Alexis Ohanian, and a slew of former US players, including Mia Hamm, Julie Foudy and Wambach.

They were granted one of the NWSL expansion franchises in 2020. Eni Aluko, the former England international, was brought in as sporting director. Their home would be the BMO Stadium, where LAFC also play. Ahead of their first season in 2022 they signed Christen Press, double World Cup winner with the USA in 2015 and 2019, her teammate in the former tournament Sydney Leroux, and New Zealand captain Ali Riley. Their first NWSL game was on 29 April, 2022. They beat North Carolina Courage 2–1.

The extraordinary thing about Angel City is not their on-pitch results, their status as a new NWSL team or even their players. It's the money. In 2023, the second year of their existence, Angel City were responsible for 38 per cent of the revenue generated by NWSL clubs that year. They brought in $31.2 million that year.

Put that next to the men's game and the basic numbers don't look that impressive. LAFC brought in $116 million in 2022 and Forbes valued them as the first MLS franchise worth over $1 billion in 2023. But the fact that Angel City went from a standing start to generating over a third of the money in their particular division serves as an illustration of something Nortman has said many times: that women's football is 'the biggest value-creation opportunity I have seen in my career.'

'We are building something bigger than a game; a platform where mission and capital coexist,' Portman told The Athletic's Meg Linehan shortly after Angel City launched. 'We want to build a fanbase that not only shows up for our team on the field, but also something for our larger community to show up for. Together we can leverage our platform, players and even our organization to show up and get young girls and boys more access to sports.'

It's easy to see why getting involved is so intoxicating. For someone like Nortman, whose career to this point has been largely based around the idea of using money to make more money, a field that many 'normal' members of society have trouble understanding and are thus morally suspicious of, the opportunity to align profit and principles is an incredibly rare one.

'It's the first place in my life where people are paying attention through joy and greed,' says Nortman, over Zoom from her California home. 'It's the first place where I have seen all my non-profit interests and my for-profit interests align.'

A few months after I talk to Nortman, the predictions about how quickly things move, and how rapidly the value of a club like Angel City can shoot up, become real. The takeover of the club by Bob Iger and Willow Bay, $250 million, doubled the previous record for a women's football club. The fact that the previous record of $120 million, the price paid for San Diego Wave by investment firm Levine Leichtman Capital Partners, was only set in March, emphasises the point that women's football is a growth industry, and is growing incredibly quickly. Ron Burkle, the previous owner of the Wave, had paid $2 million for an expansion franchise fee only three years earlier. You have to move pretty fast.

One day in June of 2023, Victoire Covegina Reynal was putting the finishing touches to a sales deck for her new project.

She had been planning to take a sabbatical, but then came up with the idea for Mercury/13, an investment group that aimed to raise $100 million and eventually take over up to 13 women's football clubs. It was a big idea, and time was of the essence, so it was pretty important to get the deck right.

Later that day, she gave birth to her daughter.

'Women's football waits for no one,' she says by way of explanation a few months later in the bar of a very plush central London hotel, smiling in the manner of someone who has found her calling.

Covegina Reynal started off in fashion PR, before becoming an agent representing a collection of MLS players, and then founded an app called Gloria, the idea of which was for football fans to connect in a similar way that fitness enthusiasts use Strava. The app was bought by German-based media company OneFootball in 2022 and Covegina Reynal was appointed as their vice-president of women's football.

But a few months later when they came to make cuts, their women's coverage was among the first areas on the block. It served as a moment of clarity for Covegina Reynal, who quit and planned to take that sabbatical, the eventual aim to do something more personal, something to further women's football and not be getting 'the scraps' from organisations for whom men's football was the default.

The sabbatical didn't last long. A week, in fact.

'I was reading a book about City Football Group – I thought "What about a multi-club investment group just for women's football teams?"' she says. 'Take all the good stuff about multi-club, and you just cater to women's football. I would build a structure where I'm never going to be left just getting the scraps. I would be able to do all the great things that I know women's football can do. I told my husband: "I'm going to start a multi-club women's football group and I'm going to raise $100 million." He looked at me and said "What about your sabbatical?"'

The reason that Covegina Reynal had to postpone the sabbatical, and not take the time off that would be entirely understandable for a new parent, was not just that she was driven by an ideological flash of light, but that there was a financial imperative. That imperative being the women's game represents a bigger opportunity for profit than the men's, simply because there is so much further to go, so much more opportunity for growth, but it soon might be too late.

'The only way to grow the women's game is to make it financially sustainable,' she says. 'Depending on grants or getting a percentage of the budget from the men's club is not sustainable. If it becomes independent, and financially sustainable, the women's game will grow.'

She illustrates the difference between men's and women's football by likening the former to a long-standing 'heritage' business, like a venerable old bank, whereas the latter is more like a start-up, which more often than not begins with a small group of people who believe they have spotted something that the established order have missed.

Nortman agrees: 'Women's sports feels like an emerging market: maybe it's a global market of about $1 billion. Deloitte did a report on men's sports which said it was about half a trillion. The idea that it is a fraction of a per cent is crazy.'

The point of all this is the belief, firmly held by Covegina Reynal, Nortman and pretty much everyone else involved in the game, that women's football is an area where people no longer have to choose between doing 'good' and making money.

'The reason why, commercially, women's football is becoming more interesting than men's in some cases is that women's football is inherently a gender-equality movement,' says Covegina Reynal.

'It's a once-in-a-generation opportunity for a brand to support such a movement. It's gold dust for them. Especially for brands that cater specifically to women – beauty or fashion or pharma, baby products or fertility clinics – you have so many categories of brands that basically have made women their main consumer. For them to get associated with women's football is telling their consumers: we care about you, and we care about you getting empowered and worthy.

'There have been several examples of brands that have embraced and have done really well. For example Bumble, and the Taylor Swift tours, the Barbie movie: these are brands that went straight to women and said "You matter and we care about you." Women went and spent their money on them. That's the opportunity on the commercial side that the women's game has.'

Nortman differs very slightly. When I ask if she also thought that the women's game was inherently a social movement, she says: 'I think it's a cultural movement. I want to create a space where every kind of person can come in and there is a social justice element to it that's really important. But there is an element to it that's really easy: you will always do better if you involve women. You have women in the locker room, in the boardroom – you're just going to do better if you don't have the same old group doing things. But you can still bring the male allies in.'

To illustrate why Covegina Reynal couldn't wait until a slightly more practical time to launch her venture, consider this speed of inflation: if you wanted to enter an expansion team into the National Women's Soccer League in 2019, the franchise fee was $500,000. In 2021, that had gone up to $5 million. In 2023, when a consortium representing a new team in Boston wanted in on the action, the price was $53 million. There is no missing decimal point in that number. 'Those jumps – you don't see them in other industries,' says Covegina Reynal.

Those jumps have a lot to do with Angel City. Nortman is keen to point out that one of the reasons for that rapid growth in NWSL franchise fees is partly because of the money that they have been able to bring in. And not just teams who have the advantage of Hollywood megastars as their owners.

'The reason the franchise values have gone up,' says Nortman, 'is because there are examples – Angel City, San Diego, Kansas City, Washington – who are all independent and female-led. It's not an accident that it went up.

'We've far out-performed the expectations we had. [In our first year we had] three to four times the revenue projections; we doubled the amount of tickets we thought we'd sell. But I think bigger than the financial results … we did it for all these reasons that were our life's work. This was the first time in my career when women had come together to build something so meaningful, in the city we all lived in – Julie and I grew up here, Natalie is a long-term resident – to show the world that [we were] not just bringing capital to women's sports, but capital aligned with the values we want to see in women's sports. It's female-owned, female-led.'

But the other thing, and the one that has provided inspiration to groups like Mercury/13 and perhaps underpins the idea that women's football can be such a remarkable growth area, is that they did things the 'wrong' way around.

Mario Malave, Covegina Reynal's co-founder and co-CEO, explains: 'The conventional flywheel is that you invest money to drive on-pitch success, then you monetise that success. What Angel City proved is that you can do things the other way around, flipping the sequence of commercial and on-pitch success. They built a brand, an entity, a culture, a community.

'We think we can create a story, rethink your social media strategy, and all of those gains we can reinvest into better players and infrastructure. It starts with commercial and then goes into success, from where you can get that virtuous circle going.'

While Angel City has the significant PR boon of being co-owned by some astonishingly famous people, they act as a sort of proof of concept, of the idea that you don't have to take over an existing – and expensive – team to make money. You can't do that in men's football, or at least it's much, much more difficult. You can't do that in men's football, or at least it's much, much more difficult.

The most comparable example is Inter Miami, David Beckham's MLS team, who played their first game in 2020 and by 2024 were valued at around $1 billion. The difference is that was made possible by Beckham's deal when he moved to LA Galaxy as a player, which included a clause allowing him to buy a franchise of his own for $25 million. That was a bargain price in 2014, when Beckham exercised the clause, given that the fee for New York City FC the previous year was $100 million. But it looked like daylight robbery in comparison to the team that will start life in San Diego in 2025, the franchise fee for which was a reported $500 million. Plus, Inter Miami had to sign arguably the greatest player of all time, Lionel Messi, along with three of his former Barcelona pals Luis Suarez, Jordi Alba and Sergio Busquets, in order to reach their valuation.

The US has always been ahead of the rest of the world when it comes to the popularity and commercialisation of the women's game, but it still acts as a useful bellwether for the rapidity of its financial growth. In short, there's money in them hills, but you will have to get in pretty quickly if you don't want to pay staggering amounts for the opportunity to speculate.

'What keeps me up at night, as an investment manager,' says Malave, 'is that we're too slow and all of a sudden we're paying ten times the price for the same team. The risk is that we overextend ourselves: we don't want to over-promise and under-deliver.'

The franchise fees are one thing, but to a point they are arbitrarily set numbers, based partly on growth but also essentially a product of market forces: the cost of something is whatever someone is capable of and prepared to spend on it.

More solid indications of the monetary rise can be seen in the sale prices for the San Diego Wave and Angel City, but also in the financial results of the biggest and most powerful clubs in Europe, when it comes to women's football. For the 2022/23 season, Barcelona reported revenues of €13.4 million – a year-on-year increase of 74 per cent. Real Madrid's was up 416 per cent, from €1.4 million to €7.4 million. Arsenal's €5.3 million represented a 138 per cent rise. Across the board, the 2024 Deloitte Money League – the annual report into the wealthiest football clubs in the world – reported that the top 15 revenue-generating clubs in Europe brought in an average of €4.3 million in 2022/23, 61 per cent up on the previous year.

You can see why people like Covegina Reynal and Nortman were so keen to get involved quickly. The amounts themselves look fairly puny compared with men's teams – that average figure of €4.3 million is about what Manchester United brought in for an agreement with Chivas Regal to be their official spirits partner - but the potential for growth is extraordinary.

The commercial potential for the women's game is only just starting: Covegina Reynal talks about making sponsorship agreements and partnerships with brands specifically aimed at women, which has started – the stadium in which Manchester City play their games, formerly simply known as the Academy Stadium, is now the Joie Stadium after a deal was struck with the baby-care brand, for example – but is still in a fairly embryonic phase.

———

That said, it's not just new or independent women's teams that have this potential, according to Covegina Reynal and Malave. When, at the end of 2023, Sir Jim Ratcliffe and his INEOS group bought just over 25 per cent of Manchester United in return for a significant say in how the football side of things was run, it was viewed with a degree of suspicion: how was this going to work? How was it possible that there could be two powerful competing forces, along with the Glazer family, who had significant says in how the club was run?

But the idea of different people running different parts of a football club might not be so alien to the women's game in years to come. One thing that Covegina Reynal and Malave predict is that a number of 'legacy' football clubs who have women's teams that, quite frankly, the traditional ownership doesn't really pay that much attention to, will essentially outsource the running and commercial exploitation of those teams.

That is an irritation for some, but an opportunity for others. A group like Mercury/13 could come in and essentially take over the women's side of the club without completely cleaving it from the rest of the organisation, but have the time, motivation and expertise to run it in a more commercial way.

'We know that about 95 per cent of the women's teams around the world are under men's teams,' Covegina Reynal says. 'But there are some big independent clubs: we're starting with them because it's a cleaner approach from a legal and operational standpoint. But the aspiration is to be able to get into a position where we can separate the women's teams from their men's counterparts. That will look very different in different countries and different leagues.

'We've been surprised to see some of the biggest clubs in the world coming to us and saying "Will you take over our women's team?" The more you have conversations with them, you realise that the mindset around women's football is that it's a rounding error in their profit and losses. It's something that is viewed as a cost centre and more than anything else a distraction.'

Malave adds: 'These clubs are sitting on these massive brands that are being underutilised on the women's side. There's then a classic innovators' dilemma: it's like when tech companies are sitting on a massive cash cow that is earning them a tonne of money, but they don't want to reinvest some of that money into that wild idea that one day could, in the future, be way bigger than the cash cow they have. That's similar to the women's game.

'Their top player makes in a week what the women's team costs in a year. It's not a priority for the business. So then we come in and say "It's not going to be a rounding error for us: we can come in and take over the whole thing, run it, staff it, give it the direction to free you to focus on what you want, but also give you the benefit of the potential that we think it has."'

———

I speak to Malave and Covegina Reynal at the start of their project, when they were in the process of acquiring their first club, FC Como in Italy. But they are by no means the first to get into the multi-club ownership game in women's football.

Michele Kang had really no intention of getting into football. In fact, she didn't know much about the game at all, to the point that her friends chided her for not knowing who Lionel Messi was. Kang was born in South Korea, but moved to America to study economics at the University of Chicago and then Yale. She worked for Ernst and Young before making her money with a company called Cognosante, which she said was designed to 'disrupt the status quo' in the US healthcare system.

As she entered her 60s, she anticipated spending more time doing philanthropic work, but in 2020 she was invited to join the ownership group of Washington Spirit, the NWSL side. Intrigued, and despite not having any connection with the game, she saw it as a form of community service, and spent time with the players and management at the club.

In 2021 the Spirit were embroiled in a crisis, centring around allegations of verbal and emotional abuse, and a toxic working environment, against former head coach Richie Burke. He was fired, but over the following year or so calls grew for the club's owner, Steve Baldwin, to cede complete control of the Spirit to Kang. These calls came from the fans, but more significantly from the team's players, who released a fairly remarkable statement in October 2021.

'Let us be clear,' the statement said. 'The person we trust is Michele. She continuously puts players' needs and interests first. She listens. She believes that this can be a profitable business and you have always said you intended to hand the team over to female ownership. That moment is now. Please sell to Michele at a reasonable price.'

Eventually Baldwin did as they asked, and Kang became the sole owner in March 2022. But she wasn't stopping there: in April 2023 she joined Eagle Football Holdings, the investment vehicle of the American investor John Textor, who owns stakes in Crystal Palace, Botafogo, Molenbeek in Belgium and, most relevantly for Kang, Lyon.

From there she began the process of taking control of the phenomenally successful Lyon Féminin who, thanks to being one of the first women's teams to receive significant financial backing had – at the time of Kang's takeover – won 16 French league titles and eight Champions Leagues. Kang took 52 per cent of the team and became its CEO, a deal that was finally completed in February 2024.

Meanwhile, she also acquired London City Lionesses in December 2023. They were, at the time, the highest profile women's team in England that wasn't officially linked to a men's team, having become independent from Millwall in 2019.

Her ideas align with those of Nortman and Covegina Reynal: the women's game could be sustainable, and then profitable, if people took it seriously as a business. 'I give full credit to people who carried the teams,' she told *The New York Times* in 2023, referring to previous NWSL team owners. 'But [Washington Spirit] was being viewed as a charity or a non-profit, and business disciplines were not applied from where I stand.'

Kang, while being a businesswoman looking for some sort of return on her investment, seems to direct her focus towards the betterment of the sport and her resources into providing the sort of structures that are taken for granted in the men's game, but have often been an afterthought in women's football.

'As my head of performance says, women are not small men, so they should not be trained based upon the training manuals developed by men,' she said, when her purchase of a stake in Lyon Féminin was confirmed in 2024. 'I wanted a dedicated staff, focused only on women. When they get up in the morning, they only think about women athletes, not men and women.'

She expanded on this in a 2023 interview with ESPN, discussing how her plans would start with the Washington Spirit but then disseminate through the rest of her clubs.

'We're going to create some sort of an innovation lab. Staff will go back and forth and will train the trainers.

'Other teams will have their own team [of staff] and we will localise. ... It will be all shared and then we'll figure out how to spread those methodologies so that everyone can benefit from what we are investing in.'

Part of the reason for Kang bringing multiple clubs together, rather than focusing solely on the Spirit or Lyon, is economy of scale – not uncommon in the multi-club model, but it's particularly relevant when you're trying to do something more than simply win football games. In order to do everything she wanted to do, to accelerate the research and investment into women's football, it made much more financial sense to do the work once and apply it to several different clubs.

'One could argue that trying to do it at one team's level is probably unsustainable,' Kang told ESPN. 'This is not a money-making business and there is still a ways to go in breaking even. So you need some scale to continue to invest, not just for one team but more teams.'

———

If, after reading all of this, you are moved to invest in women's football, either for philosophical reasons or to make a nice bit of money, then bad luck: it's probably too late. Kang and Covegina Reynal and Portman and Malave and Nortman have all got there before you.

This is a revolution in the way football ownership is thought of. The traditional structures are being reimagined, and innovation that simply isn't realistic or possible in the men's game is happening.

The concept of reverse-engineering a fanbase is a fascinating one, and something that is much easier to do in the women's game, simply because there is more space, and the structures of the men's game – or at least the top of the men's game – are so rigid. A team like Hashtag United in the lower leagues of England, who began life as the team of YouTuber Spencer Owen, did a similar thing by starting with a following before coming up with a team, but a team like Angel City is on another level entirely.

This is partly governed by how American sports are structured: by purchasing an expansion franchise licence for the NWSL, you can get straight into the top level of the sport in the country, whereas if Hashtag United's men's team were to reach the Premier League it would take them decades. Their women's team, however, could get to the WSL much quicker.

It's important to reiterate that none of the people discussed here have got into the football ownership game out of the goodness of their hearts, or because they just want to be activists. They want to make money, and have moved into the game at a time when it's more possible than ever to do that.

The people involved are all competitive, against other clubs in their orbit, but also against each other. There seems to be a nodding respect between Nortman and Covegina Reynal and Kang, but not a great deal more than that.

That said, women's football ownership does seem to be, for want of a better phrase, a more pleasant space. It's more collaborative, according to the people involved in it: Nortman speaks about sharing best practice, and even their 'playbook', with other people looking to invest in the NWSL and bid for new franchises.

'It's not just about "building my team" in a deeply competitive, sharp-elbowed way,' she tells me. 'Women's football requires a tonne of heavy lifting and best-practice sharing. It's the reason the NWSL is doing so well.

'Of course we're competitive in some ways, but I get comments after being on stage with another owner, saying "You don't hear two men's owners talking to each other and complimenting each other; authentically understanding that the way you compete in women's sports is by sharing."'

Covegina Reynal also thinks that simply by involving more women in football club ownership things can and will change.

'[Football club ownership is usually] an ego-driven exercise. Now we're trying to reposition ownership as more than just an ego-driven thing. That's by bringing in mostly women to invest. When a woman makes a lot of money, the first idea in her head is not to buy a football club. The women who have joined the Mercury/13 journey – they see this opportunity to not only own a club, but also how can that club have a social impact that goes beyond their local community?'

It's not a competition. People are not necessarily measuring themselves against men's football, and it's obvious that it will take decades for the women's game to get close to commensurate levels of money and exposure. But women's football has been, at best, patronised and ignored for most of the game's history, if not actively banned as it effectively was in England for 50 years. Its time is now.

'We get to break the rules and rewrite them,' says Covegina Reynal. 'For me, it's very exciting: in a moment in my life when I should potentially be on maternity leave, I'm running this monster because it excites me.

'If you ask me how I will know I've succeeded in ten years, it will be if I'm getting phone calls from the biggest clubs in the world, asking "How did you do it – teach us." That's not the only reason to be proud, but it will show how this world has to have an open collaboration and dialogue between women and men.'

9

STRANGE TALES FROM THE WORLD OF FOOTBALL CLUB OWNERSHIP

*'If Gaddafi's money was able to progress Palace …
then one would have to take that into consideration.'*
SIMON JORDAN
FORMER CHAIRMAN OF CRYSTAL PALACE

One of the central questions that this book is trying to address is: what makes a good football club owner?

Each section, dedicated to a different approach to football club ownership, tries to detail the pros and cons of each, and attempts to understand the nuances, while recognising that there is not necessarily a definitive right or wrong way to do things.

For this chapter though, forget all that. However you want to approach the idea of owning and running a football club, don't follow what these people have done. Think of the next few pages as cautionary tales, not inspiration.

Whatever you want from the owner of your football club, just trust me on this one: you do not want these people to own your football club.

———

George Reynolds used to carry a business card around with him.

It read: 'George Reynolds, managing director, chairman, gentleman, entrepreneur, adventurer, maker of money and utter genius.'

Some of those things were undeniably true. He was certainly a chairman. He was absolutely an entrepreneur. He definitely was a maker of money. The rest we'll leave as a matter of debate.

But weirdly the card left off some other things, like 'safe-blower', 'tax-evader' and 'harasser'. Because Reynolds was not unfamiliar with the long arm of the law: he spent four years in prison in the 1960s for taking part in a number of robberies in which his task was taking explosives to the safe; he was given a three-year sentence years later for not throwing entirely straight dice with HMRC; and in 2019 was convicted once more for harassing a Durham county councillor over a planning application for some holiday lodges.

Maybe there just wasn't enough space on the card.

Still, he didn't seem especially ashamed of his prison background: his autobiography was called *Cracked It!* and in 2001 he appeared on the pitch at Darlington, the club he owned for five rollercoaster years, wearing a mock prison suit, complete with (fabric) ball and chain, with which he did keepy-uppies.

Reynolds came from humble beginnings, but his brushes with the law were from a young age: he was caught stealing cigarettes as a boy, and in his early 20s served his first prison spell for stealing watches. It was during that stint that he was sent to solitary confinement for calling the governor a Nazi.

He also spent a night in the cells on a separate occasion, because, according to his autobiography, a small grass monkey that he had acquired while in the Merchant Navy had broken free of its restraints and somehow got its hands on a hammer, with which it smashed a series of windows. It's at this point in reading the book that you do wonder whether 'fantasist' could have been added to that list of descriptors on his business card, but who are we to doubt the word of such an upstanding citizen?

He was a man with fingers in many pies and at various points combined those pies: he acquired an ice cream van as a sort of legitimate day job, and used the van to store the equipment for his slightly less respectable nocturnal gig of safe-blowing. Apparently the gelignite, his explosive of choice, needed to be kept chilled, so he moved aside the choc ices.

The safe-blowing business turned out to be quite lucrative, especially when – according to him at least – you're pretty good at it: years later Reynolds made the exceptional brag that he was the 'third-best in Europe'. Congratulations to first and second, hard luck to fourth place: maybe you'll do better in the play-offs.

Lucrative, yes, but ultimately restrictive: one job, that he described as 'too tempting to ignore', earned him a four-year sentence in Kirkham Prison. After his release, he took the advice of the jail's priest, who suggested he went into the legitimate business world, if only because he was 'no bloody good at crime, George: you're always getting caught.'

After his release he went straight and got into the worktop business: Direct Worktops was not only incredibly successful, but Reynolds was very popular with his workforce. Implausibly, he was once a guest on Oprah Winfrey's TV show to talk about how he would occasionally buy his employees cars and pay off their mortgages. He did well enough to purchase a yacht he called 'Secret Love' and eventually sold his business for around £41 million.

Yacht polish aside, he needed something else to spend his money on. 'Darlington Football Club had, to put it bluntly,' he wrote in his autobiography, 'more ups and downs than a tart's knickers.' That charming turn of phrase was a pretty decent indicator of how the next few years would go under Reynold's tenure, after he completed his takeover in 1999.

It did start reasonably well: the crowd welcomed him with open arms, he paid off the club's £5.2 million debt and he promised to build them a new stadium. However, ten days before the start of the 2000/01 season, manager David Hodgson walked out after key players were sold and not replaced. Reynolds, on something of an economy drive, had also cut the remaining players' bonuses and made top-earner Neil Heaney's wage public.

His enthusiasm for a quarrel didn't stop in the dressing room: Reynolds not only banned the local newspaper's correspondent from Darlington games, but turned up at his house, unannounced, to complain about his articles. His wife Susan once bizarrely hinted there was some suspicion that their players were throwing games.

After a local radio host named Paul Gough pooh-poohed the idea that Paul Gascoigne would sign for the club for a reported £1,000-a-week, Reynolds held up a banner which read 'Goffy is gay.' In his autobiography, there's a page entitled 'What managers, footballers, the media and fans know about running a football club as a business': the rest of the page is blank.

An amusing gag, no doubt, but it proved ironic considering what happened next. Firstly, the attempt to sign Faustino Asprilla in 2002 will go down as one of the finest examples of a football chairman having his pants very firmly pulled down by a player and agent using them for their own means. Reynolds agreed not only to pay Asprilla wages of around £7,000 a week, but also promised him a cut of the gate receipts from every game he played in, a free car, free accommodation for him and a free flat for his driver.

Asprilla was paraded around the pitch at Darlington's Feethams ground before a game, the deal apparently done. But, alas, early one morning Asprilla bolted, flying to an unspecified destination in the Middle East where a more lucrative contract was apparently waiting for him (although if there was one he didn't actually sign it: he eventually joined Atlético Nacional in Colombia).

'I have put seven hard weeks into this and went to tremendous expense,' Reynolds sobbed. 'He reneged on the deal with us. I can fully understand why the football industry is in such a mess. Where are the days of the gentlemen's agreement, the shake of the hand and the binding contract?'

Where indeed? Reynolds did have one more club in his bag, though: that new stadium. But while it was the thing that Reynolds thought was going to save him and the club, it ultimately sank them both.

Darlington were in the third tier of English football at the time and would typically get attendances of around 5,000 for their games at Feethams, capacity 8,500. It therefore didn't seem entirely necessary to build the club a new home with a capacity of 25,000. Still less necessary for that new home to have Italian marble flooring in reception, escalators, state of the art urinals and £2 million spent on the seats alone. The whole thing cost a whopping £25 million and towards the end of the build Reynolds was forced to borrow nearly £4 million on what we'll call 'unfavourable' terms: one of the loans stipulated that if Reynolds and Darlington missed even a single payment, the interest payable would shoot up to 30 per cent.

The inevitable happened and in December 2003 Reynolds put the club into administration with debts in the region of £20 million. Most of that was down to the cost of the stadium, but the list of debtors made for pretty bleak reading: £240,000 to a local electrical firm; £10,035 to Durham University; £42,000 to a series of utility companies; £9,040 to St John Ambulance, who provided emergency medical presence at games.

This was their first of three administrations. A charity game was held in 2004 that raised just enough money to keep the club going but the club tumbled down the divisions and were in the Conference North by the time they finally went out of business in 2012. In their place a phoenix club, under supporter ownership, called Darlington 1883, emerged and remain to this day. They play their games at the rather more modest, 3,200-capacity Blackwell Meadows ground.

As for Reynolds, in 2005 he was convicted of tax evasion after he was found with £550,000 in cash in the back of his car. It turned out that he hadn't paid a penny to the exchequer in six years and had declared that his state pension was his only income. He was released from prison in December 2006 with an electronic tag, but was sent back a few months later for breaching the terms of his parole. He later started a business selling, in his words, 'adult bedroom furniture' – S&M gear to you and me. He was in trouble with the law one more time, with that conviction for harassment in 2019, for which he was fined £600. He died in 2021.

Ken Richardson was cut from a similar cloth. Just like Reynolds, he was a brash character who arrived at a lower-league club in the north of England with the promise of great things ahead. And like Reynolds, when he left a few years later things were on fire.

The difference was that Reynolds left metaphorical flames. With Richardson, they were literal.

Richardson had made his money in the potato sack business, as the founder of East Riding Sacks, but by the time he arrived at Doncaster Rovers in 1993 he already had a rather chequered reputation. His first foray into the sporting world was in racehorse ownership, but in 1984 he was at the centre of a bizarre episode that ended in him being banned from the sport for fraud.

Richardson and trainer Stephen Wiles entered a horse called Flockton Grey in a race for two-year-olds at Leicester. The horse romped home, but suspicions were raised, particularly after a large number of bets had been placed on the horse at 10/1. The Jockey Club investigated and discovered that the horse was actually a three-year-old called Good Hand, and thus had a significant size, strength and speed advantage over its competitors. Richardson and his associates had placed bets of around £20,000 on the horse and, despite spreading their wagers around a number of bookmakers to try and cover their tracks, they were found out.

Wiles had his training licence withdrawn and was banned for five years, while Richardson was found guilty of conspiracy to defraud, given a nine-month suspended prison sentence, and forced to pay around £45,000 in fines and legal fees. He was also banned by the Jockey Club for 25 years from involvement in horse racing, so he had to find something else to entertain him.

That something else turned out to be Bridlington Town, a non-league club on the north-east coast of England, which he took over in 1991. Despite starting out reasonably well, investing heavily in their Queensgate stadium and winning the FA Vase in 1993, things went rapidly south after they were forced to play home games at Doncaster's Belle Vue ground, some 130 miles away. They were relegated but apparently decided to fold, for reasons a little unclear, rather than play in the Northern

Premier League Division One. They reformed in 1994 and are still going.

By that time Richardson already had his feet under the table at Doncaster, initially billed as a 'consultant', but in effect he was in charge given that his company, Dinard Trading, had acquired a majority stake in the club.

He made big promises, claiming that Doncaster would be in the top flight inside five years, but his conduct began to ring alarm bells. He scrapped, then reinstated, the club's reserve and youth teams. He appointed his daughter and niece to the board. He threatened to pull Doncaster out of the league at one point.

He got through six permanent managers (and two caretakers) in four years, but that didn't matter quite so much because most of them weren't actually allowed to pick the team: that was the preserve of the club's self-declared 'benefactor'. One of those managers, Sammy Chung, arrived at the ground one Saturday to take charge of a game, only to discover he had been replaced by Kerry Dixon. Richardson hadn't thought to let him know.

All of which isn't ideal, but was a mere amuse-bouche to the farce and criminality that was to follow. More or less from the moment he arrived, Richardson seemed determined to get Doncaster away from their admittedly 'rustic' Belle Vue home. He advertised the land it was on for sale in the press, the slight catch there being that neither he nor the club actually owned it: the council did.

Alarm bells thus rang in June 1995 when a portion of Belle Vue's main stand went up in flames. In the end only a smallish section actually burned down, when it could have been much worse, but rats were smelled. A few months later, Richardson was arrested for conspiracy to commit arson, his big plan seemingly to torch the place in an attempt to either get the insurance money, or to hurry along the plans to redevelop the ground, on the basis that if it was replaced by a smouldering pile of wood and metal, then you'd struggle to argue it should just stay as it is.

The case didn't end up going to trial for a few years, but when it did the results were spectacular. It emerged that Richardson had offered a former SAS trooper named Alan Kristiansen £10,000 to do the necessary. The 'plan', such as it was, was to spray the building with petrol and set it alight, which he did, but fire engines got there before the whole stand could go up.

However, the best-laid plans did go slightly awry because Kristiansen didn't do a brilliant job of covering his tracks, leaving a rucksack and a selection of petrol cans at the scene. Even more absurdly, he also left his mobile phone there, but not before calling Richardson to leave a message saying: 'The job's been done.' How the police ever cracked the case is a mystery.

Kristiansen admitted arson, but Richardson denied conspiracy to commit criminal damage by fire. However, his defence wasn't well received in court: prosecutor Roger Keen QC called Richardson's evidence 'the worst concoction of waffle, piffle and flannel' he had ever heard. He was found guilty and sentenced to four years in jail. He had sold the club a few months earlier and it was eventually taken over by John Ryan, who made his money in cosmetic surgery, and who stayed until 2013.

Ryan, as an aside, became the oldest man to ever play for a British professional football club when, age 52, he came on as a substitute in a game against Hereford United in 2003. If nothing else, it should tell you that someone capable of a sideshow like that was infinitely preferable to the old guy. Richardson died in 2023.

Still, all of this is relatively minor compared with actual warlords and dictators.

Most fans would probably consider it 'not ideal' if the owner of their club was subject to a lengthy report by Human Rights Watch. Particularly one that was titled *Widespread Torture in the Chechen Republic*, which detailed systematic illegal detention with no recourse and a range of 'disappearances' of Chechen citizens.

To the majority of the world, Ramzan Kadyrov is a monster. To the fans of FC Akhmat Grozny, he is the boss.

The club was historically known as Terek Grozny, but was renamed in 2017 after Kadyrov's late father and a predecessor as president, Akhmat, who was killed by Chechen separatists in 2004. But that was just one of the many ways in which the club changed after Kadyrov took over in late 2010.

Kadyrov had always been a football fan, but his focus sharpened after Russia was awarded the 2018 World Cup. He not only saw the potential for the sport as a propaganda tool, but also decided that Chechnya should host games at the tournament. 'Kadyrov set on a mission,' wrote Miriam Elder in *The Atlantic*. 'He would prove, in spectacularly Kadyrovesque fashion, that Chechnya was so peaceful, so normal, so great that even the world's best soccer players were jumping over themselves to go there.'

The first move was to get a big-name manager. Víctor Muñoz, the former Barcelona and Spain midfielder who had previously managed Villarreal and Real Zaragoza in his homeland, was initially hired, but he didn't take charge of a game. The official reason was that negotiations over his contract broke down, but you would forgive him for having second thoughts about working under Kadyrov.

Ruud Gullit, apparently, had no such qualms. 'At the beginning there was no way I was going to come,' Gullit told the journalist Alex Kay-Jelski a few months after he was appointed. 'I talked about it, thought about it and then I met the president in Geneva … The money is good, I'm not going to lie. I'm here for that and the adventure. And every day is an adventure …'

Gullit neatly sidestepped the issue of having to deal with a dictator by … not dealing with him. 'I don't have to deal with Kadyrov. He doesn't pay me. A sponsor pays me so I can distance myself from it. Politics and football don't mix.'

Gullit could try to ignore Kadyrov all he liked, but the president's spectre loomed. 'When we lose, children cry,' Kadyrov once said, and soon enough Gullit's performances – and complaints about the lack of transfer activity and training facilities – led to his dismissal, weeping children presumably comforted. 'We parted as friends,' said Kadyrov, which is probably just as well for Gullit.

Meanwhile, Kadyrov was exploring another way to use football: by inserting himself into a series of fixtures stuffed with more celebrities. He arranged a game between a group of Chechen players – including himself – and a side featuring several former Brazilian greats, including Dunga, Cafu and Romário. In another, he coaxed Diego Maradona into playing.

A new stadium was built, where Kadyrov hoped to host those World Cup games. By this point he had become quite hands-on: in 2013, Terek were given a one-game stadium ban after he, incensed at some refereeing decisions, took control of the microphone and bellowed over the PA: 'The ref's been bought off! You're an ass!'

He later said sorry. Well, sort of. 'I apologise to the whole football world for what I said in the heat of the moment. But not to the referee, he deserved to be called corrupt.'

In 2017, Kadyrov announced the rebranding of Terek to Akhmat – and made quite a fuss of it too: to their opening game under their new name, Kadyrov invited Ronaldinho, who it was claimed travelled to Grozny to take in the match unpaid. 'Too special, come from so far and receive so much affection!!!' he said afterwards on Instagram.

By this point, hopes of hosting that World Cup match were gone, so Kadyrov had to settle for Grozny being a training base for the Egyptian national team at the tournament, a decision that horrified Human Rights Watch. While there, Kadyrov once again went about the business of getting his picture taken with a famous footballer, this time apparently waking Mohamed Salah up from a post-training siesta to drag him in front of an 8,000-strong crowd and raise the Liverpool forward's arm up like a prize boxer. Was that connected to Egypt's limp exit from the tournament in the first round? Impossible to say.

The interesting thing about Akhmat/Terek Grozny is: they're no good. Usually, when someone powerful but unpalatable is in control of a football club, the fans hold their noses and either cope with or ignore it because of the great success they're enjoying. But the club's trophy cabinet is pretty dusty: they only have their 2004

Russian Cup to show for it all. Other than Gullit, the flashy names didn't even arrive: there was talk of signing Diego Forlán in 2011, but that didn't materialise.

Instead, they are just a bog-standard Russian Premier League club, finishing somewhere between fifth and 13th in every season since wining promotion back to the top flight in 2008. It seems like a pretty rum deal: if you're going to have a warlord as your owner, the least you can expect is a couple of trophies out of it.

If Crystal Palace fans thought Ron Noades, their famously combative former owner who once appointed himself as caretaker manager, was a bit spicy, then how might they have reacted if Colonel Muammar Gaddafi had taken over their club?

Because at one point, that did look like a possibility. The Libyan dictator (official title: Brotherly Leader and Guide of the Revolution) was a keen fan of football, as well as state oppression and the sponsorship of terrorism. His son, Al-Saadi Gaddafi, was famously on the books of a few Italian clubs who wanted a bit of publicity in the mid-2000s, and in 2002 Gaddafi Snr acquired a five per cent stake in Juventus. But he wanted more and made an enquiry to Palace's then chairman, Simon Jordan, about taking control of the south London club.

In his autobiography, Jordan said the approach was one that he 'didn't particularly take too seriously,' but at the time he did concede that the money Gaddafi would bring might be just the thing that Palace needed to progress. Even if he did solemnly admit that such a takeover would come with 'a degree of stigma'.

'Gaddafi is not a name which necessarily inspires enthusiasm from the British public,' said Jordan at the time. 'At the end of the day, many people might see Roman Abramovich's involvement at Chelsea as less than palatable, but he is moving the club forward. If Gaddafi's money was able to progress Palace and allow them to compete at the top of the tree and be a successful football club, then one would have to take that into consideration.'

Harry Redknapp once said that a club's fans would welcome Saddam Hussein as their owner if they were successful: maybe he was right.

———

There's a tank outside Red Star Belgrade's Marakana stadium. The ground – officially called the Rajko Mitić Stadium – is embedded in the side of a hill just to the south of the city centre, looking over Belgrade as if the club is guarding its home town.

From that perspective, maybe the tank is appropriate. Next to the entrance to the club museum, however, it does look a little incongruous, to say the least. The club were accused of 'morbid provocation' by parking such a naked symbol of the bloody Yugoslav wars outside their home, but they were adamant that it represented no such thing and everyone was just being terribly sensitive.

Still, this perhaps explains why it wasn't quite as big a deal in Serbia as it might have been elsewhere that, for four years, a man who was on Interpol's most-wanted list for over a decade, and who was indicted for crimes against humanity, controlled one of the country's clubs.

In an ideal world, Željko Ražnatović would probably have preferred to be Red Star's president: after all, the man who is better known as Arkan, one of his very many aliases, was initially the leader of a group of the club's ultras. Indeed, he recruited many of the men who would become part of his Serb Volunteers Guard – or the Tigers, as they were also called – from the terraces, and they would become one of the most terrifying and notorious paramilitary groups of the Yugoslav wars.

Both Arkan and the Tigers became particularly infamous after an incident in the Croatian city of Vukovar in 1991, when it was alleged that he oversaw the massacre of more than 250 people. 'He was charming, extremely smart and deceptively evil,' Ron Haviv, an American photographer who witnessed some of Arkan's crimes, told *The Observer* in 2000. 'Egotistical, baby-faced and he considered himself the saviour of the Serbian people. He was a likeable guy, except that he was a pathological killer.'

Arkan made his reputation as a criminal of various stripes in the 1970s and 80s, robbing banks and jewellers, committing casual acts of violence and generally holding sway over the Serbian underworld. As such, he was recruited by Slobodan Milošević for his influence over the sort of corners of society that the government couldn't reach.

And many of those corners existed in Serbian football clubs. Arkan naturally wanted to influence as many people as possible and thus attempted to gain access to the Red Star board. Unfortunately for him, even they baulked at the idea of having someone like him in their midst, so he turned his attention to FK Obilić, a hitherto nondescript club from a suburb of Belgrade not far from Red Star's stadium. They had spent most of their history in the lower reaches of the Yugoslav leagues, but after the break-up of the country they shifted up the food chain a little.

Arkan bought the club in the summer of 1996 and their fortunes changed. Not just because of the funds that the wildly wealthy warlord injected into them, but also because, frankly, many opposition players were too scared to try their hardest against a team owned by someone who tended to solve problems with a bullet.

Arkan used his connections in high places to grant him an official coaching licence, which afforded him permission to sit in the dugouts during games (although you'd like to see the steward who would tell an actual warlord 'No, you do not have the correct paperwork' as he made for the touchline), the sight of which in itself was apparently enough for many opponents to soil themselves and perhaps not put in 110 per cent that afternoon. But there were also anonymous phone calls in which the words 'bullet' and 'knee' were mentioned, and referees were also intimidated.

Obilić won promotion to the top tier in 1996/97 and the fairy tale was complete the following season when they won the league title, finishing two points ahead of Red Star and becoming the first – and at the time of writing only – team to break the Red Star-Partizan Belgrade duopoly in Serbian football. They may have received a little more help: their final game of the season was against Partizan, who were well behind in the league and apparently did not try quite as hard as they might in the game, thus ensuring that their hated rivals Red Star would miss out.

This meant that Obilić were entered into the Champions League qualifiers, where they were exposed as being firmly out of their depth after drawing Bayern Munich, who beat them 5–1 on aggregate. Arkan wasn't able to attend the leg of the tie in Bavaria: there was still an active warrant for his arrest in Germany after some criminal activities in the 1970s.

Years after his death, it also emerged that Arkan had planned to assassinate Lennart Johansson, the former president of UEFA, because he wouldn't allow a wanted warlord to represent Obilić on official business in those Champions League qualifiers. 'There's nothing you can do when someone mentally unhinged wants to kill you,' Johansson deadpanned in a Serbian documentary in 2008.

Being an owner of a Serbian club was a dangerous business in the late 1990s and early 2000s: a number of club chairmen were murdered in this time, as well as Branko Bulatović, the general secretary of the Serbia and Montenegro Football Association. And in 2000, Arkan became one of those killed: one January afternoon he was drinking in the lobby of the Hotel Continental in Belgrade when a masked man burst in and opened fire. Arkan was shot in the head and, despite apparently being alive when he was taken to hospital, he was declared dead later that day.

A surreal postscript to the whole grizzly story was that Arkan's widow Svetlana – a Serbian singer and TV personality more widely known as Ceca – was left in charge of Obilić: Arkan actually officially stepped down from his role at the club in 1998 and Ceca replaced him, taking over completely after his death.

The team went into decline over the next few years, eventually being relegated in 2006. As for Ceca, she was embroiled in a criminal crackdown after the assassination of Serbian prime minister Zoran Djindjic in 2003 and, as part of those investigations, evidence was discovered that she benefitted to the tune of around $3.5 million from the transfer of ten players from Obilić. She managed to get away with just a fine and a brief period of house arrest after being found guilty in 2011.

Obilić now doesn't really exist, as a professional entity at least. They slid down into the Belgrade regional leagues and only an amateur women's team actually plays any football under their name. Their stadium is still used for some other teams and if you walk past it these days you can see an image of Arkan, military beret on his head, on one of the walls outside.

Suddenly a tank doesn't seem quite so bad.

Another club who had a brush with a dictator were Notts County: the story of how they were taken over with promises of going from League Two to the Premier League in five years, signed a Premier League winner and a former England manager, and then somehow got mixed up in a scheme to win a mineral mining contract from North Korea is absolutely extraordinary. But a neat way of summing it up is that, despite the proximity of one of the world's most notorious and oppressive regimes, Kim Jong Il isn't even the villain of the piece.

Plenty of clubs will argue that they have been the most put-upon and stressed in the country when it comes to their ownership and general fears over their existence, but at the very least you have to listen to County's case.

The world's oldest professional football club, established in 1862, and the team whose black and white stripes inspired Juventus's colours, almost went out of existence a couple of times in the first decade of the 21st century. In 2003 the Football League had threatened to expel them entirely had they not got their financial house in order pretty sharply, having been in administration for an extraordinary 18 months. One of the reasons for such a lengthy spell in financial limbo was that the former long-term chairman, Derek Pavis, didn't own their entire Meadow Lane ground outright, but oddly he did hold the long-term lease to just the West Stand. Untangling that legal ball of twine took a while.

In the end it took an extraordinary effort on the part of some fans, including staging a collection in which a bucket was literally passed around supporters of County and neighbours Nottingham Forest, plus receiving contributions from a small group of generous benefactors. The club were saved, but three years later would be in trouble again, at which point the supporters' trust stepped in and took control.

With this in mind it was perhaps hardly a surprise that in 2009 news of a takeover by a group called Munto Finance was greeted with joy and, in some cases, disbelief by the fans. This group claimed to be backed by the Bahraini royal family and, as this came a year after Sheikh Mansour had purchased Manchester City and lavished millions on the squad, even the faintest whiff of something similar was enough to convince many. 'Whatever happens it can't be much worse than what is happening at the moment,' one County fan, Don, told the BBC at the time. If it was a sitcom, the person he said that to would have looked straight down the barrel of the camera and raised an eyebrow. Because it would turn out to be much worse.

Still, they weren't to know that at the time: as far as they were concerned, not only was the club saved but they were rich. The chairman at the time, John Armstrong-Holmes, travelled to Bahrain with a representative of Munto, Nathan Willett, as well as a man who used a gold-topped cane, Russell King. King was never officially involved, because King was never officially involved in any of his 'ventures' down the years, but he was the man pulling the strings, and the man issuing all the reassurances that things were exactly as they seemed. When Armstrong-Holmes requested some sort of proof that these people did actually have the cash required, a bank guarantee was produced for £5 million from First London bank. All seemed kosher.

Once in charge, Munto started to spend that money and with some gusto. Or at least, they spent the promise of that money. They recruited Sven-Göran Eriksson, former England manager who only a couple of years earlier had been in charge of Manchester City, to be their director of football: he was given a five-year contract worth around £10 million (although much of that was in shares of a company called Swiss Commodity Holdings, owned by King, which will become important later) and tasked with taking them to the Premier League in that time.

He began by signing Kasper Schmeichel, at the time one of the more promising goalkeepers in the top flight at Manchester City, for £1.4 million. More modest signings – but still ambitious for that level – included the forwards Lee Hughes and Luke Rodgers, and midfielder Johnnie Jackson, all of whom dropped down a division. But they were all appetisers until Sven served up the main course.

In August, a few days before the end of the transfer window, County signed Sol Campbell on a five-year contract worth a reported £40,000-a-week. Campbell joined on a free transfer having played for Portsmouth in the Premier League in the previous season, and had played for England only 18 months earlier. 'Career-wise this sits perfectly for where I am at the moment in my life,' he said at the time. 'I didn't really have to think too much about it.'

Things started off brilliantly. They won their first two league games, against Bradford City and Macclesfield Town, 5–0 and 4–0 respectively. The fans were giddy. Eriksson had thrown himself into the job with enthusiasm. Campbell, after shaking off an injury, made his debut in September, away to Morecambe.

However, that's when things started to look slightly squiffy. Shortly afterwards Campbell walked out of the club and his contract was cancelled by mutual consent. At the time it wasn't really clear why, but the assumption was that he just changed his mind about playing in the fourth tier of English football. As it turned out, he had caught a whiff that things were not all well and in fact warned some of the other players that the promised money might not have been there. His single game cost Notts County a theoretical £250,000.

The penny was dropping elsewhere too. 'It is hard to pinpoint exactly when things started not to add up at Notts County,' wrote Eriksson in his autobiography. 'Maybe it was the day I heard we had not paid the milk bill.' Initially, the large number of unpaid bills piling up at the club were written off as 'cashflow' issues. But soon people started to ask questions.

And those questions almost always seemed to land back at King's past. It emerged that King was a serial and convicted fraudster: in fact, he had spent time in prison, sent down in 1991 for insurance fraud when he tried to claim £600,000 for an Aston Martin car that he said had been stolen, when it was actually in a garage he had rented. He was also behind the collapse of a group of children's toy shops called Zodiac, which went out of business in 1990 despite King and the directors of its parent company, Celebrity Group Holdings, dramatically expanding their number of stores in the preceding couple of years.

But perhaps his most notorious act of fraud came a few years before he arrived in Nottingham: he became partners in a Jersey-based company called Belgravia Financial Services with a local businessman called Duncan Hickman. King essentially executed a Ponzi scheme, taking money from investors but simply using some of it to pay other investors, the rest to fund his own luxury lifestyle.

When Hickman suddenly died from an aneurysm in 2008, the scheme was at risk of being exposed, so King attempted to blame it all on his deceased partner. Hickman's wife Gill was forced to sell their house and a number of their possessions in order to pay back the money that King said Hickman had stolen. King, meanwhile, had £671,213 transferred to his private bank account and absconded to Bahrain with his wife.

As it turned out, he spent his time there cooking up his next job and that job was Notts County. Once his feet were under the table, things took a turn for the implausible: Willett and King asked Eriksson to visit North Korea with them, telling him that Swiss Commodity Holdings, the company in which most of Eriksson's wages were tied up in shares, was attempting to close a deal to mine huge amounts of minerals in the country. They insisted that Eriksson's name would impress those they were negotiating with; furthermore, while they were there, the North Korean FA apparently needed some advice.

Against his better judgement Eriksson went, but things didn't go to plan. First, the 'advice' the FA wanted was for Eriksson to help fix the draw for the upcoming World Cup, for which North Korea had qualified. 'What did you say?' was Eriksson's understandable response. 'I thought they wanted balls or shoes,' he later told the BBC podcast *Sport's Strangest Crimes*. 'The amazing thing is that they didn't think I couldn't do it – they just thought I didn't want to do it.'

Then things started getting nasty: apparently King and Willett had promised the North Koreans a large amount of oil, as a way of – if you'll excuse the pun – greasing the wheels of the mineral mining deal. The oil did not materialise, so the North Koreans decided that this lot were not to be trusted. For a while it was touch and go whether they would even be let out of the country. In the end they were: King, a man of significant proportions, apparently ran off the plane when they eventually landed in China.

Things weren't going well back in Nottingham either. In fact, the whole thing was collapsing around their ears. Bills were still not being paid, everything from the aforementioned milkman to Eriksson's chauffeur. It turned out that the whole takeover had essentially been a bizarre and elaborate method of trying to obtain that North Korean mining contract, the idea being that owning the oldest football club in the world would give them an element of credibility and star power.

You wonder how they ever thought it was going to work. Even if they had closed the deal, and even if they had managed to actually mine those minerals when they were very much not a mining company, they wouldn't have been able to take them out of North Korea thanks to international sanctions. And even ignoring all of that: who tries to pull off a gigantic mineral mining heist by calling Sven-Göran Eriksson?

Probably the short answer is that they never really intended to do any of that: even before the trip to Pyongyang, they attempted to value Swiss Commodity Holdings at $1.9 trillion – that's *trillion* – on the basis that all those reserves of minerals were now just a few JCB diggers away from being theirs. The plan was to take any money raised when they floated the company on the stock market and run.

They did part of that: King fled, once again, to Bahrain, leaving County in the soup. The club was put up for sale, but as the extent of the debts run up by King and Munto Finance became clearer, finding a buyer was proving tricky. In the end, local businessman Ray Trew agreed to take the club for the nominal fee of £1, while assuming all their debts, which amounted to around £7.3 million.

Weirdly, the tale did have a (sort of) happy ending. County went on an incredible unbeaten run and won promotion as champions from League Two. And, eventually, King got his comeuppance: after almost a decade in Bahrain he was extradited to Jersey in 2018 to face trial over the Belgravia scandal and the following year was convicted of stealing that £671,213. He was sentenced to six years in jail, of which he served two.

Eriksson, bless him, summed up the whole thing in a cartoonishly 'Sven' fashion. He told the BBC: 'We started very good and we ended very bad.'

10

THE REAL-LIFE CONSEQUENCES OF A BAD OWNER

'The love of football has been kicked out of me.
I don't watch football, I don't look out for results,
or anything. I have no involvement in football
whatsoever. Steve Dale did that to me.'
GORDON SORFLEET,
FORMER BURY EMPLOYEE

Sometimes football is cut off from the real world. It's entirely possible to lose perspective completely and think anything that happens in this isolated little island matters above all else. Hopefully, most of us can sense that coming: we can feel that little tingle at the back of our brains and we know when to snap out of it.

Most of the time this manifests itself in our reaction to a bad result. A day, maybe even a weekend, can be ruined as we sulk at yet more dreadful defending from a corner, or fume at a terrible refereeing decision, as all the while our loved ones roll their eyes. Hopefully, we eventually realise what is important and wise up.

Where it becomes slightly more difficult is when this parallel universe starts to have a more tangible impact. It's easy enough to think about most of the stories in this book as only having a material impact on football: a points deduction here, a relegation which makes some fans sad there. Maybe a rich owner's plans don't quite come off and they lose a bit of money, but they shrug and write it off as a bad job, taking comfort in the rest of their cash.

But when things go bad at a football club, when the effects of a bad owner really start to bite, people suffer. Actual, real people. These are the stories of a few of them.

———

The dividing line between football and the rest of life isn't an imaginary one, in England at least. It is quite literally the law, legislated by the football creditors rule. This is a provision rooted in the 2002 Enterprise Act, which included an adjustment to company administration procedures, which meant HM Revenue and Customs could no longer claim preferential treatment when it came to recovering funds from a distressed company.

Using this, the football authorities implemented a rule for when clubs go into administration, which said that 'football creditors' have to be paid first when debts are being settled if the club wants to retain its membership of either the EFL or the Premier League.

In practice, this essentially means that players are first in line for their money, followed by other club employees, including management, then other clubs and whichever league the club is part of, if debts are owed. This means that the tax man has to wait in line, cupped hands outstretched like a Victorian urchin, to try to recover whatever money it can. HMRC has attempted a number of times to challenge this, but has been unsuccessful.

Clubs getting out of paying tax is irritating to the general public, to say the least. But the rule also pushes well down the list anyone else a football club owes money to. And in reality, they're so far down it that they're unlikely to ever get anything more than pennies on the pound.

Take Portsmouth. The various forms of chaos that Pompey have found themselves in over the years will inevitably have left some destruction in its wake. Between Milan Mandarić relinquishing sole control of the club in 2006 and the supporters' trust taking over in 2013, the club were seemingly in permanent financial crisis and went into administration twice.

Not great for the club, given that they incurred points deductions for both of those periods, plus another for further financial issues in December 2012, losing a total of 29 points in three different seasons. That resulted in their relegation from the Premier League to League Two, which obviously is far from ideal from a football point of view, but the consequences of their money problems go far beyond that.

In 2010, just after they had been put into administration for the first time, a list of the people they owed money to emerged. It included agents, to whom nearly £10 million was owed, as well as the players, former owners and of course HMRC. But it also contained a long list of other businesses.

Canterbury, their former kit suppliers, were due a whopping £1.4 million. Portsmouth City Council were owed £28,690.70. The club's own supporters' group were due £300. Some £2,701.91 was owed to St John Ambulance. The Scout Association were expecting £697. A pretty heathy phone bill of £5,748.40 was owed to Vodafone. A youth football club called Highbury Hawks were owed £912. Dairy Crest were owed £313.31: given that Notts County had a similar problem during the Munto Finance debacle, perhaps it's a sure sign of things going really wrong when you can't pay the milkman.

And then there were a series of smaller local businesses. A carpet cleaning company was owed £792.66. A florist, £995. But the one that stood out on the list was a firm called TWC Joinery and Shopfitting, who seemed to be owed £54,777.93.

This was a local company run by a man named Terry Clark, who was not only a Portsmouth fan but one who had been vice-president of the supporters' club a few years earlier. Thus, it meant a little bit more when he was asked to do some work for them.

He was employed by the club to fix various aspects of Fratton Park – a charming old ground, but one that even its most strident defenders would probably call 'ramshackle' even now, never mind when all of this was happening. Before the start of the 2009/10 season the Premier League decreed that the dressing rooms had to be expanded, so the club called Clark. They wanted a new toilet block to be built for one of the hospitality lounges, so the club called Clark. They needed a new staircase for the fire escape, so the club called Clark.

But the invoices started to stack up and Clark's gradually got shuffled further and further down the list of priorities as the financial situation worsened. When the club eventually went into administration for the first time, in February 2010, Clark was still trying to get his money.

He told *The Times*: 'I was promised by Daniel Azougy [the club's former finance consultant] in November that I would be paid in instalments over the next few months. They made one payment of £8,000 and I haven't been able to get hold of anyone since.

'Yesterday I was lucky enough to get through and I was told "You're a small fish. There are lots of other people ahead of you." I've done so much for the club over the years and this is the thanks I get.'

Clark also spoke to *The Observer* around this time: 'They've taken advantage of me because I love Portsmouth. I've followed the club for 50 years – my dad took me when I was four years old. I've done my bit for the club over the years, sponsoring its youth development programme, introducing new clients to them, because I only want the best for Portsmouth. They played on my loyalties because I would never put any pressure on.'

Maybe you could argue that this wasn't an example of the callous treatment of a loyal fan. Maybe it's unrealistic to expect sentiment to be taken into account in situations like this. Maybe this was just how things worked, that administrators are employed to save, as best they can, a business that in this case was a football club, and thus the jobs of many other people. Maybe people like Clark are merely collateral damage in a broader, incredibly unfortunate situation.

But 'collateral damage' is just a polite way of saying, in this situation at least, that someone has been betrayed by one of the few institutions they have any sort of emotional connection to. And for what? Basically because a collection of speculators and chancers tried to make money from a football club, failed, and then walked away when it all went south.

Clark never got the rest of his money. TWC Joinery and Shopfitting went into administration itself in January 2011, just under a year after Portsmouth did. From reading TWC's administrators' report, it's clear that the money owed by the football club wasn't the sole, or perhaps even the main, reason that the company was in trouble, but what small business could easily cope with not being paid nearly £50,000? The company was liquidated in December 2011.

Once upon a time there was a person like Gordon Sorfleet at every lower-league club in England.

His official job title was press officer at Bury, but in reality he was the guy who just did whatever needed doing. He managed the ticket office. He dealt with the catering sometimes. He sorted out the matchday programmes. At that level of the pyramid, there isn't such a thing as 'not in my job description'.

Sorfleet was a lifelong Bury fan who started working at the club in 1999. In 2002, Bury almost went to the wall: the ripples of the ITV Digital collapse, which knocked so many clubs off course, sent them into administration. But along with some other Bury staff members and the supporters' trust, they managed to raise enough money to keep the club afloat, and then some.

So successful was the fundraising drive that Sorfleet was selected by UEFA to win their supporter of the year award, presented at their annual gala dinner in Monte Carlo. 'Me and the wife went,' he says now. 'I got the award and the next thing I remember was Zinedine Zidane clapping me on the shoulder and saying "Well done mon ami".' Sorfleet's wife Christine nearly derailed Roma's season by accidentally stepping on Francesco Totti's toes.

Sorfleet's name was inscribed on the award, but the next day he went to UEFA and requested that it be redone to reflect the fans' contribution. It's trite to say it, but people like Sorfleet are the very best of England's smaller football clubs: without them, football at that level would not survive.

Sorfleet was just entering his third decade at Bury when Steve Dale bought the club in December 2018 for a symbolic £1. Bury had significant debts, but Dale didn't realise the extent of them and within a couple of months it became clear that the financial situation was so dire as to threaten the future of the club.

'He got lucky the first month he was there because the TV money came in and a transfer sell-on clause came through,' says Sorfleet. 'Once that dried up, he realised he had a problem because he couldn't fund the club. He couldn't even fund his car: he turned up in a fancy Rolls Royce and it wasn't taxed.'

Those funds helped them pay a tax bill in February and narrowly avoid a winding-up order by HM Revenue and Customs, but as it turns out that was simply delaying the catastrophe that everyone could see coming. Around a dozen people were made redundant, leaving only six permanent members of non-playing staff, including Sorfleet, to somehow try to keep things ticking over.

Dale started making odd decisions, like buying a massive screen to put in the corner of Bury's Gigg Lane ground, on the basis that he could bring revenue in by selling adverts on it. But the fact that he nearly doubled the advertising rates meant that most of the people who would want to buy space could no longer afford it.

Wages were not being paid on time, if at all. The entire March payroll wasn't paid, which led the EFL to express their 'extreme concern' about the situation. If the league was worried, imagine how the regular employees felt.

'Stress levels were through the roof,' Sorfleet says. 'I didn't see a penny for six months. It had serious consequences. I got to one point where I was about £8,000 in debt. I was borrowing money left, right and centre. My son bailed me out a lot because he would just hand over his wage to keep the house going and keep the family going. Bills still have to be paid: I still have to pay the rent and the council tax.'

Was there any sense that Dale knew about this and, more pertinently, did he care? 'None whatsoever. To him it was just an asset that needed closing down quickly.'

The parlous financial state of things led to the sort of farcical situations that carry with them a grim sort of comedy, which of course are not funny at all. In what has emerged as a theme for distressed clubs, Bury couldn't afford to pay the milkman. Sorfleet had to scrape together some money from the petty cash for the company that provided the matchday programmes, who refused to print them unless they were paid.

Dale became less and less of a presence at Gigg Lane, and more of one in the national media, giving interviews in which he pleaded ignorance about the state of the club when he bought it. 'To be fair to him it wasn't all his fault,' says Sorfleet. 'He just didn't have the resources to get it out of the mess it was in. That was plainly obvious from day one. He was in over his head.'

At one point a couple of investigators from HMRC turned up to interview Dale about an unpaid tax bill. The appointed hour came and went, so Sorfleet called Dale to see where he was. He instructed Sorfleet to tell the investigators that his dog had died and he was too upset to come in. This was the third time he had used that excuse, so either he had a very unlucky pack of dogs, or he wasn't entirely shooting straight dice.

The club technically limped on until August 2019, when they became the first club since Maidstone United in 1992 to exit the league for non-sporting reasons. But for Sorfleet, the end was much sooner than that. He was made redundant on 30 March, informed via a letter that his 20-year association with the club he had supported all his life was over. After Sorfleet left, the only person still regularly doing any work at the club was the groundsman, who kept showing up to make sure the pitch stayed in reasonable order.

'I'm still bitter about it,' says Sorfleet. 'Very bitter. I'm still owed £11,000.'

These days Sorfleet is a delivery driver who sounds much happier with his lot than when he had to deal with Steve Dale on a regular basis. Bury regenerated, a 'phoenix' club formed by fans eventually joining forces with what remained of the original Bury, who now play their games at Gigg Lane. Sorfleet offered to help out, but he was ignored. He went to a couple of games, but it wasn't the same. He hasn't been back since.

'The love of football has been kicked out of me. I don't watch football, I don't look out for results, or anything. I have no involvement in football whatsoever. Steve Dale did that to me.'

In 2010, the Pakistan cricket team played a Test series against England. One of the most exciting elements of those matches was the emergence of a young fast bowler called Mohammad Amir. Tall and thin but powerful, and with a beautifully natural action, Amir was only 18 but looked like he had been doing this for decades. He had the skill and sporting brain of a seasoned veteran, handily packed into the body of a magnificent young athlete. Anyone who saw him that summer will tell you he was a force of nature. It was impossible not to get excited about his future.

Then one Sunday morning, in the middle of the Lord's Test match, a story emerged in the now defunct *News of the World* newspaper, reported by the infamous investigative journalist Mazher Mahmood, that said Amir was one of three Pakistan players who had been involved in spot-fixing to benefit supposed betting syndicates in far-flung places. The players were not fixing the result of the game, but small events within the match: Amir would bowl a no-ball at a certain point, which would have been gambled upon.

The bribes were handed out by a man called Mazhar Majeed, who represented the three players – Amir, Mohammad Asif and then Pakistan captain Salman Butt – who were involved in the corruption. The following year Majeed was sentenced to 32 months in jail for conspiracy to allow others to cheat at gambling and conspiracy to accept corrupt payments.

That was the headline part of the *News of the World* story, but Majeed was also recorded as saying he had bought a football club – Croydon Athletic, who played in the Ryman League (the division below the National League South) at the time – for the sole purpose of laundering money.

Majeed had taken over the club in 2008, when they were struggling in the Ryman League Division One South, and thanks to the money that he put into the club they became one of the wealthiest teams in their league and started climbing the divisions, with the help of players like former Ipswich Town and Southampton midfielder Jermaine Wright. In 2010 they won promotion to the Ryman Premier League for the first time in their history and were unbeaten at the start of the following season, before the revelations about Majeed brought everything crashing down.

'He said that if we got promoted again, he had a plot of land where he could build a 20,000-seater stadium,' Neil Smith, who was Croydon assistant manager at the time, told Kent Online in a 2019 interview.

Majeed had also brought in the club's chairman, David Le Cluse, who started attending games after his pest-control company had solved an issue at Majeed's house. Le Cluse took his role in November 2009, replacing former chairman David Fisher, who himself had been arrested in an unrelated fraud case. The following summer Fisher was found guilty of stealing around £500,000 from his employers.

While the rest of the sporting world was scandalised by the cricket-fixing, a corner of south London was horrified that their club had been used by Majeed. He was arrested the day after the *News of the World* story was published, but because he had essentially financed the club and after his arrest his assets had been frozen, nobody knew what would happen next.

'My whole world just dropped,' said Smith. 'I was just like: "What happens now?" All of a sudden there's no money. Everything stopped – no money could go out or in, nobody was getting paid. What do you do? The players have got families. We had a game against Concord Rangers and the boys were just sat in the dressing room crying, because the club was over in our eyes.'

'I just don't know,' said Le Cluse at the time, when asked whether the club could survive. 'The situation is constantly changing and we're just taking one day at a time at the moment. We're in a crisis but we're doing our utmost to save the club.'

With the uncertainty around the club's future and where the money to keep it running was going to come from, players began to leave. The managerial team too. 'We were trying to find a new buyer and it was utter chaos for the next two weeks,' said Smith. 'We had the FA phoning up and I just had to distance myself from it. Innocent or not, I can't be a part of that. That's why we took a step away.'

Le Cluse in particular was working frantically to keep Croydon in existence. He had not even been in his job for a year, but he had become a passionate supporter as well as the club's chairman. Le Cluse didn't have any money in the club personally, but it was thought that the affair had personally cost him as much as £50,000 through business deals that had collapsed because of the adverse publicity.

Investigators from HMRC visited the club to check whether the money-laundering was confined to Majeed personally or whether Croydon had a case to answer too. The control of the club eventually passed to Majeed's sister-in-law, but by that point the fate of the football club had been put firmly into perspective.

On 2 October, Le Cluse was found dead in his garage, having taken his own life. He was 44.

'He was very upset at the allegations and the club getting involved,' Tim O'Shea, the Croydon manager at the time, told *The Times*. 'It probably hit him harder than most because of his personal friendship with Majeed. He wanted nothing more than for the club to succeed and he was probably upset and affected by it more than anybody else.'

Majeed was sentenced to two years and eight months in jail in November 2011. He later pleaded guilty to charges of tax fraud relating to his property company and was given a further two years in jail in 2015. After his release, he reinvented himself as a boxing promoter, and was involved in fights that featured Amir Khan, Kell Brook and Chris Eubank Jnr.

Croydon Athletic were given a ten-point deduction after a series of financial irregularities related to the scandal were discovered in 2011. Most of the players and management staff had by this point left, and the club was unable to fulfil a series of fixtures. The club was dissolved in December 2011. A new club, AFC Croydon Athletic, was formed by fans and entered the Combined Counties Football League in 2012.

11

WHY DO PEOPLE OWN FOOTBALL CLUBS?

'Ego is the only reason [people buy football clubs] ....
The belief that they can do it better than it's been
done for the last 50 years.'
DAMIAN IRVINE,
CEO OF EBBSFLEET UNITED

It was all change at FC Twente in 2023. General manager Paul van der Kraan had announced he was leaving, as had technical director Jan Streuer and head coach Ron Jans. There was a leadership vacuum and someone was needed to steer the ship.

It so happened that Joop Munsterman, the former owner of the club, was a guest on a local radio station shortly after the departures had been announced. The presenter asked if Munsterman would be interested in returning to Twente.

'No, of course not,' replied Munsterman. 'I'll never be involved in football again. I've closed off that world.'

And you can't really blame him. Munsterman had worked his way up the ranks at Wegener, a Dutch media group, after starting as a cleaner when he was 16 years old, eventually becoming CEO of the company and making millions.

He was from Enschede, a small and relatively sleepy city in the east of the Netherlands where it's easy to become pretty well known if you have made something of yourself, and had supported Twente since he was a boy. He became chairman of the club in 2004, bankrolling the greatest era in their history. Under Steve McClaren Twente won their first and to date only Eredivisie title in 2010, also enjoying four straight seasons in the Champions League.

Like Leeds United in the late 1990s and early 2000s, they lived the dream. Alas, the comparisons to Leeds didn't end there: they had also overstretched themselves financially and, following their failure to qualify for the Champions League in 2012, Munsterman and fellow director Aldo van der Laan entered into a number of ill-advised deals, including a series of third-party ownership (TPO) arrangements with sports investment groups Doyen Sports and Vijai.

This amounted to the companies lending Twente the money to buy players in exchange for a 'stake' in the player's transfer rights. This sort of thing used to happen quite frequently and, assuming the player did well/appreciated in value, could be both extremely useful for the club and lucrative for the investment groups.

However, it didn't quite go to plan. James Montague, in his book *The Billionaires Club*, wrote that 'when the Wikileaks-style website focused on football finance, Football Leaks, released copies of Twente's TPO agreement, it was clear that a desperate Munsterman had ceded too much control to Doyen, giving them an automatic say on some transfers if an offer was made at the right price.'

UEFA were not impressed and banned Twente from European competition. By 2015 the club were in serious financial trouble, almost going bankrupt, and the Dutch FA docked them a total of nine points over two seasons after not meeting a series of financial targets. They were relegated from the Eredivisie in 2018.

By that point Munsterman had resigned, his name mud, only a few years after taking Twente to their most glorious point. The consensus seems to be, from people who know him, that Munsterman is not a bad guy, just someone who made a few ill-advised decisions, then made a few more ill-advised decisions to extricate them from the problems caused by the first set of ill-advised decisions. Now though, he's a pariah.

———————

It's cases like Munsterman's that lead you to pose the question: why would anyone want to own a football club? Is it really worth the bother, the stress, the potential damage to your reputation?

If money is your goal, there are many easier ways to make your fortune. The old line that the best way to become a millionaire through owning a football club is to start off as a billionaire has plenty of truth to it.

But one thing the world is not short of is people queuing up to either buy, or invest in, football clubs. So why do they do it?

The first answer is that, despite the trail of bedraggled former owners left contemplating what to do with all that extra room in their wallets, it is possible to make money in football, if you're smart and lucky. Which is how you make money in any other walk of life, really.

The most obvious way is to buy a club for one price and then sell it later for many multiples of that price, relying on the value of football clubs to increase as they steadily have been doing for the last few decades. Take Liverpool: John Henry and what is now called Fenway Sports Group (FSG) paid £300 million for the club in 2010, when it was at a low point and the previous owners desperately had to sell. In 2023 Forbes valued the club at £4.3 billion. The world of football finance is very complicated and there are lots of impenetrable numbers and statistics floating around, so let's cut through the jargon and interpret those figures to assess Liverpool's value 13 years after FSG bought it: it's worth loads more.

FSG sold a minority stake in the club in September 2023 and, although that was used to pay down bank debt incurred during the Covid-19 lockdowns and for various other reasons, they still controlled the club. There have been background rumblings about Liverpool being for sale for years, without anything ever coming to fruition, but although Henry told the *Financial Times* in June 2024 that FSG 'generally do not sell assets', we can assume they will cash out at some point. And when they do, even taking into account the money they may have invested themselves, they will walk away with billions.

There's Chelsea too. Roman Abramovich paid £140 million for the club in 2003, then 19 years later the consortium led by Todd Boehly paid £2.5 billion for it. Of course, Abramovich spent millions on transfer fees, infrastructure and paying managers off in his time at Stamford Bridge, but had he been able to profit from the sale of the club rather than being forced to sell because of his links to Vladimir Putin, he would have made a very nice profit indeed.

'The idea that these clubs are going to be yielding assets, as in paying a dividend every year, is not the way they work,' Deloitte's Dan Jones told *The Wall Street Journal*. 'But from a capital growth point of view [owning a club] can make sense. To an extent, they are a rare asset, just like a fine art painting, classic car or a collection of fine wines.'

These are two of the more high-end examples, and buying a Premier League club is now out of reach for all but the wealthiest, but there is potential for profit lower down the ladder, as can be seen by the increasing number of Americans either buying or investing in English Football League clubs.

November 2023 saw Castle Sports Group, the investment vehicle of Floria-based businessman Tom Piatak, buy League One club Carlisle United. A year earlier Brad Galinson, a property developer also from Florida, took over League Two Gillingham. A couple of years before that, Rob Couhig bought a 75 per cent stake in Wycombe Wanderers. There are now so many Americans who either own or have significantly invested in EFL clubs that there's a WhatsApp group for them all.

There are plenty of reasons that an English football team is so attractive to an American investor, from the global popularity of the sport to the vast amounts earned through broadcast rights deals, but another is the structure of the league pyramid. In the major US sports, there is no movement between divisions, meaning that unless you have enough money to buy a team already in the NFL or NBA or MLS, there is no immediate way of progressing a team into the top level. The only way of getting in is to wait for expansion and even those costs are huge. The owners of the new MLS team in San Diego paid $500 million for their franchise when it was announced in May 2023, while the fees for new NWSL teams are growing exponentially.

Thus, the idea of paying a relatively low amount for a small club that has the theoretical potential to rise through the levels of a sport is extremely appealing.

Also, remarkable as it might seem to the average English fan settling down to watch a game between teams that have sleeve sponsors, training kit sponsors, main shirt sponsors and official partners for everything from cryptocurrency to instant noodles, there is still a perception among some American investors that football – even in the Premier League – is under-commercialised.

'The US is a lot more commercially savvy,' says Christina Philippou, lecturer in accounting, economics and finance at the University of Portsmouth. 'If you go to NFL games, they sponsor everything you could possibly even imagine. Everything is "sell, sell, sell, sell." European markets aren't like that, football isn't like that.

'There are really, really strong revenues, particularly in the Premier League, but then the profits aren't particularly good. There's a lot of losses, even in the promised land of the Premier League. I think that's quite attractive to a lot of Americans who go "Hang on a minute, they're really underselling this stuff."

'There is so much more potential on the commercial side, there's potential to make more money, but also there's potential to manage cost better and therefore kind of increase the profit margin even if you keep revenues where they are.'

Omar Chaudhuri, chief intelligence officer at Twenty First Group, who among other things use data and analytical models to advise people or groups who are looking to buy football clubs, adds: 'They see inefficiencies in the way that clubs are operated, particularly compared to what they see in the US around the revolution you've seen in baseball, around "Moneyball"-style analysis.

'Their view is that European football is under professionalised and that there are opportunities to get a competitive edge through just being smarter.'

This is also partly the explanation for the number of slightly incongruous American sportspeople who have invested money in English football teams. As discussed earlier, Tom Brady is a minority partner in the group that took over Birmingham City in 2023 and his fellow former NFL star JJ Watt, along with his wife and former USA international Kealia, bought a stake in Burnley the same year.

The idea here is to capitalise on the broader concept of the Premier League and English football as a 'brand', but help to direct some of those with a non-specific interest into becoming long-distance Burnley fans.

Watt told ESPN: 'America is craving football content. There's a large group of people that still don't have a great knowledge base, so they're still trying to find their squad. They're still trying to find who they're supposed to support. I think it helps us a lot that more eyeballs come over. We just direct those eyeballs up to Burnley.'

Beyond American attitudes to maximising the commercial potential of the game, there are other ways of making money through owning a football club. But it's tough and you have to be smart.

'Typically people don't make money from professional football clubs, largely because costs have escalated at a quicker rate than revenue growth,' says Rob Wilson, football finance expert and head of the finance, accounting and business systems department at Sheffield Hallam University.

'The only real way you can make money is by being resolute in your objectives and very, very hard-nosed when it comes to negotiation on player transfers. The industry is perpetuated by this kind of thirst for playing talent, who actually aren't always that talented. So you would typically have three or four clubs perhaps going after the same player and that then just increases transfer fees.'

Wilson argues that those teams who are disciplined in how much they will pay for talent are the ones more likely to be able to sell that player on later for a profit. All of which features a colossal number of variables, most completely out of the control of an owner. So it becomes a risky game.

Another reason for buying a club is to use the reflected glory of the spotlight football provides to promote your other businesses. Venky's, the group of Indian chicken producers that bought Blackburn Rovers (with calamitous results) in 2009, partly did so to promote their poultry business – albeit slightly haphazardly. They told the journalist Nick Harris that they wanted to capitalise on the publicity brought by their entry into the Premier League by opening a chicken takeaway shop in London, and when he asked where they might want to do this they somewhat ambitiously said: 'Oxford Street'. At the time of writing, the Oxford Street branch of Venky's chicken is yet to open.

Rather more successful was Vichai Srivaddhanaprabha's purchase of Leicester City in 2010 for around £39 million, which increased the international profile of his airport duty free business King Power. Indeed, King Power's revenue increased yearly until the Covid-19 pandemic essentially shut down international air travel and thus their business, and while the efforts of Jamie Vardy can't account for all of that growth, it undoubtedly helped. His son, Aiyawatt Srivaddhanaprabha, took over as both CEO of King Power and chairman of Leicester after Vichai's tragic death in a helicopter crash in 2018.

Josh Wander, CEO of the multi-club ownership group 777, sees their ownership of football clubs as, in part at least, a way of gaining a series of new captive audiences. He told the *Financial Times* in 2023 that fans 'want to be monetised' and that: 'The vision for this football group is that one day we're not selling hot dogs and beers to our customers; [it's] that we're selling insurance or financial services or whatever.'

———

There are of course other, less tangible, reasons to own a football club, all based around the idea of prestige or influence.

The more innocent end of that scale is the owner who simply purchases a club because they can, the classic rich man's plaything, because it confers a kind of status: look at me, I own a football club, and I am bathing in the reflected glow of its glory and the plentiful thanks of a local community.

But more often these are people who are trying to gain something other than money by owning a club. That could be publicity and popularity to influence a political career, perhaps, like Silvio Berlusconi: the late former Italian prime minister undoubtedly loved football, and in fact was a revolutionary thinker in his own way with some of the methods he introduced, but his stewardship of AC Milan afforded him a profile that few other politicians could match.

In fact he didn't get into politics until 1994, eight years after he took over Milan. Would he have remained a relevant figure in Italian public life for the next two decades-plus without the involvement of football? It's doubtful.

Then there's Roman Abramovich. For a while, the assumption about this low-key Russian billionaire that nobody had previously heard of was simply that he had so much money that he didn't know what to do with it. The story that he fell in love with football after watching the Brazilian Ronaldo tear Manchester United apart in the 2003 Champions League was broadly believed.

Later, of course, it would emerge that Abramovich's ties to Vladimir Putin were a little closer than most realised, and that his purchase of Chelsea had as much to do with soft power and the idea of public protection as it was him having an extremely expensive plaything.

And then we come to the nation states. We've discussed sportswashing and the reason that the governments of Qatar and Saudi Arabia and Abu Dhabi have purchased football clubs elsewhere in this book, but it's worth considering them again.

These states becoming so intimately involved with the world's most popular sport is partly to do with the diversification of their economy, the idea that the fossil fuels that have left them with more money than God will one day run out, so they had better think of some alternative ways of making a profit.

But more than that, it's so that the world thinks of something other than the unpleasant parts of what those countries do. Saudi Arabia's move into sport, most notably golf, F1 and latterly football, is to recruit people to their cause, to ensure that their image is improved, to distract the world from the human rights abuses that they have and are perpetuating.

This is the power of football harnessed for purposes that it was never meant to be for. People have been using the game to further despicable ideologies for decades, going right back to Mussolini and the World Cup in Italy and beyond. But rarely has it been so naked, and so prominent, as it is today.

It must also be said, dear, pure, innocent reader, that some of the people who own football clubs, or might want to own football clubs, don't always do it for causes as noble as geopolitics.

Another potential reason for someone to buy a club – which, we have to stress, is very much not typical – is money-laundering. So much so that in January 2024, the European Union specifically included provisions related to football in some new money-laundering laws, which among other things would give journalists and anti-corruption groups access to a list of anyone who owned 25 per cent or more of a club.

And not without reason. A report, published in 2016 by the pressure group Transparency International, outlined the theoretical ways that someone might wish to use a club to wash money gained through illegitimate means.

'It is achieved through a variety of means,' said the report, 'notably manipulating club accounts by inflating income from ticket sales, buying empty spectator seats, inventing a fake revenue stream and engaging in the developing of property near stadiums. The international market for transferring players can also be a vehicle for money-laundering, as the overvaluation of a player is similar to the money-laundering protocol of inflating invoices for goods and services. Another vehicle for money-laundering is the use of tax havens and the ability to use front companies and shadow directors as football club owners.'

And it's not just in theory, either: it does actually happen.

A documentary by Al Jazeera in 2021 exposed a series of middle men attempting to help investigators, posing as Chinese investors, buy Derby County for the explicitly expressed purpose of laundering some supposedly ill-gotten funds.

The UK's then security minister Ben Wallace told a panel of MPs in a 2023 Treasury Select Committee meeting that at least one English football club was under investigation for money-laundering. 'The sports industry is as susceptible as anything else to dirty money being invested or their organisations being used as a way to launder money,' Wallace said.

In Belgium, a police investigation called Operation Zero led to clubs bringing in new safeguards to prevent money-laundering through the country's clubs. Some 57 people were charged in 2022, at least in part thanks to the evidence provided by former agent Dejan Veljković. 'This is not a surprise, but our hearts as soccer fans bleed,' said the CEO of the Belgian Football Association, Peter Bossaert.

A UEFA-commissioned report, compiled by the Centre For Sports Studies in 2018, warned that a handful of nefarious agents were using the transfer market to channel funds. 'There is a dirty mentality in football with a lot of people trying to find ways of enriching themselves and taking advantage of all of this money that's circulating – especially through the transfers,' the report's author, Raffaele Poli, told *The Guardian*.

Now that we've got that unpleasantness out of the way, it is worth mentioning that not all football club owners are doing it for nefarious or financially-driven reasons.

Take Steve Gibson, who was head of the consortium that saved Middlesbrough from oblivion in 1986 and has been the club's chairman and owner since 1994. Gibson made his fortune in the haulage business and became the club's youngest ever director when he joined the Middlesbrough board aged 26 in 1984.

He frankly doesn't need the hassle of running a football club, he doesn't rely on it financially and he has had a variety of approaches to buy Boro over the years, most of which have received relatively short shrift. So while he equally isn't doing it out of the goodness of his heart, you can be pretty sure that if it was a club other than the one he has always supported, he probably wouldn't still be there.

A similar, if perhaps less celebrated, figure is Peter Coates, who along with his son John owns Stoke City. Coates and his family own and run Bet365, one of the biggest gambling firms in the UK, who recorded revenues of £3.39 billion in 2023. Coates has bought Stoke twice: once in 1986 and then again in 2006, when he returned to the club after being essentially hounded out in 1999, selling to an Icelandic consortium.

Again, Coates has no financial reason for staying at the club, but because they're his home-town team he remains. 'Me and my family, we don't look at Stoke as a business,' Coates told *The Guardian* in 2015. 'For us it's something important for the area and something we want to do.' Of course, you could interpret this as a form of sportswashing, depending on how dim a view you take of the gambling industry, but if so it would be a particularly localised form of it. It also presumably doesn't hurt that Bet365 can put their logo on Stoke shirts and their stadium, but again, if they wanted to properly go down that path, they would probably aim a little higher than Stoke.

You also have the local sugar daddy owner, someone like Jack Walker, who bankrolled Blackburn Rovers to the 1995 Premier League title, or Jack Hayward, whose money allowed Wolverhampton Wanderers to rise from the fourth tier of English football to the top. These are local boys done good who tip their money into the club and don't expect it back, and are just happy to see their team succeed.

In some rare cases the financial and the altruistic motivations combine, which as discussed earlier is the case in the women's game, where the key figures in that ownership landscape see both the potential for doing good and for making some money.

'It's the first place in my life where people are paying attention through joy and greed,' says Kara Nortman, one of the co-founders of Angel City in the NWSL. 'It's the first place where I have seen all my non-profit interests and my for-profit interests align.'

Sometimes, though, it's easy to overthink these things.

Damian Irvine is the CEO of Ebbsfleet United, but has a wide and varied history in sports administration, having been involved with Notts County, Wycombe Wanderers and a few National Rugby League clubs in his native Australia.

Thus, he has encountered many different owners from many different backgrounds in his time, and in his opinion there is one basic motivating factor behind anyone who owns a football club.

'There's only one reason – and they can come up with all different sorts of potential motivations to mitigate the real one.

'But ego is the only reason. It just really comes down to ego and the belief that they can do it better than it's been done for the last 50 years. There is some real honour in that, where they think "I hate the way it's being done, I can do it better."'

You can see why football could appeal to someone who has been successful in another business. The one thing that everyone knows about the business side at the top level of modern football is that there has never been more money washing around in it, but barely any clubs make a profit. There's a simple disconnect there and it says to someone who has made money elsewhere that the industry as a whole must be doing something wrong, and that they will do things right.

But then they get into the game and they start doing the same things, overpaying for the same players, spending 140 per cent of revenue on wages, sacking a manager after six games ... and the cycle continues.

It works both ways too. As fans we always think that this owner is the one who will guide us to the promised land, that they're not like the other owners. They will spend money, but sensibly. They will be patient with managers. They won't put the ticket prices up. Everything is going to be great.

In many ways football clubs are the roguish cad who has left a string of broken hearts in their wake, and prospective owners are the naifs who say 'I can change them.' Cut to a couple of years later and everyone is in tears, hope is lost and nobody is ever able to love again.

Until the next one comes along ...

12

WHAT MAKES A GOOD FOOTBALL CLUB OWNER?

'What makes a good owner? Accepting ... you are there to honour the tradition, the culture, the history, the heritage of the football club.'

NIALL COUPER,

CEO OF FAIR GAME

It seems like a simple question, really.

Everyone probably has a decent idea of what makes a good football club owner. Or at least, everyone has an idea about some of the virtues a good football club owner should have and some of the weaknesses they shouldn't have.

But boiling that down to a list of qualities, to a handy cheat sheet for the aspiring owner looking to thrive in the game, is rather more difficult.

For a start, defining what 'good' means is not as straightforward a task as you might think. Does 'good' mean someone who facilitates on-pitch success for their club? Does it mean someone who has a strong relationship with the fans? Can an owner be 'good' if their team wins a lot but they are using their status as an owner to perpetuate other, unpleasant or immoral things outside of football? Does 'good' simply equal longevity?

Does 'good' simply apply to an owner's personal success? If Owner X buys Club Y for Amount Z, then three years later sells Club Y for Amount Z times five, does that make Owner X 'good'?

The difficulty in defining an owner's goodness or otherwise is perhaps no more clearly emphasised than in the case of Mike Ashley.

The former owner of Newcastle United was initially reasonably popular when he bought the club in 2007: he tried to paint himself as a man of the people, showing up in the away end at games in his replica shirt, at one point filmed downing a pint of beer in one gulp during a game against Arsenal (an amusing side note: because you're not allowed to drink alcohol within sight of the pitch at Premier League games, Ashley was admonished for this stunt but tried to explain it away by claiming the beer was non-alcoholic. At the time, non-alcoholic beer was not served at Arsenal). He also brought the beloved Kevin Keegan back to the club in 2008, to replace the rather less than beloved Sam Allardyce.

However, it all went wrong the following season, when Keegan resigned after he – in his own words – 'came up against a wall of incompetence, deceit and arrogance,' the final straw coming when Newcastle signed two players, Uruguayan winger Nacho González and Spanish forward Xisco, without Keegan's knowledge, signings that turned out to be favours to an Argentinian agent.

Ashley promptly put the club up for sale and from that point he was despised by the Newcastle fans, who viewed him as a cold businessman with no sense of what they wanted from their owner. More unpopular managerial appointments and two relegations to the Championship in the subsequent years hardened opposition to Ashley, but if you were to show an accountant the bare facts of his reign, they would probably nod approvingly.

In those years Newcastle were run self-sustainingly, rarely paying irresponsible transfer fees for players and often turning impressive profits on them: Moussa Sissoko was bought for around £1.5 million in 2013, then sold for £30 million to Tottenham Hotspur in 2016, while Gini Wijnaldum came in for £14.5 million and a year later went to Liverpool for £25 million. Books were balanced, wages were kept under control, lavish spending was rare.

Ashley will always be pretty high up on any 'worst owners ever' list, for understandable reasons, but from a certain perspective he was the very model of a shrewd club custodian.

Also, take Fenway Sports Group. Any outsider would probably regard them as superb owners of Liverpool: they arrived at a club in the middle of an existential crisis, a club that had been bought from the Moores family by Americans Tom Hicks and George Gillett, who made brash promises that weren't kept, ran out of money then fell out with each other. This was an institution on its knees, with poor results on the pitch and a fractured relationship between the board and the fans off it.

After a slightly rocky start, they appointed Jürgen Klopp, probably the second-most transformational manager in the club's history after Bill Shankly, paired him with a brilliant player-recruitment team who for a stretch between around 2018 and 2021 got basically every significant transfer decision right. All of which was rewarded with their sixth European Cup/Champions League triumph, their first English league title since 1990, a very tidy collection of other trophies and arguably just as importantly a connection between the supporters, manager and players that none of them will ever forget.

And yet they remain significantly unpopular with a certain section of the Liverpool support. Some complain that they didn't spend enough on transfers to truly capitalise on that 2019/20 Premier League title win, but the more grown-up criticisms were based on a few spectacularly tone-deaf decisions. One was a proposed ticket-price increase in 2016, when the club announced it would charge £77 for the most expensive seats at Anfield, up from £59. In response, fans walked out in the 77th minute of their game against Sunderland, prompting the club to back down on the price increases. Another was their response to the Covid-19 pandemic, when they furloughed around 200 non-playing staff in April 2020, another decision that they reversed after significant unrest.

But it was probably their involvement in the proposed European Super League that was the biggest dividing issue,

Liverpool being one of the clubs that signed up for the doomed project in April 2021.

In response a collection of Liverpool supporters' groups combined to release a statement that said: 'A breakaway Super League will not only stamp on football's competitive ideals, but will take with it Liverpool's history and stature, tainting our name, for what? The pursuit of money. As current custodians of our club, Fenway Sports Group have talked so often of the importance of fans, only to disregard them to fill the coffers. Shame on you.'

Again, Liverpool backed down, with principal owner John Henry saying: 'I hope you'll understand that even when we make mistakes, we're trying to work in your club's best interests. In this endeavour I've let you down. I'm sorry, and I alone am responsible for the unnecessary negativity brought forward over the past couple of days. It's something I won't forget.'

And so, the examples of Ashley and FSG show that neither on-pitch success nor maintaining a steady financial ship are, on their own at least, enough to make an owner universally popular. So what does?

The truth is that, because 'what makes a good football club owner' is such a complicated question, there is no definitive answer. So I won't provide one here. Apologies if that was the reason you bought this book. Sorry, no refunds will be on offer. Congratulations for getting this far, though.

What can be done is to lay out a few suggestions, a few of the possible answers that should not be regarded as absolute answers.

In the Premier League, the archetypes of what constitute a 'well-run' club are the likes of Brighton & Hove Albion and Brentford: self-sustaining organisations that seem to combine patience and smart decision-making; clubs that have the ability to regenerate. These are stable institutions, not ones that go for a flashy approach; ones that do things in a sensible, understated, arguably even quite cold way.

Is it a coincidence that they are both clubs run by local boys (Tony Bloom at Brighton and Matthew Benham at Brentford), fans who made money then took over their clubs and have run them in a prudent way? Probably, but it does speak to the characters of both men that, even as fans, they have been able to run their clubs in fairly unemotional ways, not afraid to sell important players when it makes business sense, not afraid to change managers when they think there's someone better available.

I asked all the people I have interviewed for this book what they regard as the qualities that make a 'good' owner, and here are a few of their suggestions.

'Passion is my number one belief,' says Nasser Al-Khelaifi, chairman of PSG. 'You have to believe in your club and believe what you're doing. You have to run into work every day. I often say, when I stop loving what I do is the day I quit. I deal with all the things that are thrown against me because I love what I do – I love football and I love PSG.'

'Someone who really, authentically cares about building their team, but also the ecosystem,' says Kara Nortman, co-founder of Angel City in the NWSL. 'I think that's the most important thing: it's not just about "building my team" in a deeply competitive, sharp-elbowed way. Women's football requires a tonne of heavy lifting and best-practice sharing. It's the reason the NWSL is doing so well.

'Another thing is self-awareness – which we all think we have – about understanding what we're best at, which phase are we best at. Me and my colleagues are really well suited to this phase of women's football. But in ten years, when we're at a stage where everyone's worth as much as the Milwaukee Bucks or the Golden State Warriors … it's about what you need now versus what you need in the future …'

Martin Hollaender, from multi-club group Orlegi, offers: 'Take into consideration all the stakeholders of the club. Create value for the club, but also for its surrounding society. A good ownership is one that has the guts and the nerve to be able to think long term.

To have the stability – emotionally and financially – to invest long term.

'When you have a visible owner, that helps. You need to be on top of your management as an owner.'

Christina Philippou, lecturer at the University of Portsmouth and football finance expert, suggests 'Somebody who is cognisant of the fact that they will probably need to be pumping money over a very long period of time.' Rob Wilson, who occupies a similar role at Sheffield Hallam University, says: 'I think financial sustainability should be the priority, supported with an understanding and intelligence of your key stakeholders.'

Niall Couper is the CEO of Fair Game, an advocacy group that, in their own words, seeks to improve the governance of football in England and Wales. 'Accepting that you're a custodian,' he says. 'Accepting that you are the latest owner of a tradition that goes back decades and that you are there to honour the tradition, the culture, the history, the heritage of the football club of which you are temporarily in charge. Having that at your core is really important because that means you then care about your community, you care about your fans, because that's what your role is.'

And Spencer Owen, founded of Hashtag United, says: 'It's about having the long-term sustainability of the club at its heart, to be sure you're not chasing short-term goals or ego. You're trying to create something that lasts. Beyond that, it's about having an identity. What makes your club special?'

What of the managers? They are, after all, the ones who have to spend the most time working with a club owner; the ones whose careers are in many ways defined by whoever is upstairs. They exist at the whim of the person in the big chair.

'A good chairman believes in you,' says Tony Pulis, a managerial veteran who took charge of ten clubs over a 28-year career and had his share of lively employers. 'He gives you the time to change the club's course and build a winning mentality. He doesn't listen to outside noise and is strong enough to ride the waves that follow bad results.

'Unfortunately today there are too many people in between the owner and manager, but back in the day it was in my view important to have a real strong relationship between the two most important people at the club.'

———

And what about the fans? What is most important to those of us who watch games every week, and invest time, money and more of our emotional wellbeing than is probably healthy into this game and the teams we love? It's very hard, if not impossible, to get a truly representative answer, but I conducted a survey of just over 1,100 fans to ask a series of related questions in order to get some sort of idea of what they think is important.

A couple of quick caveats: this survey was conducted around the time when the protests against Reading owner Dai Yongge were at their peak, so there was probably an over-representation of their extremely dissatisfied fans. Nottingham Forest fans were probably also slightly over-represented, given that they are my team and some of the participants came forward in response to me posting the survey on X.

Nevertheless, while not pretending to be definitive it provides a decent cross-section of the football community, and thus might give us some indication of what fans care about when it comes to their owners.

I gave seven selections for the type of owner that, in an ideal world, fans would like for their club: fans/supporters' trust; a single wealthy benefactor; a multi-club group; a nation state; an investment group like Fenway Sports Group; other, inviting them to fill in their answer; and finally 'I don't care as long as the team is doing well.'

By a massive distance, the most popular answer was fan ownership: 54.5 per cent, in fact, suggesting that the utopian ideal of a club governed from the stands is still alive and well, despite the structure of English football being such that it's very difficult for this kind of model to deliver consistent on-pitch success and to climb the leagues.

Perhaps this is related to the satisfaction scale: the most frequent answer to the question asking fans to rate their happiness with their ownership from one to ten was ... one: 194 of the respondents were as dissatisfied as it's possible to be, in fact. This is where the Reading caveat comes in: 65 of those were from Royals fans, clearly a significant over-representation considering they are a moderately sized League One club.

As a rule, fan ownership comes in when a club is in a bad way, which is a practical consideration (usually there's nobody else viable who wants to take control), but also one that is perhaps explained by a 'back to basics' factor. If a club is in trouble, it's usually because mistakes have been made or decisions taken that aren't in the best interests of a club: from that point, the idea of fans taking control, a group who it is assumed will have those interests at heart, becomes attractive.

To illustrate that point, of those Reading fans who rated their happiness with the ownership at one out of ten, 28 voted for fan ownership as their preferred model. The next least satisfied group were Manchester United fans, who even after the Glazers sold 25 per cent of the club to INEOS and Jim Ratcliffe are not likely to forgive their long-time overlords in this lifetime. A total of 44 United fans selected one out of ten, 35 of whom wanted a fan-ownership model.

After fan ownership the next most popular answer, quite a way back on 12.9 per cent, was 'I don't care as long as the team is doing well,' suggesting that more fans than we might like to think actually don't pay much attention to the name above the door. Which is an understandable reaction: for most fans supporting a football club is an escape from their daily life, a diversion that ideally would extend to watching the games and being part of the community that exists within every fanbase. Not many people really *want* to care who owns their club – they are just forced to.

After that 11.2 per cent wanted a single, wealthy benefactor, and the remainder of the responses were split between a variety of other competing suggestions and nuances.

As for those who are absolutely delighted with their owners, 13.5 per cent rated themselves as nine or ten out of ten in the happiness stakes. Of those, the dominant forms of ownership were supporters' trust teams (Exeter City, AFC Wimbledon, the new version of Bury), teams that are owned or controlled by businesspeople who also happen to be fans (Brentford, Brighton) or people who have spent a lot of money on the team (Manchester City, Newcastle).

Interestingly the only club whose supporters registered both ones and tens on the happiness scale was Newcastle: fans that don't approve of their takeover by the Saudi Investment Fund are in the minority, but they are there.

I also asked what qualities fans would ideally like to see in an owner, and the answers were wide and varied. The idea that the owner recognises that they are actually not really the owner, more of a custodian who currently has the responsibility of caring for this valuable community artefact and knows they will one day pass it on, was also a common theme.

If not fan ownership then an owner who is a fan was mentioned more than once: Steve Gibson's name cropped up in a number of answers as the ideal owner. But then again an individual figure doesn't have to be present: one respondent said their ideal owner should be 'forgettable, not a topic of public discourse'.

However, three main themes were consistently raised throughout the answers. One was money: both having it, but not spending too much of it. We can be as worthy as we like and talk about the community institutions and having an affection for a club all day, but it's an undeniable fact that money matters for an owner.

It should go without saying that the way an owner spends money is more important than how much they spend, and not every fan is asking for lavish amounts of money to be thrown at their team (although many wouldn't say no if you offered that to them). An owner should not spend more money than they or a club has: it's the sort of thing that sounds like the most obvious point in the world, but it's one that a troubling number can't seem to stick to.

Another point was based around the idea of honesty and clear communication: it turns out that if you speak to the fans, whether that's in person, through interviews or just clear and concise statements, setting out what you plan to do with the club, then they're more likely to like and trust you.

The third prevailing sentiment was that an owner should be consistent, have a plan and stick to it, be patient. That doesn't even necessarily mean that they should not be too trigger-happy when it comes to sacking a manager, just that they should be clear about their expectations and not change course at the first sign of things going slightly awry.

Again, this shouldn't be taken as a definitive view of what all fans think, but perhaps more as a guide, a nod towards general opinion. As with everything else, you probably can't get a result that gives you an absolutely accurate version of what fans think: you could stand outside every ground in the country with a clipboard and still not achieve that. But at the very least it's worth listening to the people that were there before most owners arrived and will certainly be there after they have gone.

So what does make a good football club owner? As has hopefully been made clear, there isn't one particular answer to the question.

Much like the old adage that a team can't win the league in September, but they can lose it, there are a number of things that an owner shouldn't do, or that make a bad owner. Don't spend money you or the club don't have. Don't spend no money at all. Don't treat your fans like idiots. Don't sack managers at the drop of a hat. Don't commit fraud. Don't launder money. Don't attempt to set fire to your club's stadium in an ill-conceived attempt to collect an insurance payment. Don't be a monstrous warlord.

Most of these things you would like to hope that no human being would need to be told, but as some of the stories in this book prove, you can't rely on people to do the self-evident stuff at the best of times, never mind when they get that first sugar rush of power that comes with owning a football team.

Being a sensible owner of a football club should perhaps, on the face of it, not be the most difficult thing in the world to do.

But it's really, really difficult, which is why so many fail and so few remain popular. The owner of a football club should be prepared to fail, should be prepared to get things wrong, should be prepared to face fierce criticism. They should also be prepared to do everything right on paper, but for none of that to actually work in practice, and thus be regarded as a colossal dud.

Because ultimately the most tangible way in which an owner's success is defined is whether their team does well on the pitch. An owner can put in place all the sound processes and business practices and sensible methods they like, but if that doesn't equal the 11 players on the pitch winning games, then cries from the stands of 'sack the board' will grow louder and louder.

It's an incredibly tricky game, one that is devilishly difficult to win. You wouldn't blame someone for reading all of this and deciding that it simply isn't worth the trouble, and thus you do start to have a certain amount of sympathy for anyone who tries it.

Then you think about some of the stories in this book and that sympathy starts to dissipate.

13

THE FUTURE

'What's the next big innovative way of making content, or gamifying football? There's plenty of room for clubs to try some more experimental things, and some more experimental leagues.'

SPENCER OWEN,
HASHTAG UNITED FOUNDER

There is a crisis in football club ownership in England.

In January 2024, the chairman of the English Football League Rick Parry gave evidence to a parliamentary committee about the state of football finance and governance, and he issued a stark warning about the present and future of the game.

Parry outlined the startling fact that, at the time he was speaking, two-thirds of the clubs in the EFL were insolvent and were in danger of disappearing completely. 'The clubs want a better future, they want a better system because they know the current system is broken,' Parry said.

If football was any other industry, a significant proportion of clubs would have gone out of existence by now. It's only because of their status as community institutions – plus the many prospective owners who think they can succeed while others have failed, which means there's usually a willing queue of suitors – that most are still around.

Which is an absolutely absurd state of affairs, given how much money is in the game. In 2021/22, Premier League clubs collectively earned £5.5 billion in revenue, but only seven of them reported pre-tax profits. Over the preceding ten years, according to football finance expert Kieron O'Connor who writes the Swiss Ramble blog, only three clubs turned a profit: Tottenham, Liverpool and Burnley.

This tells you two things: firstly, that it is perfectly possible to both run a football club in a loosely sensible financial manner while at the same time remaining competitive and even successful on the pitch. But secondly, barely any clubs are actually doing it.

The Premier League will be fine, ultimately. Particularly with their profit and sustainability rules starting to have the desired impact in terms of being a deterrent for clubs spending wildly on transfers, given the punishments handed to Everton and Nottingham Forest in the 2023/24 season. The total of 12 points that Everton and Forest were docked between them for breaching those rules made many clubs, to quote one Premier League director, 'shit themselves.'

The EFL is a different story. In June 2023 Deloitte reported that in the previous season the average – *the average* – wage-to-revenue ratio among EFL clubs was 108 per cent. That's 72 clubs who were spending more money only on player wages, never mind anything else, than they were bringing in. The most egregious case was Reading who, as mentioned earlier, had a wage-to-revenue ratio of 216 per cent in 2020/21. That looks like a typo, but sadly it isn't.

All of this tells you that a large number of the people who own football clubs are either acting recklessly or they simply don't know what they're doing.

Either way, it tells you that something needs to change. So what does the future look like?

———

To stick with the financial theme for a moment, everything will be fine in the Premier League if things continue on the up and up, if revenues continue to grow and clubs can thus keep pace with the rapid rate of inflation that exists within football which, like so many other things to do with the game, isn't reflected in the real world.

But the line on the graph might not keep going up. You only have to look at the television broadcast deal for the Premier League that was signed in late 2023. On the face of it, the Premier League could slap themselves on the collective back because they had achieved an increase on the previous deal: Sky and TNT Sports agreed to pay £6.7 billion over four years starting from 2025, which is up from the £4.9 billion in both of the previous two cycles.

Well done everyone, good job. The number is going up, and going up is good, so ... champagne?

Well, cork it for a minute. For a start, the previous deal was only over three years and only accounted for 200 matches per season. The 2025 deal guaranteed at least 267 live games would be broadcast, which over four seasons means 1,068 games in total. So in its most basic terms, the cost to the broadcasters per game has actually gone down from £7.8 million to £6 million. It's even less than when the market seemed to peak, which was in the 2016–2019 cycle, when each game worked out at around £10.2 million.

And that doesn't take into account inflation: £4.9 billion in 2019 equated to a little over £6 billion in 2023, when the new deal was agreed, making it even less of a step up.

The overseas rights are worth another £5 billion and the Premier League is still well ahead of the other major European leagues on that count, so it's not as if belts need to be significantly tightened. But it is an indication that not absolutely everything is on the up and up in the world of the Premier League, and thus the idea of constant growth in the central column of the division's income is just not true.

So will this deter people from trying to buy football clubs? Not likely, but will it persuade them to run them differently? Well, you'd like to think so, but clubs haven't proved they are able to act responsibly thus far, so perhaps not.

It's easy to think that the Premier League's status as the dominant financial force in the game is set in stone now, but empires fall just as quickly as they rise.

'I think the temptation is always to say it's set,' says Omar Chaudhuri, chief intelligence officer of analysts Twenty First

Group. 'But I always look back to Serie A and where that was 30 years ago: the belief would have been then that Serie A has all the best players in the world, best coaching, best football culture, probably best stadiums at the time – and then look where it is now. So I think that's a cautionary tale for the Premier League.'

As the game currently is, it's tricky to identify properly what could topple the Premier League. But it could be anything really: one of the 'legacy' European Leagues might have a resurgence, it could be the Saudi Pro League, it might even be MLS.

Or it could be the European Super League. Since the initial attempt to launch the Super League fizzled out before it really began in 2021, it has been a slightly peripheral part of the footballing consciousness. But it will come back and it could have a significant impact on what owning a football club looks like in the coming years.

'Football needs change,' Bernd Reichart, chief executive of A22, the company that was formed to 'sponsor and assist' the Super League, told me in early 2024.

Apart from presenting an alternative European competition to the Champions League, the concept of the Super League is that it allows the clubs themselves much more say in how their competitions are run.

'I think it's just fair to assume,' says Reichart, 'that the ones who are organising and managing the competition are the ones who share or bear the whole burden of economic risks.

'It's the clubs who invest and take economic risks when they buy or transfer players, when they invest in their infrastructure, when they develop a women's team, when they build academies, when they manage their fan relations.'

This speaks to one of the key flaws (although they would probably not perceive it as a flaw) of the Super League idea – that it would further stratify the football world, making the rich even richer and the poor insignificant. The clubs at the top already get most of the money, but it would appear that is not enough.

Another central tenet of the Super League is the idea of longer-term participation in European competition. The initial proposals outlined a closed shop, a centralised group of mega clubs that couldn't be relegated from it, but after the backlash against that aspect of it was so great, further plans were altered slightly to create a three-tiered structure, with promotion and relegation.

That, in the view of Reichart, provides greater stability for clubs, because it allows them to plan and budget for longer in those competitions.

'It is just tough to compete. It wouldn't be responsible if I bet on a continuous European path year after year because actually, I can fail. You're not retaining your talent and you're not actually building infrastructure and you're not trying to grow as a club.'

From a philosophical point of view, the idea of the Super League, or indeed any competition that isn't based on sporting merit, becomes something other than football and is thus something to be suspicious of. But it's hard to get away from the idea that it might be extremely attractive to football club owners: we know this, because the owners of 12 clubs threw their weight behind the concept in 2021.

'It [the Super League] would be a big group of clubs who run and manage the competition,' says Reichart, 'who are co-shareholders in the distribution platform that is generating the revenues. I'm convinced that every owner or every potential owner, if they look at a competition where they have an intermediate influence on the governance, will see it is highly attractive compared to the influence, or non-influence, they currently have.'

He might be right. The idea of the whole thing might make your skin crawl, and we can howl at the moon all night hoping it isn't so, but he might be right.

———

For some, the great hope for the English game is the new independent football regulator, announced by the UK government in 2023.

This regulator will, in the words of the government, 'have powers to monitor and enforce compliance with requirements in financial regulation; corporate governance; club ownership (owners' and directors' tests); fan engagement and club heritage protection; and approved competitions.'

You wonder why this sort of thing hasn't been in place for years. The answer might be that, much like any area of previously unchecked capitalism that has been allowed to go about its business merrily enough, the people being regulated aren't keen to be regulated.

'Our game has challenges, of course,' Richard Masters, chief executive of the Premier League, solemnly wrote in *The Times* in February 2023. 'But English football is an incredible success. This has been achieved largely without the intrusion of cyclical political pressures and heavy-handed regulatory intervention. So while we accept the case for reform, it is vital the government does not inadvertently throw away the advantages that have been so carefully developed.'

The question then becomes: how big is the stick going to be? Is the regulator going to have any power to stop rogue owners before they've had the chance to do real damage? How much power can the regulator have before it is deemed to constitute government interference, which is a very big no-no as far as FIFA are concerned?

For it to make any difference at all, it must have the authority to do certain things that will have an actual impact. For example, when it comes to ownership, the regulator must be empowered to withdraw the licence of someone who has proven themselves to be an incompetent or malign owner, to force the sale of the club into some form of escrow so that it can be saved.

This can't be arbitrary. There must be some red lines that are crossed to trigger such a drastic move. It could be, for example, after a certain number of times that an owner has failed to pay staff on schedule, or breached financial sustainability rules in an egregious manner.

There are problems with this. Who is 'the owner' of a club? The name on the documents isn't necessarily the name of the person who makes the decisions or even ultimately provides the funding. The legalities of it are, to use considerable understatement, tricky.

But something drastic has to be done in order to make the game, and the way it is run and financed in general, more sustainable, never mind to address the more extreme cases and save some of the clubs that might be in immediate danger.

One of the methods of reform that has been frequently trumpeted is the idea of redistributing wealth, to ensure that some of the people further down the food chain get a bigger slice of the fat cash pie that football gorges itself on.

The problem is that a greater redistribution of funds throughout the football pyramid like this will only go so far. This is because, in so many words, football club owners as they currently think simply cannot be trusted to be prudent. They are like a toddler who wants some cake, eats all that cake, then demands some more cake, which they eat, and then some more cake, before eventually they're sick all over the kitchen floor.

Actually, it's probably better for someone to explain that in a slightly more adult fashion.

'The functional problem at most clubs is they're paying too much out in wages,' says Rob Wilson, from Sheffield Hallam University. 'I'm really nervous about an independent regulator almost forcing what they call a fair distribution model.'

Wilson's argument, put simply, is that if you give most EFL clubs more money it won't necessarily be used to run things in a more sensible and prudent manner, but will just lead to a souped-up version of the current problems. They will take that money and spend it just as recklessly, if not more so.

'I wince every time somebody says fair distribution, because fair distribution is not giving Port Vale, for example, an extra £5 million a year out of the Premier League deal that just says they can go and spend more money on player wages.

'This may help with a couple of things, but it isn't going to change anything, as long as the mindset of clubs stays the same.'

Where a regulator could have an impact is if this sort of financial redistribution is brought in, but with rules in place on where owners can actually spent the extra money.

'Let's say a Championship club currently gets about £9 million in solidarity payments,' Wilson says. 'You increase that to £15 million and you say "We're going to restrict you to only spending £2 million of that on player wages."

'The other £13 million has to go into infrastructure, stadium redevelopment, academy-system coaching, sports science – all of that stuff that creates a much higher performance environment, and produces much more talented players out of the academy that you can then use to trade and improve your own financial position.'

Perhaps more than any regulation, the main thing that has to change is the attitude of more, more, more; of gambling to reach a higher level simply by spending. That might be a little further off.

———

'I think football will be far more global and far more interconnected,' says PSG chairman Nasser Al-Khelaifi, when asked about the future. 'European football should keep its traditions – I have stood up for UEFA and the traditional models of European football. However, it needs to modernise. Every other successful sport and successful businesses are based on global interconnectivity. European football should move a bit in that direction and I think it will.'

The ownership model that Al-Khelaifi represents probably doesn't need to worry too much. Football has shown absolutely no appetite for curbing the introduction of more state owners into the game, so there's really very little reason to think that if another wealthy government wants to buy a club, they will be prevented from doing so.

What of the other structures, though? This book has looked at a number of different types of ownership models, so it's worth considering which ones we might see more of in the future.

It's become pretty clear that the area of football with the biggest cause for optimism is the women's game, both in terms of financial expansion and the general concept of it being a positive that women's sport is taken more seriously. The potential for growth is extraordinary, in both a financial, cultural and social respect, and those who have already got into the game have done so because they know that the line on the graph is going up and up and will only get steeper.

'I hope so,' says Victoire Covegina Reynal, when asked if the level of investment in the women's game is going to increase. 'There are big investors already. Women's sports as a whole has become *the* big thing. The 2023 World Cup was a success and so many other athletes have had visibility. It kind of becomes a no-brainer. We get to break the rules and rewrite them.'

As well as more investment in the women's game, perhaps we will see more women invest in the women's game. 'I think more female ownership in football would be really welcome,' says Chaudhuri. 'It's a very testosterone-heavy space. European football is so fractious: you look at all these different bodies, whether it's leagues or the European Club Association or UEFA and Super League, whoever else is in there. It's all very, very male and very fractious.'

In the men's game, buying in at the top level has become almost impossible, because the prices have reached extraordinary levels. So Chaudhuri believes that we will see more and more outside investors look to clubs in the EFL, where they believe there is more growth potential.

'You can buy in the bottom half of the Premier League, but you constantly face the risk of going down, so is it worth the premium that you pay there?' he says.

It's not just owners that could be heading to those smaller clubs. It's possible that a broader disillusionment with the Premier League and/or top-level football more generally will drive more fans to smaller clubs, thus increasing their fanbases and making owning those clubs even more attractive.

'We're going to get more disillusioned Premier League fans,' says Maggie Murphy, former CEO of community-owned Lewes. 'We're already seeing them here, coming from Brighton, who I think are a well-run club, coming to us because they feel detached. I think some fans feel a bit more like a client or a customer than a fan or an owner.

'I think the fan-ownership model will only appeal to clubs like Bury who have gone bust and committed people have tried to build it from the ashes. That's exactly what happened at Lewes: six owners came together and decided to go with community rather than corporate ownership. Because it is really hard.'

The chapter in this book about multi-club ownership outlines the strengths and weaknesses of that model, but it feels unstoppable.

Of the 20 clubs that competed in the 2023/24 Premier League season, 15 had links in some way to other sports clubs, 13 of which were other football clubs. Those links ranged from a full, structured multi-club organisation like the City Football Group, to someone like Bournemouth owner Bill Foley holding a minority stake in French club Lorient, to the slightly looser link between Newcastle United and the Saudi clubs also owned by the Saudi Public Investment Fund.

This sort of empire-building is only going to increase. 'The outcomes of being in a multi-club structure are so significant that I think it should be part of any owner's agenda,' says Martin Hollaender, from the multi-club group Orlegi. 'If not, they will be up against it.'

Perhaps we will see more people from a non-traditional background get into the ownership game, like Spencer Owen, who founded Hashtag United, a team that built a following from the internet before actually playing a game.

'People often ask how they can do what we've done,' says Owen. 'You can't recreate it, but what you can do is think: what's the next platform? What's the next big innovative way of making content, or gamifying football? There's plenty of room for clubs to try some more experimental things, and some more experimental leagues.'

So should we be optimistic about the future of the game? Can we be hopeful that the people who own football realise that they have a broader responsibility to the game, to their clubs, to their communities?

Yes and no. To address the negative first: we've outlined the often parlous state of the game's finances, but there is a moral black hole at the heart of football ownership too.

Anyone who thinks there was a golden age where only nice people controlled football clubs is a dreamer, drunk on a heady nostalgia for a time that never existed, as some of the details in this book's chapter about the history of ownership will show.

But there was a time where people did not, for the most part, have to worry about what their football club was being used for. The specific motivations of individuals may have been malign, but they were just that: individuals. They may have been using their position for some personal gain, but that was straightforward: if you didn't like your club chairman because he had his fingers in the till, or was trying to gain political favour, or just because he wore a stupid tie, that was a straightforward decision. You might even have been able to make enough noise to force him out.

Now, the question of whether the people who own our football clubs are agreeable or not is fraught with the kind of things that football fans shouldn't have to consider. Most of us fell in love with the game at an early age, watching this extraordinary sport and the power it could have over otherwise rational human beings, and were drawn in, intoxicated by the spirit and atmosphere of the whole thing. It helped us build bulletproof personal relationships, helped us relate to parents or form lifelong friendships or even find a partner. On a more basic level it was just fun, an escape, a couple of hours every week where you could forget about the real world and its unpalatable complications.

It should be uncomplicated. But it has been made extremely complicated. Should fans really have to worry that the owner of their football club might be using it for money-laundering? Or to distract attention from killing a journalist in an embassy? Or to sell you insurance?

Football is such a colossal part of modern society, such a huge cultural force, that those who control it have an opportunity to use it for good. It would be very easy to look at the state of things and think there is no hope, that we just have to accept that things are the way they are and that's it.

But the heartening thing is that there are people out there who are doing that.

People like Maggie Murphy and Stefan Schubert and Julian Tagg and Kara Nortman and Dale Vince and Spencer Owen show that there is a different, and positive, way of doing things.

There are people out there who will harness football for good reasons, who will use it to combat sexism and misogyny, or promote climate change awareness. There are people who will defend the soul of their club, who won't accept it being used as a marketing tool for something else completely. There are people who are able to think about things differently and will carry on in the face of the world turning its nose up because they're not conforming to traditions.

In an industry as unregulated as football, money will always be a key motivator for many who try to get involved, the ultimate endgame as they buy their lottery ticket, hoping to hit the jackpot. But there are ways to go about it, ways to chase that money, without destroying your club at the same time.

You can use football as a valuable part of a local community that genuinely contributes to it rather than just taking up space. You can use football to empower women in a patriarchal society. You can use football to encourage people to think about the climate crisis and how they can live their lives in a way that isn't going to make the planet cave in. And you can use football to bring people from all corners of the globe together in an online community.

There are reasons to be hopeful. You just have to look a little harder for them.

BIBLIOGRAPHY

Calladine, M. – *No Questions Asked: How Football Joined The Crypto Con* (Independently published, 2024)

Conn, D. – *The Beautiful Game? Searching For the Soul Of Football* (Yellow Jersey, 2005)

Eriksson, S.G. – *Sven: My Story* (Headline, 2013)

Foer, F. – *How Football Explains The World* (Arrow, 2006)

Goldman, R. – *The Sisterhood: The 99ers And The Rise Of US Women's Soccer* (University of Nebraska Press, 2021)

Herbert, I. – *Tinseltown: Hollywood And The Beautiful Game – A Match Made in Wrexham* (Headline, 2023)

Hopcroft, A. – *The Football Man* (Collins, 1968)

Jones, A. F. – *It's Always Sunny In Wrexham* (Independently Published, 2023)

Jordan, S. – *Be Careful What You Wish For* (Yellow Jersey, 2012)

Keegan, K. – *My Life In Football: An Autobiography* (Macmillan, 2018)

Keoghan, J. – *Punk Football: The Rise of Fan Ownership in English Football* (Pitch Publishing, 2014)

Lipton, M. – *White Hart Lane: The Spurs Glory Years, 1899–2017* (Weidenfeld & Nicolson, 2017)

Maguire, K. – *The Price Of Football* (Agenda Publishing, 2020)

Midgley, D. and Hitchens, C. – *Roman Abramovich: The Billionaire From Nowhere* (Willow, 2004)

Montague, J. – *The Billionaires Club* (Bloomsbury, 2017)

Preston, J. and John, E. – *Watford Forever*, (Penguin, 2024)

Reynolds, G. – *Cracked It!* (Blake Publishing, 2003)

Robinson, H. – *The Men Who Made Manchester United* (Pitch Publishing, 2023)

Robinson, J. and Clegg, J. – *The Club: How The Premier League Became The Richest, Most Disruptive Business In Sport* (John Murray, 2019)

Slack-Smith, D. – *Killing The Game* (Ignition Sports Media, 2018)

Spurling, J. – *Rebels For The Cause: The Alternative History Of Arsenal Football Club* (Mainstream Publishing, 2004)

Szymanski, S. and Kuper, S. – *Money And Football: A Soccernomics Guide* (Bold Type Books, 2015)

Tejwani, K. – *Wings Of Change* (Pitch Publishing, 2020)

Thomas, D. and Smith, M. – *Bob Lord Of Burnley: The Biography Of Football's Most Controversial Chairman* (Pitch Publishing, 2019)

Vince, D. – *Manifesto: The Battle For Green Britain* (Ebury, 2023)

Vine, P. – *Visionary: Manchester United, Michael Knighton and The Football Revolution* (Pitch Publishing, 2019)

White, J. – *Manchester United: The Biography* (Sphere, 2008)

Williams, J. – *Red Men Reborn: From John Houlding to Jurgen Klopp* (Pitch Publishing, 2022)

ACKNOWLEDGMENTS

Who Owns Football? is the second book I have solely written. The first one was about sporting mascots and, while it was undoubtedly enjoyable to write profiles of oversized Muppets and interview the bloke who plays Harry The Hornet, this book was slightly more labour intensive.

For that I have to thank my agent, Melanie Michael-Greer, for thinking the same author who wrote that could tackle this. The same goes for Matthew Lowing, Sarah Skipper and everyone at Bloomsbury Sport, and thank you to Bill Edgar for the meticulous editing and for patiently coping with my casual attitude to punctuation.

Thank you to everyone who gave their time to be interviewed and for those who helped facilitate those interviews, including but not limited to David Sugden, Stefan Schubert, Maggie Murphy, Alejandra Depalma, Rob Wilson, Preston Johnson, Niall Couper, Hillary Messenger, Raphael Honigstein, Ruth Pintner, Lina al-Hathloul, Nick McGeehan, William Bi, Koen Verdruye and Spencer Owen.

I also have a day job at The Athletic, and the people at that job would have been perfectly justified in saying 'not a chance, son' when I first mentioned this project. So thank you massively to Alex Kay-Jelski (despite abandoning us), Laura Williamson and especially Kevin Coulson.

For moral and editorial support and advice, thank you to Daniel Storey, Sarah Winterburn, Matt Stanger and Adam Bate, to whom I am also thankful for the distractions that to an untrained eye would look like procrastination and bullshit, but are actually vital discussions about the state of the game that have informed this work hugely. Or something like that.

Speaking of bullshit, thank you to Mick, Gary, Mary, Dave, Bambi, Al and Andrew for often unintentionally providing some very welcome distractions in the bleaker days of writing. And on a related note, thank you to the good people at Prestige Wine Merchants on the high street near my house. A valuable public service.

Thank you to my mum, Sharon, my dad, Chris, my sister Ellie and my nephew, Sam: thank you for giving me the choice between going to the circus and going to the football all those years ago, thank you for being so excited about this book, but mainly thank you for being so wonderful. A more loving and kind family surely doesn't exist, and I am incredibly lucky to have you.

It feels slightly absurd to thank a cat that, despite years of encouragement and hundreds of books in the house, hasn't even bothered to try learning to read. But in the long hours of being strapped to my desk, having a tiny furry moron purring or snoring away in the corner was enormously comforting. Thanks Clough.

Finally, and most importantly, thank you to Laura, for your support, encouragement, care, for answering my stupid questions about grammar and for tolerating my remarkable ability to relate every life event back to football. I'd be lost without you and I love you very much.

INDEX

INDEX